I was intrigued by your <u>Nothing But Winners</u>, and kept reading the lines to see how many were in my joke file. I found none. You have a lot of material I didn't recognize. Congratulations.

Bob Hope
Comedian

If you have to give a speech there's nothing better than a couple of good one-liners to spice it up a little. This book contains not one but 6,000 examples of <u>everything</u> you need to know about one-liners!

Ed McMahon
"Tonight Show"

Henny Youngman will envy <u>Nothing But Winners.</u> The best - and funniest - collection of one-liners I've ever read. Enjoy, Enjoy.

Larry King
Talk Show Host And National Columnist

"This is the aircraft carrier of jokebooks. It's a dynamite collection of funny material. Uptown all the way!"

Al McGuire
NBC-TV

Delightful book! I have an idea I'll be quoting from it frequently.

Paul Harvey
Paul Harvey News

"It's funny and will be useful!"

Mike Wallace
CBS-TV

NOTHING BUT WINNERS

By Pat Williams
THE GINGERBREAD MAN
THE POWER WITHIN YOU
WE OWED YOU ONE!

NOTHING BUT WINNERS

by

Pat Williams and Ken Hussar

Over 6,000 one-liners, alphabetized and
categorized for easy reference

Illustrations by Mary Cosby

TriMark Publishing Company, Inc.
Wilmington, Delaware

DEDICATION

This book is respectfully dedicated to our long-suffering wives, Jill Williams and Carolyn Hussar, who have endured the not-so-funny times of research, writing, typing and editing. Humor is a serious business. Therefore, it should be noted, that our "Wife" and "Mother-in-Law" sections are fictitious and meant in a spirit of fun (well, most of the lines, anyway).

CONTENTS

NOTHING BUT WINNERS

INTRODUCTION

Laughter is like an animate super glue that serves as a quick bond between an audience and speaker. The great joke, delivered with confidence and savvy, is a two-edged instrument that entertains the crowd, and at the same time, encourages the speaker through the listeners' audible, approving response.

This, if you will, is an eclectic book of one-liners. In our travels, we have collected tens of thousands of jokes from banquet speakers, books, humor services, magazines, newspapers, radio, and television, which, in turn, produced a huge file. From that file we have selected about 6,000 of the funniest ones that we have successfully used with our audiences--proven winners. It is our hope that you will agree with our immodest assessment that this is the most complete resource of useable humor in terms of quantity and quality.

Robert Orben, today's best and most prolific one-liner writer, has said, "To the writer who accused me of plagiarism by innuendo, I say this: When you take material from one writer, it's plagiarism--when you take it from many writers, it's research."

Another humorist, Dr. Herb True of Indiana, writes: "There isn't much new or original material around. Feel free to borrow the proverbs, sayings, the joyous jokes of others, then change, adapt, personalize and make the material your own. An old joke is one that isn't funny. A new one is any joke that hasn't been told in your original way."

It is within this context that we present these choice lines, claiming no originality, save the way in which we have cataloged and organized the material.

As you use these lines, we suggest you read the book about fifteen minutes a day, checking your favorites for later reference. If you attempt to digest too much in one sitting, there is a danger that you might skim over a super line.

Once you have selected your favorites from a particular category, organize them in a sequence that will build to your biggest laugh-getter.

Finally, practice, practice, practice. The "Audience Repartee," "Introductions," and "Roast" sections provide you with a bunch of quick laughs that will help you gain immediate rapport with the group you are addressing. By planning and rehearsing the lines, your wit will seem effortless and spontaneous.

We express our profound thanks to Sylvia Koch, production supervisor for this project, whose diligence, efficiency, and enthusiasm were necessary ingredients in making this book a reality, and to Mary Cosby, the gifted artist from Chattanooga, whose crisp and imaginative illustrations provide creative lead-ins to the alphabetized sections.

To give you a foretaste of what is to follow, here are some lines to whet your appetite:

ADAGE: It's not whether you win or lose, it's who gets the blame.

BASEBALL: Those fans are really something! When the team held its Easter egg hunt, the fans booed the kids who didn't find any eggs.

BASKETBALL: We're not really fast. Yesterday we had three loose balls roll dead in practice.

BOOK: I figured that if I ever got wealthy or became a celebrity, I'd write a book about it. Unfortunately, I couldn't wait that long.

BUTTERFLIES: I'm so nervous. This may look like a bow tie to you. I assure you it isn't. One of the butterflies in my stomach got out.

CAR: Never buy a car that is being sold at the bottom of a ravine.

COACH: If losing helps build character, he has all the character he'll ever need.

EXERCISE: I was going to start my weight lifting program yesterday, but I wasn't able to lift the barbells out of the trunk of my car.

GOLF: I've been hitting the woods great, but I have a terrible time hitting out of them.

MARRIAGE: They're a perfect couple. He's a hypochondriac and she's a pill.

MORNINGS: When I awaken every morning, the first thing I do is stumble to the bathroom, breathe on the mirror, and hope it fogs up.

MOTHER-IN-LAW: My mother-in-law can talk faster than most people can listen.

POST OFFICE: The post office advertises express mail. They guarantee they'll lose your letter the same day.

SENIOR CITIZEN: He's so old, he needs jumper cables just to get started each day.

SMALL TOWN: Our population is only ten. No, make that eight. One guy died last week and I'm out of town.

SPORTS: The only thing duller than track is field.

UMPIRE: Fans expect an umpire to be perfect on opening day and to improve as the season goes along.

WEATHER: It was so hot yesterday, I saw a squirrel picking up an acorn with an oven mit.

WIFE'S COOKING: The recipe said to grease the bottom of the pan. So my wife turned the pan over and greased it.

WIFE'S DRIVING: My wife failed her driver's test because of one tiny mistake. She ran over the guy giving her the exam.

And the lines get stronger as you continue to dig into this book. It is our feeling that you now have in your hands the best collection of jokes ever assembled. Deliver them with confidence, timing, and enthusiasm and your audiences will declare you a winner and champion as a speaker.

Best wishes,

Pat Williams

Pat Williams

Ken Hussar

Ken Hussar

ACCOUNTANTS

Detective: "So, you're looking for your bookkeeper. Is he tall or short?"
Boss: "Both."

"Our firm is looking for a new accountant."
"I thought you just hired one a week ago?"
"Yeah, he's the one we're looking for!"

Be aware of the accountant who tells you he can get you a great tax break by putting all your money in his name.

My accountant has devised a wonderful system for reducing our bills. It's called microfilm.

Our firm has a bookkeeper who's shy and retiring. He's about $400,000 shy. That's why he's retiring.

Old accountants never die, they just lose their balance.

He's such a financial genius that the American Association of Accountants just named a loophole after him.

Our accountant is really sharp. In fact, right now he's standing out in the lobby by the gumball machine with two pennies and his pocket calculator.

He doesn't keep very good records. His bookkeeping would give Mother Tums indigestion.

Our new accounting firm is Kool and Laid Back. I am a little concerned. Their motto: "Hey, pal, close enough!"

I have a fabulous tax advisor. What he doesn't know about taxes could fill a prison cell.

My accountant started my day off badly by calling me. "I'm leaving the firm to go to work for the government." I asked, "What are you going to do?" He answered, "I'll be making license plates."

I was gripped with terror as I read the finance magazine's report of The Ten Richest People in America, and I saw our accountant was one of them.

ADAGE

Two frogs are talking to each other: "Time's fun when you're having flies."

It's a small world, but I wouldn't want to paint it.

A woman's place is in the home and she should go there directly from work.

There is more than one way to skin a cat. None of which I want to hear about.

Early to bed and early to rise makes a man healthy, wealthy and apt to get his own breakfast.

If at first you don't succeed, so much for sky diving.

Like the little skunk said when the wind changed, "Now it all comes back to me."

My wife's motto: "If the shoe fits, try on six or seven other pairs."

Most people can't stand prosperity...but then again, most people don't have to.

Live each day as though it were your last and someday you'll be right.

If at first you don't succeed, find out if the loser wins anything.

You can't live on borrowed time--except when it's been left on a parking meter.

Never put off for tomorrow what you can put off for good.

Let a smile be your umbrella and you'll get a mouthful of rain.

"You always hurt the one you love," said the porcupine.

Show me a man who walks with his head held high, and I'll show you a man who hasn't gotten used to his bifocals.

You can lead a horse to water, but don't expect him to put the shower curtain inside the tub!

There is nothing so simple that it can't be made more difficult.

To err is human, but when you wear the eraser out before the pencil, you're overdoing it!

If at first you don't succeed, you're running about average.

Remember, a trip of a thousand miles ends with a million steps.

Don't try to keep up with the Joneses...drag them down to your level... it's cheaper!

If you want to do something that will live forever, sign a mortgage.

If it's filed correctly, it won't be anything you're looking for.

Opposites attract. Just try driving north on a southbound street.

Lightning never strikes twice in the same place. Of course it seldom needs to.

Show me a man with both feet on the ground, and I'll show you a man who can't put his pants on.

If at first you don't succeed, pretend you weren't trying in the first place.

If at first you <u>do</u> succeed, try to hide your astonishment.

Remember, a bird in the hand makes it awfully hard to blow your nose.

People who live in glass houses always have to answer the doorbell.

You can't fool all the people all the time, but those turnpike signs come pretty close.

Two can live as cheaply as one--that is if one has lockjaw.

"The man who treats himself has a fool for a physician," but at least he doesn't have to wait three weeks for an appointment, or read old magazines in a doctor's office for two-and-a-half hours.

Be alert. The world needs more lerts.

Anyone who says, "Nothing could be finer than to be in Carolina in the morning," has lived a very deprived life.

Sticks and stones may break my bones, but words can never hurt me--unless somone hurls an unabridged dictionary at me.

Nice guys finish last. So do people who read and follow instructions.

Remember, wives, "A stitch in time" only encourages your husband to bring you more sewing.

"The way to a man's heart is through his stomach." Who said that? I think it was a guy in his tenth year of medical school.

Today is the first day of the rest of your life. And this poses a problem for those of you who are job hunting. Nobody likes to hire beginners.

Remember, today is the tomorrow you worried about yesterday--but not nearly enough.

When you walk through a storm, hold your head up high...and you'll get a stiff neck and soggy shoes.

Be true to your teeth or they'll be false to you.

A journey of a thousand miles usually begins with leaving the plane tickets on top of the kitchen table.

The sooner you fall behind, the more time you have to catch up.

It's not whether you win or lose, but who gets the blame.

"Summertime and the livin' is easy..." Tell that to a guy who sells sleds door-to-door.

If at first you don't succeed, welcome to Club Real World.

The man who can smile when everything else around him is going wrong is probably retiring next week, anyway.

Like my wife always says: "It isn't the thought. It's the gift that counts."

Remember, nothing lasts forever—with the possible exception of TV telethons.

He who laughs last is probably busy writing down the joke.

If your parents didn't have any children, chances are you won't either.

For every action there is an opposite and equal reaction--especially on Mondays.

A little learning is a dangerous thing. Just ask any kid who comes home with a bad report card.

It's hard to feel fit as a fiddle when you're shaped like a cello.

One good turn gets most of the blanket.

Remember, money can't buy poverty.

You're only young once, but you can be immature forever.

There are bigger things in life than money. Bills, for instance.

Behind every famous man is a woman telling him he's not so hot.

"One for the money, two for the show, three to get ready, and four to go...and ten for the babysitter when you get home."

If you can keep your head while others around you are losing theirs, you'll be the tallest guy in the room.

A woman's work is never done--thanks to daytime TV.

The happiest days of your life are the school days, providing your children are old enough to attend.

To make a long story short, don't tell it.

I've seen the future and it's much like the present--only longer.

If the early bird catches the worm, why doesn't the dumb worm sleep late?

Remember, money isn't everything. It isn't plentiful, for instance.

It's no disgrace to be poor, but it is mighty inconvenient.

People seldom think alike--until it comes to buying wedding gifts.

Next to being young and pretty, your best bet is to be old and rich.

If money talks, why isn't it screaming for help?

Just when you think you can make both ends meet, somebody moves the ends.

Where there's a will there's a lawsuit.

A sure sign of summer is when the chair gets up when you do.

People who say, "I slept like a baby" usually never had one.

He who eats more than he sleeps is fat and tired.

If you could have everything, where would you put it?

If at first you don't succeed, failure may be your thing.

A friend in need is a pest.

If you have nothing to do--don't do it here.

Where there's smoke, there's toast.

Beauty is only skin deep, but ugly goes clear to the bone.

The future isn't what it used to be.

He who hesitates is not only lost, but miles from the nearest exit.

If I had known I was going to live this long, I would have taken better care of myself.

We have seen the light at the end of the tunnel, and it is out.

Honest criticism is hard to take, particularly from a relative, a friend, an acquaintance, or a stranger.

To err is human, but all the time?

Never try to teach a pig to sing. You not only waste your time, but you also aggravate the pig.

Motto: Lousy salesmen have skinny kids.

Beat the system--unplug the computer.

When the going gets tough, the tough go shopping.

You can fool all of the people some of the time, and some of the people all of the time. And I think that's usually enough.

The difference between genius and talent is that genius gets a weekly paycheck.

It is better to have loved a short girl than never to have loved a tall.

Things improve with age? Did you ever attend a class reunion?

Light one small candle. It's better than paying a huge electric bill.

Laugh and the world laughs with you. Cry and your contact lenses fog up.

If you can keep your head when all others around you are losing theirs--it could be that you're the cause of it.

Remember--home is where the payments are.

With age comes wisdom--but sometimes age comes alone.

Start the day with a smile and get it over with early.

If you want a job done, give it to a busy man. He'll get his secretary to do it.

It's tough to plan for the future when you're too busy fixing the things you did yesterday.

There is no such thing as a <u>little</u> garlic.

No task is impossible, unless you appoint a committee to do it.

Live each day as if it were the first day of your marriage and the last day of your vacation.

Children and parents should never be in the same family.

Kids teach you thrift. You learn to do without everything you want.

Ask not for whom the bell tolls. You'll know when you get the phone bill.

The only thing that comes to him that waits is whiskers.

Nothing is impossible until it is sent to a committee.

A clean tie will always attract the soup of the day.

The severity of the itch is inversely proportional to the length of the reach.

 # ADAM AND EVE

Adam and Eve had the perfect marriage. Adam could never talk about the way his mother used to cook, and Eve could never brag about all the guys she could have married.

Do you realize that Eve was the only woman in history who, when invited to a party, could honestly say to her husband, "I have nothing to wear."

He has such bad luck with women that he wishes that Adam had died with all his ribs in his body.

Remember, it wasn't the apple on the tree that caused all the problems...it was the pair on the ground.

ADULT EDUCATION COURSES

Making Paranoia Work for You
Creative Suffering
Overcoming Peace of Mind
You and Your Birthmark
Whine Your Way to Alienation
Money Can Make You Rich
Talking Good: How to Improve Your Speech to Get a Better Job
I Made $100 in Real Estate
Underachievers' Guide to Very Small Business Opportunities
Filler Phrases for Thesis Writers

ADVERTISING

I discovered that I was middle-aged the day they showed a commercial for persistent backache, heartburn and receding hair, and I realized I was listening to it.

An example of truth in advertising would be a company that comes up with a name that befits the flavor of packaged soups---like Cream of Envelope.

A businessman displayed a hostile attitude toward advertising. I asked why. He said, "I tried advertising once when I owned a store. It was a disaster. People came from all over, even from the next county, and they bought almost everything I had in stock. Why that nearly put me out of business."

Headache commercials are always talking about fast, fast relief. Fast? It takes twenty minutes just to get the cotton out of the bottle.

 **ADVICE**

Never wear thongs unless your toes are all pointed in the same direction.

Here's a tip to make those shoes last longer. Take bigger steps.

Three rules for successful living: Never play cards with a man named 'Slim'; never eat at a place called 'Mom's'; never call a sumo wrestler 'Fatty'.

Misers aren't fun to live with, but they make wonderful ancestors.

When administering mouth-to-mouth resuscitation, be careful not to step on the victim's ears.

Here's some advice for this year's senior class: Learn a trade while you're in school so that when you graduate you'll know what kind of work you're out of.

John Paul Getty's advice for becoming rich and powerful: "Rise early, work late, and strike oil."

Henry Kissinger said, "The nice thing about being a celebrity is that when you bore people, they think it's their fault."

Today why not dial a few wrong numbers just to keep people on their toes.

Be clever today. Write a letter to <u>Reader's Digest</u> and let them know that they may already have won your subscription.

Despite what you read in the newspapers, people do not usually die in alphabetical order.

You can teach your dog to fetch by tying a cat to a boomerang.

Be suspicious when you find that your mechanic has clean fingernails.

On a slow weekend, why not put your pet chameleon on a plaid cloth.

Remember, when you go to court, you're putting your fate in the hands of twelve people who weren't smart enough to get out of jury duty.

The best way to constantly look young is to constantly hang around very old people.

Today is an excellent day for revenge. Pay the paper boy with a wet check.

Today is also a good day to learn patience. Spend some time playing fetch with your pet turtle.

Never try to put on a pullover sweater when eating a caramel apple.

Never kiss the hand of a lady after she's been at a self-service gas station.

Never try to adjust your clothing in a crowded elevator.

Never wave to your friends at an auction.

If you dance with a grizzly bear, you'd better let him lead.

Today's helpful hint: The easiest way to refold a road map is in a ball.

Gargling the first thing in the morning is an excellent way to discover if your neck leaks after you have shaved.

The best way to keep your wife in the kitchen is to put a phone there.

If at first you don't succeed, try doing it the way your wife told you.

If you want to catch a whale, first you must find a hundred pound worm.

If you believe, "It's a small world isn't it?" try touring it by bus sometime.

Never drop your contact lens during tap dancing class.

Never start a fight with a guy who's holding a tube of Krazy Glue.

Never shake hands with a man holding a chain saw.

As you get older, it's even more important to exercise, so you'll look good at your funeral.

AFTER SHAVE

I can always tell when the boss is going to arrive. His after-shave makes it from the parking lot to the office door about five minutes before he does.

He tried a new after shave this week--Evening in Camden.

He smells like an explosion in an Old Spice factory.

A sure after-shave for men...it smells just like Tupperware.

AIR-CONDITIONING

Isn't air-conditioning wonderful? You don't have to wait until December to catch a cold. Now you can have one all year around!

My car is equipped with 4-70 air-conditioning. I roll down all four windows and go seventy miles an hour.

We've got some tough economic problems to solve like--what do we do with the tremendous concentration of wealth in the hands of the air-conditioner repairmen?

AIRLINES

I flew on Crashlandia Airlines the other day. They had no in-flight movie, but every now and then your life would pass before your eyes.

The pilot was flying low over gas stations to ask for directions.

I flew one of those small airlines...Air Newark. The stewardess was a midget. She said, "Would you like coffee, tea or condensed milk?"

Next time a stewardess asks that you put your seat in an upright position, stand on your head.

They had mistletoe hanging at the airport so you could kiss your luggage good-bye.

You know what really bothers me about airlines? That I can't afford to go to Paris, Rome and Hong Kong--but my luggage has!

We played a new game on a small airline. It was "Guess Which Wheels Won't Come Down".

It was a great airline. In case of emergency a compartment above you opens up and a rabbit's foot comes down.

The airline was really cheap. No movies. We had to watch slides of the pilot's vacation.

The pilot made me a bit nervous when I overheard him saying. "Hey, I ain't gonna try and land this big old thing in the dark."

It also makes you a bit nervous when you hear the pilot say, "Now I guess we'll find out if these cushions really float."

I flew to Europe on a low budget airline. At dinnertime they gave us fishing rods and flew real low.

An airplane was approaching a tower. The tower called, "What time is it?"

The plane answered, "What difference does it make?"

The tower: "Well, if your Eastern it's 3 p.m.. If Delta, it's 1,500 hours, and if you're Piedmont, the big hand is on the twelve, and the little hand is on the three.

Two old ladies were aboard an airliner for their first flight. One asked the cabin attendant if they would be flying faster than sound.

"No," smiled the attendant, "not this flight."

"Oh, I'm glad," said one of the ladies. "We want to talk."

Isn't it great when they say, "Passengers, we are in a holding pattern over O'Hare Airport, but we expect to land in just a few minutes." Then they start showing "Gone With the Wind."

We were going to fly on Crashlandia Airlines, but they pulled the steps away and the plane fell over.

They couldn't afford in-flight movies, so the pilot flew low over drive-in movies.

A guy walks up to the ticket window and says, "I'd like two chances on your flight to Miami."

I took a flight on Flying Leap Airlines. They have a motto: "If you want on-time arrivals, pleasant courteous service, and no hassles with your baggage--take a flying leap."

It was one of those small airlines. For entertainment they passed around a hand puppet.

There were only four people on the plane, and the stewardess told me they lost my luggage. She said the strap broke on the roof rack.

It made me nervous when I heard the pilot telling the co-pilot, "The blue parts are water...the green is land."

A plane was going up and down and sideways. A nervous lady suggested, "Everybody pray."

A guy said, "I don't know how to pray."

The lady replied, "Well, do something religious."

So the guy started a bingo game.

Captain to passengers: "Now, there is no cause for alarm, but we felt you passengers should know that for the last three hours we've been flying without the benefit of radio, compass, radar or navigational beam. This means that in the broad sense of the word, I'm not quite sure in which direction we are headed. However, on the brighter side of the picture, we are making excellent time."

The pilot's voice came over the loudspeaker. "There is a fire in engine three, but don't worry. It should be put out shortly by the Atlantic."

I guess I'm overly sentimental, but when I go to the airport to leave this city, there's just one thing I hate to lose sight of--my luggage!

If you look like your passport photo, you're not well enough to travel.

While checking in at Scare-Ways Airlines, I came with three pieces of luggage. I said, "Please send one piece to Chicago, one to Los Angeles, and one to New York."
The guy behind the counter said, "I'm sorry. I can't do that."
I said, "Why not? You did it the last time I flew."

It makes you a little nervous when the pilot gets on the plane wearing a cowboy hat and a hospital gown.

We flew in on Gypsy Airlines. They have lower fares, but they steal your luggage.

I flew on Chinese Airlines. They served us food to take out.

Don't fly on foreign airlines. I get a little nervous when I see a pair of dice hanging from the cockpit and a dent in the side of the plane.

I came in on Scare-Ways Airlines. God's gift to Greyhound.

I had some good news and some bad news at the airport today. The good news is that the first two pieces of luggage out of the baggage chute were mine. The bad news is that they started out as one piece.

The only time that most people look like their passport photos is during a hijacking.

I flew in from Denver on Hayseed Airlines. Only cost $27.00, but it took ten hours. We lost some time over Nebraska doing a crop-dusting job.

The jet age can be defined as breakfast in London, dinner in San Francisco, and baggage in Buenos Aires.

How often do jumbo jets crash?
Generally, only once.

I can't figure how airlines work, but I do get a little suspicious when I fly from Philly to Boston, and three days later my luggage arrives smelling of soy sauce.

Last year we were in L.A., and it was incredible. We circled the airport for two hours. What made it even more incredible--we were in a bus!

I wouldn't say we were flying blind, but I got a look at the instrument panel, and it was in Braille.

I should have known what kind of flight it was going to be when the pilot boarded the plane carrying jumper cables.

I got a little nervous on my last trip when the pilot walked into the tourist section and showed everyone his learner's permit.

The airline was so small you had to have the exact change to get on the plane.

My last flight was really rough. The plane kept bouncing around all night. The only person who got any sleep was the pilot. They finally landed when we ran out of coal.

A jet flew a little too close to my house. I was walking from the kitchen to the living room, and the stewardess told me to sit down.

After much turbulence, a pilot appeared with a parachute strapped on his back and said, "Don't worry. I'm just going for help!"

"What's your position?" the radio tower asked the pilot.
"I'm five-feet-ten and in the front of the plane," he called back.

A little boy was pestering the stewardess throughout the entire flight. Finally, in desperation, she opened the door and said to the kid, "Okay, it's all right for you to go out and play now."

I flew Crashlandia Airlines no-frills flight Tuesday. The stewardess walked the aisle and announced, "All right, fasten your scotch tape."

Stewardess: "You are now landing in Cleveland. Please set your watches back 100 years."

I was on a plane that was almost hijacked. A guy put a gun to the pilot's head and demanded to be taken to the place where his luggage was going.

I just flew in, and boy, are my arms tired!

Incidentally, if you're going to fly, go by plane.

The stewardess on Crashlandia told us that in case of emergency, the meat loaf could be used as a floatation device.

When I fly, I think of three things: faith, hope, and gravity.

A Crashlandia plane had to make an emergency landing at sea. "Everybody who can swim," said the pilot, "get on the right side. Everybody who can't swim, get on the left side. Now, for you people on the right wing, when the water gets to your knees, start swimming. And for you people on the left wing--thank you for flying Crashlandia."

I flew Air-India. They have three classes. First class, where you are served a gourmet dinner. Business class, where you have a buffet. And the Untouchable class, where they give you a wooden bowl, and you beg for food in the first two classes.

Our pilot was laughing hysterically. I asked, "What's so funny?"
He said, "I was just thinking about what they'll be saying at the asylum when they find out I escaped."

Two fellas travelling East for the first time on a plane stopped in St. Louis and saw a little red truck come over for refueling. The plane landed in Cleveland, and again a little red truck rushed up to it. In Albany, the same thing happened. "This plane is making wonderful time," one said.
"Yes," said the other, "and that little, red truck isn't doing badly either."

Amazing how small airlines keep popping up. I flew on a new one the other day--Air Brooklyn.

The stewardess told the passengers, "Keep your seat belts on until we stop, or you may wind up in the airport before we do."

The problem with sitting in the middle seat of an airplane is that everything gets passed over you. For instance, the person seated next to me asked, "I wonder what they're serving for dinner?"
I replied, "Wait a minute. I'll check my lap."

 # AMBITION

I never asked for much in life. I just wanted to be born into a family where soul food is pheasant under glass.

As the ambitious salesman used to say, "Another day, another dollar." However, if you're working on a straight commission, that could be an exaggeration.

 # AMTRAK

One never needs to be bored. If you have three or four spare hours, there are so many things you can do to occupy your time--like making a phone call to Amtrak.

For those of you who have never telephoned Amtrak information and reservations, they have special numbers. Those numbers are for people who like to hear busy signals.

ANCESTRY

I traced my family tree and found out that I had an uncle who died of Dutch Elm disease.

I can trace my family all the way back to Columbus. I even have a sister in Akron!

Uncle Rodney was run over by a steam roller. Aunt Shirley held up well during the services, until they lowered the envelope into the ground.

The best part of his family tree is underground.

ANNIVERSARY

We were invited to an anniversary party. The host said, "When you come in the building, just push the button for the eighth floor with your elbow."
"Why my elbow?" I asked.
"Well, you're not coming empty-handed, are you?" the friend replied.

My wife and I are celebrating our tin anniversary. Seven years of eating out of cans.

I bought her a mink outfit: A rifle and a trap.

ANTIQUES

The popularity of antiques is really something. Right now there are 25 million Americans who have things that are old, funny-looking, don't work, and are kept around for sentimental purposes. Some of them are called antiques--and the rest are called husbands.

ANXIETY

Nervous? I feel like a pizza on the way to Orson Welles.

I won't say how insecure people are getting, but Dial-a-Prayer just added two more numbers.

APARTMENT

Tour guide: "This building has been here for over three hundred years. Not a stone has been touched, nothing has changed, nothing replaced."
Tourist: "They must have the same landlord we do!"

I don't want to complain about the way our landlord is maintaining the building, but yesterday I slipped on the ice--in front of our bathtub.

This past winter my great landlord set the thermostat up to 78 degrees. And next winter he promises to hook up the thermostat.

APPEARANCES

I have another big appearance coming up this weekend. I've been asked to be grand marshal at my neighbor's garage sale.

APPLAUSE

I can see that you are an intelligent audience and that you are saving your thunderous ovation for the end of my speech.

ARMY

They ask such silly questions like, "If you were in command at the Alamo, what would you do?"
I said, "Fire the architect."
They said, "Why?"
I said, "No back door."

A small boy was leading a donkey by an army camp. A couple of soldiers wanted to have some fun with the boy. "Why are you holding onto your brother so tightly?"
"So he won't join the army!" was the reply.

I just tried on my old army uniform, and the only thing that fits is the tie.

One great thing about the army--you never have to decide what to wear.

You get a little worried about some of the guys that show up at the draft board. Especially the ones that try to pronounce the eye chart.

While he was in the army, he saved the entire regiment. He shot the cook.

I remember when I was in the army not doing well on the rifle range. I told the sarge that I felt like shooting myself. He said, "Take along a couple extra bullets."

He was the only guy on Normandy Beach with a blanket and a beach ball.

He was a great military strategist. He used to fire on his own troops just to confuse the enemy.

(to soldier facing firing squad) "Are there any last requests?"
Soldier: "I suppose re-enlisting is out of the question?"

He served on a submarine in the Navy and went to sleep with the windows open.

I remember my uniform. What a fit! I'd stand at attention, and my uniform would stand at ease.

You remember the war. It was in all the papers.

In combat, I ran so fast that the tongues of my shoes were panting.

The Army classified me as 2-F, 2-F. "Too feeble to fight."

Evan was a veteran of World War II, but the notes don't specify which side he was on.

He learned some things in the Army that have sustained him thoughout his entire adult life. For instance...little potatoes are easier to peel than big potatoes.

When war was declared, he was the first guy in town to go down to the front...window and wave goodbye to the troops.

I went into the army in 1964 when the Selective Service wasn't being too selective.

I spent hours and hours doing all kinds of vital things to defend democracy--like policing the lawn.

As I remember it, we had deadly enemies in World War II, Japan Germany, Italy, and cigarette butts. But not necessarily in that order. I used to have a nightmare about that lawn. One time I dreamed the Germans flew over and it was awful. They made a direct hit on that lawn--not with bombs--with candy wrappers.

We used to have a saying in the army. If you had a difficult intellectual problem, always ask a sergeant. He'd know a private in his company that could solve it.

You know what I liked about the army? They gave you your own clothes. When I was in the army they had 14 million men and three sizes--too big, too small, and out-of-stock.

I think the army's idea of uniforms was to make the enemy over-confident. I had a coat so long, it came with shoelaces.

In those days everything you wore was olive drab. One day I fainted on the lawn, and it took them three days to find me.

The shoes they gave us were absolutely waterproof. If it rained, not a drop leaked out.

The army always had the right knack for putting the right man at the right job. They drafted a brain surgeon whose hand was so steady he could cut to within a thousandth of an inch, and the army really used him. On Sunday, he was the guy who cut the roast beef.

You have no idea what the food was like. For punishment they gave you seconds.

What does an army cook do when he retires, anyway? Every recipe he knows ends up with, "Serves 3,000."

A platoon was taking a few minutes to eat a meal of lukewarm, grayish looking stew. A sergeant poked at it with his spoon and said, "If my wife could see this, she would be mad."
The soldier next to him said, "Why would she be mad?"
The sergeant took one more look at the awful stew and said, "I think it's her recipe."

In ROTC he was voted the most likely to become the Unknown Soldier.

He joined the Navy to see the world and spent four years in a submarine.

All the time he was in the war, his wife kept sending him nagging letters. He couldn't even enjoy the war in peace!

Our drill sergeant was really tough. He was so tough he wore a toupee...that he kept on with a nail!

Being in the army was always kinda tough; someone was always telling you what to do, where to go, what to wear, what to say. Of course, there's another institution that allows civilians to experience the same thing: it's called marriage.

When I joined the army my uniform jacket fit fine, but my trousers were just a little loose around the armpits.

The sergeant said, "This bullet will penetrate two feet of solid wood. So remember, keep your heads down."

I used to wonder why army clothiers were inspired to make army fatigues that olive color. Then I saw army food.

Tough sergeant: "Private, I bet that when I die you'll come to my funeral just to spit on my grave."
Private: "No, sir, I promised myself that when I get out of the army I'll never stand in line again."

I was classified 5-F. That means that if the U.S. was invaded, the Army would send me overseas.

He blew up six ammo dumps, seven factories, and a ball bearing plant, and then they shipped him overseas.

In the army, he was always where the bullets were the thickest--at the munitions depot.

At Fort Benning, they named an obstacle course in his honor.

ATTENDANCE

Attendance at one of our games was really bad this year. Only 45 people showed up. It was such an intimate crowd that instead of playing the National Anthem, we played "Feelings".

AUDIENCE REPARTEE

(receiving award) The timing of this award is very special to me. And the reason that it's so special is that I am grateful that it wasn't presented to me posthumously.

(taking watch off and putting it on podium) Don't let this comfort you. It's a sun dial.

(when flowers align podium or are on banquet table) I don't know. I've died before a lot of audiences before, but this is the first time that anyone has been thoughtful enough to send flowers.

(when a joke dies) Look out! You're getting that glassy stare again.

(when the phone rings) Would someone please answer that? It might be the phone.

I'm like the cross-eyed discus thrower. I don't set a lot of records, but I do keep people alert.

The program is nearly over. I can sense that the audience is still with me--but if I run really fast I can shake you off.

I won't say my show was bad last night, but half the empty seats got up and left!

My act was a great success. It was the audience that failed miserably.

Please keep on clapping. One more burst of applause like that and I'll get paid for overtime.

I asked him where he had put his name tag (sticker). He said, "Young man, I don't need it. I memorized it."

I asked the program chairman how long I should speak at the Kiwanis meeting. He replied, "Well, speak as long as you want. The luncheon starts at 1:15 and we all leave at 1:45."

(after someone snaps your picture) That should be a dandy!

(after great round of applause) Lock the doors. I'm not going to let this group get away.

(after a flattering intro) Am I really that good? I want more money!

(closing) I know something you folks don't. I just finished my program.

(in hot room) Did someone just throw more logs on the air-conditioning system?

(after no applause) Well, that was a wonderful round of indifference.

(no applause) Thanks for that great burst of silence.

You know, it is possible that these jokes could be worse. They could be mine.

(to a tall man) Look at the size of this guy. If he falls down, he's out of town.

I had a wonderful evening, but this isn't it.

I've spoken to literally thousands of audiences and have enjoyed being with dozens of them.

Please laugh a little faster. My time is short.

You're my kind of audience--trapped.

That's my E.F. Hutton joke. You tell it and suddenly the crowd is quiet.

Sir, I can read your mind, and obviously I don't have to be a speed reader to do it.

(while lowering microphone) How do you like that? I've been waiting so long to speak, I've shrunk.

My act was so bad the people in the back kept hollering, "Up in front."

Sir, I'd like to leave one thought with you, but do you have a place to put it?

Here's an idea. Let's all get down on our hands and knees and look for your I.Q..

(to an audience of doctors) This is the first time that I have ever addressed an audience of doctors, so I've tried to do some of the things my mother told me to do before going to the doctor: Put on clean underwear...try to look poor...

We will now take a look at the instant replay footage so you can get a close-up of that joke dying.

Be honest now. What do you think of our chef? Really, what this man doesn't know about cooking, you could put in a stomach pump.

I feel very close to this audience--closer than I've ever felt to an audience before. So I'd like to take this opportunity to invite myself to your homes for Christmas.

I feel like a Hindu snake charmer with a deaf cobra.

(pointing to a man wearing a plaid jacket) Somewhere out on the parking lot is a '52 Dodge without seat covers.

Here's an idea. Why don't we all stroll out to the parking lot and watch our cars depreciate?

It's a borderline thrill to be here.

It's a semi-pleasure to be here.

I'm as popular as the lookout at Pearl Harbor.

I'm as popular as the watchman on the Titanic.

(bad microphone) Can you hear me? You know, I've spoken to more dead mikes than an Irish undertaker.

(when someone walks in late) Glad you could join us. Where have you been? You're lucky. I almost marked you absent.

Hey, pay attention back there. This could be on the mid-term.

If you don't understand a joke, just raise your hand and we'll discuss it.

Last night's audience was so wild. Some guy yelled, "Louder!" during the silent meditation.

All you people here that are having such a good time. What makes you so sure that you locked your front door and turned off the television?

Before we begin tonight, I have a special request. Would the owner of the convertible with the purple fenders, tutti-frutti body, feather boa hood ornament and pink satin seat covers please report to the front of the room? There is nothing wrong, we just want to see what you look like.

People have been rather indifferent to my performances lately. Last week an audience gave me a shrugging ovation.

(when a slide doesn't appear and the audience is looking at a blank screen) I love this picture. It shows the results of (name's) aptitude test.

(when you garble) And, now, I'd like to repeat that for those of you who don't speak Flub.

(response to a long question) Please repeat that. I'm sorry, I must have dozed off.

The great thing about holding an event like this at night and downtown is that there is always a place to park. If all the spaces are filled, just be patient for a few minutes until the next car is stolen.

It's been more than a thrill for me to be here--it's been an inconvenience.

This group would throw a grenade at Bambi's mother.

I'm not going to be long tonight. I've only got this jacket rented until 9 p.m..

(receiving an award) I don't deserve this award. But then again, I've got arthritis, and I don't think I deserve that either.

(after a big welcome) Wow! All I can say is exercise caution. I know guys running for Congress with less encouragement than that.

(closing) You've been marvelous, and as you leave here tonight, I'd like you to remember one thing...and that is where you parked your car.

(closing) In my speaking experience I have learned that there are two types of speakers I can do without: Those who never stop to think and those who never think to stop. I trust I haven't been either. Good night.

(to someone in a loud outfit) I like that combination. Tell me, did you choose it purposely or did the light burn out in your clothes closet?

Are there any questions? (if none) Are there any answers? Are there any survivors?

Wow, I've been sitting up here so long, that spotlight has faded my suit.

Someone came up to me after the program and said, "Boy were you terrible."
My host said, "Just ignore that guy. He just goes around repeating what everybody else says."

And so, as I come to the end of my talk, I have to tell you people what a thrill it is to look out over this audience of so many people that have never heard me speak before--and are now vowing never to make the same mistake twice.

I like your vocabulary. It's limited, but stimulating.

My last show opened up with great difficulty. The curtain was up.

It wasn't easy doing the show. The seats faced the stage.

The night after the critics' reviews, they sent the audience home in a cab.

The next night they arrested the doorman for loitering.

I don't care if they walk out on me. It's when they walk <u>toward</u> me that I worry.

When my show opened, the mayor gave me the key to the city. The next day they changed the locks.

A friend called me after the show and said, "Well, you'll never be better than you were tonight."

There is a problem with practicing your speech in front of a mirror. You'll never see that interested an audience again.

(closing) Well, it's been a wonderful evening. Kind of a shame that we spent it here.

If you think my program is monotonous, you should see my home life!

(after a long discourse by an audience member) Sir, your answer--does a question come with it?

Your train of thought, sir, does it have a caboose?

(after an involved question) Would you repeat the question? No, let me change that. <u>Can</u> you repeat the question?

I am pleased to be here tonight. If you live in New Jersey, you're glad to be anywhere.

It's certainly nice to be here in your town. The last time I was here, it was closed.

It's fun to get dressed up for an evening out, isn't it? You girls walk into the dressing room and there you are surrounded by sprays, lotions, perfumes, brightly-colored clothes...and that's just your husband's stuff.

What a crowd! There are an awful lot of people here...really awful!

(when there are a lot of empty seats) This must be a very wealthy town. I see that each of you bought two or three seats.

Oh, my goodness, look at you! Was anyone else hurt in the accident?

Thank you for giving me a piece of your mind. I appreciate it. Especially when your inventory is so low.

I'll make a deal with you. If you laugh at one joke, you'll get five free!

Is that your husband? How long has he been that way?

The last audience I spoke for was so small it looked like a testimonial dinner for (Benedict Arnold or some current unpopular figure).

(when someone precedes you with a great opening) I wouldn't give this spot to the cleaners.

I always enjoy being with a group of prominent, successful, intelligent businesspersons, and I even enjoy spending some evenings with a group like yours.

(if you're overlooked) That's perfectly okay. Now I know how the celery feels at a Thanksgiving dinner.

(when receiving an award) Getting this plaque is an enlightening experience. Up till now, I never knew Earl Scheib did engraving.

I'm not used to receiving awards. Up till now I've always taken extreme pride in my humility.

(if people get up and leave) Now that's what I like. A moving, standing ovation.

(when a joke dies) I think I'll try that one on this side of the house. This side is dead.

You might as well laugh now 'cause this isn't going to get any funnier.

I know you are out there because I can hear you breathing.

(when dishes crash to the floor) I'm sure it was nothing. Try to get back to sleep.

Let's have nothing out of you except breathing--and very little of that!

I don't have to do this for a living. I can always starve to death.

I'm sorry. I forgot your first and last name.

(when audience groans at a joke) C'mon now. You got in for nothing and that's exactly what you're going to get.

(after generous applause greets you) Not only are you kind, but you're also very perceptive.

Just remember, as I tell jokes tonight--laugh. It's not only your right, it's your responsibility.

During the middle of my most recent presentation, a member of the audience stood up and said, "Is there a Christian Scientist in the audience?"
"I am a Christian Scientist," a lady answered.
"Would you mind changing places with me?" said the man. "I'm sitting in a draft."

I don't get many laughs with my material, but sometimes the smiles can be deafening.

Well, tonight our program is improvised. That's show business talk meaning 'confused and disorganized'.

(closing) I'd like to do more for you, but my 24-hour deodorant is starting to give out.

And if the high school teacher who told me I'd never amount to anything is watching tonight, let me say one thing. "You little fortune teller, you!"

(carry out a shovel and throw it on the floor) This is just in case I die out here.

Incidentally, I am hard of hearing, so if the applause is not very loud, I won't be able to hear you.

While driving here tonight my wife and I saw a very long funeral procession. I said, "Wow, I wonder who died?"
She said, "The guy in the first car."

(after weak applause) Well, that sounded like a caterpillar in sneakers going across a shag rug.

And for those of you who came in late, "Aren't you glad?"

I've travelled far and wide as an after-dinner speaker. I found it's safer that way.

When I started in this business I had only 25¢ to my name. Now I'm $55,000 in debt.

Isn't this some place? No cover, no minimum, no talent.

Did anyone lose a large roll of bills with a rubberband around them? Well, I found the rubberband!

(to a heckler) Look buddy, pretend I'm your wife and ignore me for awhile, okay?

(when a joke flops) And I was expecting so much from that one...

(no laughs; threateningly) Remember, you could be replaced by an audience.

It's always a treat to be here in this great city (pull out card and read off name), and it's even a greater thrill to be here with this world-renown company, (pull out another card). For those of you who just came in, I'm the speaker of the evening, and my name is (pull out last card).

After the show, there was a long line of people asking for my autograph. They all wanted to see if I could write.

I don't mind if you look at your watch while I'm up here, but it really bothers me when you shake them.

(bearded man) Get a load of that beard! Were you born or trapped?

This is an important evening for me. I'm celebrating my sixteenth anniversary of using this material.

Last night I had the audience in the palm of my hand--which gives you an idea of how large it was.

Some people live on borrowed time. I live on borrowed jokes.

(when one individual laughs at a joke) Look, there will be no individual laughing here. You either laugh with the rest of the group or I'll have to ask you to leave.

(when no one laughs) How can all you people sleep out there with all these lights on?

(long banquet) This reminds me of a similar experience I had when I read the entire Sunday Inquirer from cover to cover. My suit went in and out of style four times.

True composure is laughing at your best joke--when the speaker ahead of you tells it.

I'm pleased. Tonight we've covered more ground than a Weight Watchers picnic.

I don't think I'll need the microphone. After all, with a wife, three children, a dog, and a mother-in-law in the home, I'm used to talking loudly.

(to those who came in late) Come in. Sit down. Is there anyone here that you don't know?

Wow! This room is crowded! Walking around here is like trying to play a trombone in a telephone booth.

It's been a pleasure being in a small town like this where people are not continually exposed to top-flight talent.

I still get enjoyment from being recognized in restaurants and airports. The other day, a couple approached me at the Philly Airport and said, "Aren't you (fill in your name)?" It was my parents.

(when you hear a police siren outside) Listen to that! My wife has arrived to take me home.

(bald emcee) Look at that flesh-colored hair. Now I know why they call him a polished speaker.

I have five kids, none of whom pay any attention to me. Could it be that they're in training to become an audience?

This is an English speaking audience, isn't it?

There's not much that I can say about this dinner tonight that hasn't already been said by the Department of Health.

Please don't sit too close. Some people have actually been scorched by my sizzling delivery.

(blow on the microphone several times) If there's anything I hate, it's speaking into a dusty microphone.

I apologize for being late. We had an accident at home. Our basset hound jack-knifed.

In conclusion, please take these suggestions home and sleep on them. I see that some of you already have a head start.

I want to thank you. This audience has made me feel right at home-- which gives you an idea of the kind of family life I have.

(when an audience responds with generous applause) Ah, yes, you're so right!

Thank you for your undivided attention. And now we come to the part of the evening where we give the prize for the person who drew the best doodles.

(during a long banquet) I didn't realize anything could last this long without Saran Wrap or aluminum foil.

I knew the program was in trouble when I saw my calendar watch change during the appetizer.

All my jokes are original, which means I can't remember who I got them from.

Everytime I write a new joke, some guy uses it the year before.

Don't make a fuss over me. Please treat me the same as you would any great performer.

It is great to be in this unique town. Unique coming from the Latin unus for one and equus meaning horse.

I tried to insure my jokes, but the insurance company turned me down. They said the mortality rate is too high.

(long question) Could you please review the highlights of that question? Our lease runs out in July.

(when the lights go out) Hey, I told the power company that the check was in the mail!

(camera flash) Please take another. I can still see out of my right eye.

(if there is an umpire or sports official in the crowd) Can everyone hear me alright? (to ump) Can you <u>see</u> me alright?

(joke dies) When would you like me to call you in the morning?

The program committee asked me if I needed anything, and I told them just an audience--asleep or awake, and I see that they've provided me with some of each.

There are so many celebrities here that I'm the only one I've never heard of.

As the cow said to the farmer on the winter day, "Thanks for the warm hand."

I'll keep my remarks to fifteen minutes due to throat trouble. Your program chairman told me, he'd choke me if I spoke longer than fifteen minutes.

(when joke dies) I've got millions of 'em. Don't ask me why I used that one!

(after banquet) I won't keep you long. I'm dying for something to eat.

(when one person applauds) What's a matter? Did your hands fall asleep?

When I came to my last song, the audience went wild with applause. They knew I was done.

If you keep reacting like that, I won't tell you my funny stuff!

Don't worry. Loud applause doesn't frighten me.

I don't have to do this for a living. I could always be out there sleeping with you folks.

I'm as nervous as a mailman at a dog show.

(sight gag) Pour water from pitcher into glass, then drink from pitcher. Then pour glass of water back into the pitcher.

When I got off the plane, I was met by my fan club. Mother never looked better.

(someone walking out) It's down the hall and to the left.

Please save most of your applause for later. I've got a weak finish.

(no laughs) I'm glad you're not laughing. I was looking forward to a quiet evening.

(to a man in a tux) I like your outfit. Did you mug a penguin?

Look who's here. Did you pick the lock on your cage again?

What do you do for a living? You are living, aren't you?

You're such a great audience, I'd work for nothing...Come to think of it...

First time I heard that joke, I laughed so hard tears rolled down my bib.

I'm not nervous. I'm a regular rock of Jell-o.

My wife asked, "Well did you kill the audience?"
"No." I answered, "they were dead when I got there."

Our next speaker will be right with us as soon as he slips out of his strait-jacket.

Thank you for that enthusiastic reception which you gave to our previous presenters. It's nice to perform for an audience that doesn't get out much.

I really feel badly for the 175 chickens and 7,000 peas that have given their lives to make this dinner possible.

Here's a speaker who's an inspiration to people everywhere. They figure if he can make it to the top, anybody can!

Before I go any further, I'd like my wife to stand so you can greet her. (pause and look around the room). You know, I thought it was awfully quiet after we stopped at the last service station.

(when someone leaves early) Don't you know that there's a substantial penalty for early withdrawal?

Can those of you way in the back hear me? If not, please don't holler. Just wave your binoculars.

I noticed that his speech was written on recycled paper--which undoubtedly explains some of his jokes.

And to think I cancelled a dentist appointment to be here.

I would have enjoyed your remarks if I had a better seat. The one I had faced you.

Look at Sam over there. He's nodding off again. I ordinarily just see him during working hours, and it never occurred to me that he might sleep at night, too.

I could form an attachment for you, and that attachment would fit right over your mouth.

(after long intro) Do you realize that if I were one of those speakers who needed no introduction, we'd all be getting in our cars and going home by now?

(sip from water glass) Wow! I've just got to get that recipe!

I wish I had an answer to that question, because I'm tired of answering it.

I'm as confused as a termite in a yo-yo.

Would the owner of the Mercedes with the phone, TV set, stereo and faculty parking sticker please report to the front of the auditorium? There is nothing wrong. We just want to find out how you do it!

(to heckler) Next time you give your old clothes away, stay with them.

Show some respect for that joke. It's older than you are.

AUTUMN

When fall arrives I can't help think that what America really needs is an obedience school for trees.

Ah, yes, autumn, the season when every man in America gets dressed up and has that certain air about him--mothballs.

Between baseball, football, golf and tennis matches--October is the month husbands spend the greatest amount of time watching TV. In fact one woman was concerned that if her husband died, she didn't have anything that would remind her of the way he always looked to her. So she had a picture taken of the back of his head.

Fall is my favorite season of the year in Los Angeles, watching birds change color and fall to the ground.

Autumn is the time of the year when the trees in my backyard turn red. It happens every fall when my wife spray paints the redwood picnic table.

Terror is when you open the cedar chest to pull out your fall clothes and you hear a moth burp.

DO-IT-YOURSELF
SPACE.

WRITE YOUR
OWN JOKE
HERE!

BABYSITTERS

Babysitters have very modest requirements. For instance, our baby-sitter asks for one thing: That the stereo, TV, phone, refrigerator and baby be in the same room.

The worst part about spending $75 on an evening out is that when you get home the babysitter looks like she had a better time than you did.

We've discovered a foolproof way to make sure the sitter watches our kids. Right before she arrives at the house we put the kids in the refrigerator.

(to audience) Is there a Mr. and Mrs. Smith in the audience? Please don't be alarmed. Your babysitter just called and wants to know where the fire extinguisher is.

When I was asked for a reference for our last babysitter, I said she was unpunctual, lazy and rude. How can I say anything in her favor? I guess I could always say she's got a good appetite and sleeps well.

You can always tell an experienced sitter. She's the one who thinks that the way to every room in the house is through the refrigerator.

BACHELOR

I stopped by to visit a bachelor friend, and it was really touching. There he was standing in front of the sink doing the dish.

You can always spot a bachelor at the laundromat. He's the one trying to stuff his clothes into the video game.

BALD

This next joke is so funny, you'll laugh so hard your hair will fall out. (to bald person) Oh, I see that you've heard it already.

One of the nice things about being bald is that when company comes over, all you have to do is straighten your tie.

New Schmel Hair Tonic is not guaranteed to grow hair but what it will do is shrink your scalp to fit what hair you've got.

He washed his hair this morning and forgot where he put it.

I don't care what you say about baldness. At least it's neat.

If there was a tooth fairy for hair, can you imagine what (bald person) would be worth today?

He's not bald, he just has flesh-colored hair.

He's not bald. He just happens to have the world's worst case of ingrown hair.

He's not bald. He's just too tall for his hair.

A lot of people don't know this, but last week he quietly switched from Head and Shoulders to Mop and Glo.

When he said his right ear was warmer than his left ear, I knew his toupee was on crooked.

My hair's getting thin, but then again, who wants fat hair?

There are three ways that men can wear their hair: Parted, unparted and departed.

I wouldn't say that he's bald. He just has a part that won't quit.

Ten years ago he had thick, wavy hair. Now the waves are gone, and there's nothing but beach.

He's so bald, his head keeps slipping off the pillow when he sleeps.

When the Lord makes something good, he doesn't cover it up.

Tell me, are you bald or did you just shave too high?

He keeps his hat on with a suction cup.

We read in the Bible that the very hairs on our head are numbered, and in his case, each year it gets a little easier for the Lord to take inventory.

I won't even attempt to tell him a hair-raising story.

Medical research clearly shows that there is just one thing that will prevent baldness--hair!

He looks like the lone survivor of an Indian raid that got scalped and put somebody else's hair on.

This new hair tonic is really something. Last week I spilled some on my comb, and now it's a brush.

A man enters a barber shop, hands his toupee to the barber and says, "I want a haircut and a shampoo, and I'll be back in half an hour."

Sure he's getting bald. People were certainly right when they said he'd come out on top.

I first met him on a Chicago street corner. There he was in that tan trench coat, his hair blowing in the wind...and him too proud to run after it.

I saw him down at the barber shop today...reminiscing.

There is this solace about being bald. If you find a hair in your food, you know it's not yours.

He's not bald. He just has a full head of skin.

He got that way (bald) by getting smart with the barber. When the barber asked, "How do you want your hair cut?" he quipped, "Off!"

 **BANKS**

The IRA is a terrific deal. If you put in $2,000 a year you can defer taxes on it for 30 years until you are a millionaire--and we all know that millionaires never have to pay taxes.

I'm determined that I won't go through life pinching pennies and worrying about the family budget all the time. Like I told the kids last night, "Forget the family budget. Give the parakeet another seed."

You can always tell a bank is in trouble by the little things. Like when they come to repossess your toaster.

A banker's houseboat was sinking so he sent an S.O.S.. The Coast Guard replied, "What is your position?"
The man said, "I'm First Vice-President of the First National Bank. Please hurry!"

The bank phoned and said, "Mr. Roberts, your account is overdrawn $19.27."
"Look up a month ago and see how I stood," Roberts answered.
The teller replied, "Last month you had a balance of $217.46."
"Did I call you then?" Roberts asked.

Rumors have been circulating that many United States banks are being controlled by the mob. Well, I went right to our local bank president and said, "That's ridiculous. That could never happen here, could it, Babyface?"

I would like to open a joint account with someone that has money.

I've never been overdrawn at the bank, just underdeposited.

His wife entered the bank and said, "I'd like to open a joint account. A checking account for me and a deposit account for my husband."

Credit manager: "How much money do you have in the bank?"
Loan applicant: "I don't know. I haven't shaken it recently."

The bank just threw me out of their Christmas club. They said I wasn't coming to their meetings.

A man handed a paper bag to the teller, pointed a gun at him and said, "Fill up the bag or I'll shoot." The teller said, "Okay, but you may want to straighten your tie. Your picture's being taken."

The bank has a realistic idea of my present financial situation. The latest batch of scenic checks they sent me has a scene of an automobile graveyard.

My bank is really fussy. They require identification when I deposit money.

"I'm here to see the lone arranger."
"He's on vacation."
"Okay, let me speak to Tonto, then."

The bank turned down his vacation loan. To retaliate, he bought a five-pound fish, wrapped it, put it in a safe deposit box, borrowed vacation money from another bank, and then left town for three weeks.

Teller: "I can cash your check if you can identify yourself."
Woman pulls mirror out of purse and looks in it: "Yes, that's me alright."

BANQUETS

(to a guest that always dresses casually) You can tell he's taken this banquet seriously. His socks match.

(opening) As my Dad used to say...(long pause). My Dad wasn't much of a talker.

Let's forget all our problems tonight. Relax. After all, isn't it silly how little things get to people? Right now, for instance, I could say two words that would spoil the evening for every waiter in this room. "Separate Checks."

First, I'd like to compliment the chef on this marvelous dinner. I didn't even know that Black and Decker made steaks.

(after introduction) Now I know what a stack of pancakes must feel like when the syrup is poured on.

I've been introduced by people of rank before, but this was the rankest.

(after audience has been seated for a long time) Let's all stand up and fluff our pillows.

I've been to so many chicken dinners that when I go home, I no longer sleep--I roost.

I can tell what you're thinking. Now that we're done with our ham, here comes the baloney.

 **BARBERS**

"Haven't I shaved you before?"
"No, sir, I got that scar on my neck during World War II."

Sign in a barber shop window: "We're not responsible if our barbers' opinions conflict with those of your analyst."

Sign in barbershop window: "Five barbers. Come in and enjoy panel discussions."

Doesn't it bug you when you have to sit and listen to your barber tell you how to save the world when he can't even save your hair?

I switched barbers when I saw him ordering supplies: two bottles of hair tonic, two bottles of shaving lotion, and sixteen bottles of iodine.

After being cut six times by the barber, the customer said, "May I have a razor?"

"Why?" said the barber. "Do you want to shave yourself?"

"No, just defend myself," the customer replied.

The barber asked, "How do you like your haircut?"

"It's nice," came the reply, "but could you make it a little longer in the back?"

Barber: (shaving customer) "Did you have ketchup for lunch?"
Customer: "No, why do you ask?"
Barber: "Then I must have cut your throat."

I was in the barber shop watching the barber shave another customer. Suddenly a mouse ran up the barber's leg. You should have seen the surprised look on the customer's face when it finally rolled to a stop.

 # BASEBALL

Two things kept me from being a professional athlete. When I played baseball I could never hit a curve ball. And when I played golf--I could.

I'll say one thing about the Chicago Cubs. I didn't think anything could be in the cellar this long and not be an oil heater.

Did you read on the sports pages about the ballplayer who was mired in a terrible slump--he did a TV shaving commercial, took a swipe at his face and missed!

Someone asked me why I switched from a 34-ounce bat to a 29-ounce bat. I told them, "Well, it's lighter to carry back to the bench when I strike out."

A fan yelled to me, "Hey, the only thing you know about pitching is that you can't hit it."

They once had a day for me. It was the "Pat Williams' Day Off."

I'll never forget my first baseball game. I slid into home plate in a cloud of dust. The only problem was I was coming to bat.

Baseball is the only sport where you can keep the ball if it lands in the stands. Take stock car racing for instance. You never hear stock car racing fans yell, "I've got it."

Little League coach to whipped boys: "Fellas, don't get down on yourselves. You did your best and shouldn't feel badly that you lost the game. Keep your spirits up. Besides, your parents should be very proud of you boys. In fact, just as proud of the parents of the daughters on the team that beat you."

One pitcher has been knocked out of the game so many times, when he goes to the mound, instead of a baseball cap, he wears a shower cap, and instead of a resin bag, he has soap on a rope.

I once played on a team that lost 27 games in a row. The next game, we got rained out, and the manager threw a victory party.

The manager came up to me and said, "Remember all those batting tips, catching tips and base-running hints I gave you?"
I said, "Sure I do, Skipper."
The manager said, "Well, forget them. We just traded you."

I'll say this about my baseball career. I was non-violent. Sometimes I'd go for weeks without hitting anything.

I always try to provide sound, reasoned, mature guidance for my kids. For instance, my son can't decide on whether to be a professional comedian or a baseball player. I told him to stick to baseball. He can always play for the Cubs and have the best of both worlds.

You know that your team is in trouble when your pitching machine throws a no-hitter.

Frank Howard when playing for the Washington Senators, pointed out the white seats where some of his longest homeruns landed. He was asked what the green seats meant and said, "Oh, they represent the times I struck out."

Each time I was traded, the sportswriters announced: "This is a trade that will hurt both teams."

A billboard on the outfield fence read, "The (team name) use Lifebuoy." Some wise guy sneaked in one night and painted under it--"And they still stink."

I always get the same seat at the ballpark. Between the hotdog vendor and his best customer.

I know my son's going to be an all-star pitcher. He already has a fantastic breaking ball. Just the other day, with just one pitch he broke a window, a lamp, a mirror, and a vase.

It's weird. Ten dollars can feed a third world family for a month, or an American family for six minutes at the ball park.

One player I know was thrown out of a game just for singing the National Anthem to an umpire. Not the whole anthem...just, "Oh, say can you see...?"

One of the players heckled the ump..."Hey, ump, if you follow the white line you'll find first base." At a night game, "Hey, ump, how can you sleep with all these lights on?" Or, "Shake your head--your eyes are stuck!"

A fellow walked up to the ticket window of the cellar-dwelling team and said, "I'd like four seats for tonight's game. Which do you recommend--first or third base?"
The ticket agent said, "How about second base? We're not using that this year!"

Someone asked the rookie, "What size hat do you wear?"
He replied, "How should I know. This is the first week of spring training."

The Chicago Cubs won't have to worry about getting the flu this year. So far they haven't caught anything.

Everyone expects him to lead the league in steals--especially his parole officer.

He does the things I've never seen a young ballplayer do before, and I hope I never see again.

He's got all the tools--which is a good thing, because by All-Star break he'll be a carpenter.

I wasn't much of a fielder. I used to play shortstop wearing a catcher's mask.

His son struck out so many times in the Little League playoffs that his father said, "Son, I may have to do something that I don't want to do."
"What's that, Dad?" his son inquired.
"Trade you," the father replied.

A player was asked his best position. "Sort of stooped over like this," was the player's answer.

When I signed my contract with them, they gave me a bonus which in those days was unheard of. Even today it's unheard of.

Whenever I was catching his knuckleball I would always let it bounce in front of the plate and roll to the screen. I got to meet a lot of fans that way.

I knew that our neighborhood Little League was getting too competitive when I was told that they traded my eight-year-old to Cleveland.

He just got a job where he doesn't come in contact with many people. He's the third base coach for the Chicago Cubs.

They're one of the finest teams in the country. Unfortunately, they play terribly in the city.

I was a 400 hitter lifetime. Every 400 trips to the plate I'd get a hit.

If diamonds are a girl's best friend, how come my wife gets so upset everytime I turn on a baseball game?

No wonder kids are confused these days. I saw a little leaguer being told by his coach, "Hold at third," and his mother was yelling, "Herman, come home this instant!"

This time of the year I get that uncontrollable urge to go to the ball park. It's not that I'm crazy about baseball, but I just love watered-down soft drinks and cold hot dogs.

Some ballplayers have trouble hitting their weight, but last year (egotistical player) had trouble hitting his hat size.

The coach told me my swing is improving. I'm missing the ball much closer than I used to.

Talk about hitters! I've seen better swings on a condemned playground.

When they read the roster of baseball's all-time great managers, you'll be right there listening.

Took the kids to the baseball game, and it was really exciting. Twelve round-trippers! Three on the field and nine to the concession stands.

He's the only guy in baseball who not only can read an eye chart, he can understand it!

He's been working on a new pitch. It's called a strike.

He would have been a better manager if he understood more. Of course, if he understood more, he probably wouldn't have become a manager.

Umpire: "I'll lean down and bite your head off."
Manager: "If you do, you'll have more brains in your stomach than you have in your head!"

The highlight of his career was walking with the bases loaded to drive in the winning run in an intersquad game in spring training.

He's so slow that to time him from home to first base, they use a calendar.

Pitcher talking to trainer on rubdown table after being knocked out in fourth inning: "I can't understand it. I thought I had good stuff today."
Trainer: "Well, the batters seemed to like it."

"Look, Billy," the coach said, "you know the principles of good sportsmanship. You know the Little League doesn't allow temper tantrums, shouting at the umpire, or abusive language."
"Yes, sir. I understand."
"Well, then," said the coach, "would you please explain that to your mother?"

Bob and I aren't playing major league baseball today because of sinus problems. Nobody would sign us.

He's been in the league so long that he bought his first wad of tobacco directly from Sir Walter Raleigh.

A surly and boorish umpire returned home after a long road trip. He settled into his easy chair and called his little boy over to sit on his lap. "No!" said the lad. "The son never sets on the brutish umpire."

My friend said, "I know I'm a loser. I lost my wallet. My wife is very sick. I lost my job. The Phils lost to the Dodgers. It's unbelievable-- leading by three in the eighth, and the Phils lost to the Dodgers!"

A father watched his young son practice baseball in the backyard by throwing the ball up and swinging at it. Time and time again the bat missed contact. The boy noticed his father watching, and said, "Wow, Dad! Aren't I a great pitcher?"

The coach lacked confidence in his pitcher. On the lineup card he penciled in, "Martin and others."

After watching a 450-foot homerun disappear out of the stadium, the manager said to the pitcher, "Anything hit that high and far should have a stewardess and an in-flight movie."

To a catcher, "Bill, how many games did you catch before the coach told you about the mask?"

He's the luckiest pitcher I've ever seen. He always pitches on days when the other team doesn't score any runs.

It's tough playing in New York. The first time I got into the bullpen car, they told me to lock the doors.

The only problem I have in the outfield is with fly balls.

He owes his pitching success to two things: conditioning and a fast outfield.

Kazanski played third, second, short, and right field. He was a utility pole.

Five consecutive hitters nailed the pitcher's first pitch for hits to open the ball game. The manager called the catcher to a mound conference and asked, "What kind of stuff does he have today?"
"How should I know?" said the catcher. "I haven't caught a pitch yet!"

Our team was called the Mudville Kleenex, because we were nice and soft and popped up one at a time.

This team plays poorly on grass. They are even worse on artificial surfaces. What they should do is put paper down and play on that. This team always looks good on paper.

Umpire: "Ed, if the pitcher threw an elephant you couldn't hit it."
Batter: "Bob, if the pitcher threw an elephant, you couldn't call it!"

When I hit my first homerun, one of my teammates was kind enough to drop bread crumbs so I could find my way around the bases.

I was watching the baseball game on TV and my wife said, "Speaking of something that's high and outside, the grass needs mowing."

A player yelled to the ump, "This is a great game. Too bad you can't see it!"

A scout watched a pitcher throw a perfect game, striking out all 27 batters. No one hit a foul ball until one batter topped one in the ninth inning. The general manager told the scout, "Sign the batter who hit the foul. We need hitters."

Players are so affluent these days. One manager called the bullpen and got an answering service.

Toward the end of his career, he got a little out of shape. The ump told him to stop crowding the plate and he was in the on-deck circle at the time.

 **BASKETBALL**

Our team doesn't need more shooters. It needs more makers.

Just remember that if you can hold your head up high and walk eight feet tall through the challenges of life, you'll never walk alone. There will always be a basketball scout right behind you trying to recruit you.

I asked one of the players on the employee questionnaire: "Where was the Declaration of Independence signed?"
His answer, "On the bottom!"

(about opposing coach) He's so lucky. He'll call me on the phone to flip a coin for our tournament matchups. He'd flip the coin, I'd call it, and he'd win every single time.

(high-salaried superstar) Sure, we're overpaying him. But he's worth it.

He knew his career was over when he was driving the lane and was called for three seconds.

One guy we scouted last year was so quick that he could go through a revolving door behind you and come out ahead of you.

(coach after 103-58 loss) We got beat by one bad call--the one our athletic director made to schedule this game.

Our team was so slow on the fast break that they reran the game tapes on a View Master.

Our coach doesn't use new techniques in practice. He just relies on the old, proven ones like the rack, limb dislocation and solitary confinement.

I won't say how bad our team is, but I've seen more baskets made by occupational therapy groups.

Our first round draft choice spent the off-season working as a life guard. He can't swim, but he can wade like mad.

I sure am relieved when the off-season rolls around. It gives my fingernails a chance to grow back.

An agent said that he might send a 6-11 player back to play in Europe. "But I can't send him to Italy. He played there once, and they decided that they already had enough statues."

Our center placed his right leg over his left knee and placed both feet solidly on the floor.

I know a coach who was told he could hire two assistants. He hired a psychiatrist and a hair dresser. The psychiatrist went crazy in six months. The hair dresser is still with the team.

Talk about turnovers. My high school team was called so much for travelling that we were sponsored by Triple-A.

We scouted one guard last year. His coach said, "He's the only one I know who's quick enough to play tennis with himself."

Under race he put "Mile."

This year we're going to run and shoot. Next year we hope to run and score.

There was a basketball coach who told recruits their height was of no consequence, as long as their ears popped when they sat down.

I play in an Over 30 basketball league. We don't have jump balls. The ref just puts the ball on the floor, and whoever can bend over and pick it up gets possession.

Basketball coach after his team's 90-53 loss to a superior team: "Their players put their pants on the same way our players do. It just takes them longer to pull them up."

At the beginning of the year we had a booster club, and by the end of the season it had turned into a terrorist group.

He's one of the finest officials money can buy.

I was invited to a masquerade party and won first prize. I stuffed my pockets with money and went as a free agent.

I can dribble the ball through my legs, behind my back, left-handed or right-handed. That's why I've been thrown out of every bowling alley in town.

After a questionable call, the ref said to the coach, "If you say anything, I'll give you a technical."
"What if I _think_ something?" the coach said.
"That's okay," said the ref.
The coach then said, "I _think_ you stink."

Our new center is so big, he wasn't born, he was founded.

He was so tall when he was born that his birth certificate read "June 1st, 2nd and 3rd."

The team was in a slump, so the coach thought he had better stress the basics. He picked up the ball and said, "This is the basketball."
"Hold on a minute, coach," one of the players interrupted. "Not so fast."

He accounted for 3,000 points during his career. He scored 1,000 and gave up 2,000.

My days with the team are numbered. I was recently sent on a scouting trip to the Bermuda Triangle.

Last season we couldn't win on the road, and this year we can't win at home. My failure as a coach is that I can't think of anywhere else to play.

Coach: "Where did you get hurt, Earl?"
Earl: "Right over there, coach."

The coach was telling the players what they were doing wrong: defense, shooting, rebounding. He noticed one of his players wasn't paying attention. "Dennis," he said, "Where are most basketball games lost?"
"Right here at State College!" Dennis replied.

Our coach loves the refs. He sends them cards every Christmas--in Braille.

He's also kind to the refs. He helps them feel their way into the gym before the game.

The doctor told me to stay away from places where there'd be a lot of people--so I went to a (losing team's) game.

A guy walked up to our ticket window and woke up the ticket seller. He said, "I'd like four tickets for tonight's game. By the way, what time does the game start?"
Our ticket agent said, "For four tickets, what time would you like the game to start? For four tickets we'll come over and play at your place!"

Just remember--if you can't play a sport, forget it!

We have one player whose sweat is so rare that it can cure hepatitis.

Another one of our players wore out five pairs of sneakers just from stumbling.

Team Questionnaire:

Favorite color: Scotch plaid.

Favorite sea food: Salt water taffy.

Father's alma mater: Always do your best.

Mother's alma mater: A winner never quits and a quitter never wins.

Best position: Kinda crouched over like this.

Have you lived in Orlando all your life?: Not yet.

Our center told us he made his water bed more comfortable by putting in water softener.

I asked him, "Where are the Argentinian Pampas?" and he said, "On Argentinian babies."

On our personnel questionnaire we asked "Church preference". He filled in, "Red brick."

On our team questionnaire we ask, "Who to notify in case of accident." One player wrote in: "A good doctor."

I can tell you what it's like working in the N.B.A. Picture a nervous breakdown with paychecks.

We have a minor scheduling problem that we'll have to iron out. This year, the last game of the playoffs conflicts with our home opener.

I've guarded guys who could leap before, but all the others came down.

BEAUTY PARLOR

I took a peek inside a beauty parlor. Now I know what a mummy looks like without the bandages.

In most beauty shops, the gossip alone would curl your hair.

BIRTHDAY

I was so surprised at birth that I couldn't speak for thirteen months.

When it comes to birthday parties it's easy to divide mothers into two groups: those who think that a birthday party for 24 five-year-old kids can be organized, educational and fun--and those who have had one.

You can always tell the experienced parents at a children's birthday party. They don't hand the kids napkins--they give 'em drop cloths.

I got my son a bicycle for his birthday, and I hid it where he'll never find it--in the bathtub.

BODY BUILDING

The guys at the health club call me Wonderman. They wonder why a guy with such a pitiful body would bother with pumping iron.

Last night, I sucked my stomach in so hard I threw my back out.

I have the kind of figure that looks great in tapered shirts--that is if you wear them upside-down.

Every morning I get up, bend over and touch my toes. The trouble is--I touch my toes with my stomach.

Every day my wife bends over and touches the floor seventy times. It's not exercise. She's picking up the kids' clothes.

BOOK

As our publisher once said to Tolstoy, "Make up your mind, Leo--do you want to write a book about war, or about peace?"

He feels so stupid--spent a whole year writing a book and then discovered that he could buy one for a few dollars.

I just love that book you wrote. I've been reading it night and day, and I'm now on page ten.

Novice to author: "I'm interested in writing a book. What's the best way to start writing?"
Author: "I suggest from left to right."

His publisher is publishing two of his books at the same time--his first and his last.

One publisher said my book was so bad that they had to rewrite it before they threw it away.

Another publisher wrote, "We reject not only what you sent us, but anything you might write in the future."

This book fills a much-needed gap.

I'm writing a book. I have the page numbers down, now all I have to do is fill in the rest.

I just read the book "The Miracle of Helium". I couldn't put it down.

I've written several children's books. I didn't mean to, they just turned out that way.

A first grader was listening to some high school students exchanging tips on how to read faster. The little girl offered, "I find I can read faster if I don't stop to color the pictures."

I wrote something last week that was accepted by Simon and Schuster. It was my check for The Book-of-the-Month Club.

I read a mystery book printed in Chinese. The only problem was I knew who the killer was on the first page.

This book is dedicated to my wife, without whose charge accounts it might not have been necessary.

I just wrote a book. One critic said, "Once you put it down, you can't pick it up."

He's very patient. He's waiting for the Encyclopedia Britannica to come out in paperback.

I gained fifty pounds writing my last book. Every time the typewriter came to the end of the line and the bell rang, I took a snack break.

My latest book is one that everyone will have their noses in. I'm printing it on Kleenex.

When you read my book, keep your eyes glued to the pages...that way you'll know where they are.

My latest book is titled, "500 Useful Diseases and How to Catch Them".

My new book is titled, "How Green Was My Pool Table".

I asked the critic, "Did you read my last book?"
The critic replied, "I certainly hope so."

I was going to call my new book Being Decisive, but then I changed my mind.

My latest books are titled: "The Underachiever's Guide to Very Small Business Opportunities", and "Tax Shelters for the Indigent".
Also: "How to Overcome Self-Doubt Through Pretense and Ostentation", "Burglarproof Your Home With Cement" and "Overcoming Peace of Mind".

I wasn't overly sensitive when the publisher returned my manuscript, but I did get a little touchy when he sent it by "junk mail".

My new book is titled "Everything You've Always Wanted to Know About Amnesia But Forgot to Ask".

My new book is in its fourth printing. I sure wish we had done the first three right.

I'm writing a book that's going to be in a class all by itself. It's for people who want to be unpopular, unadjusted, unsuccessful and fat.

Have you seen these children's books? They're all about Jane, Dick and Spot. Spot is a dog--and Jane is nothing to brag about either.

I was in an old book store the other day and found <u>How To Hug</u>. I thought it was a romantic novel but when I got it home, it turned out to be Volume Six of the Encyclopedia Britannica.

From the moment I picked this book up, until the moment I put it down, I couldn't stop laughing. Someday I hope to read it.

After you read this book, please don't lend it to a friend. Have him buy his own copy. If I sell enough copies, I'll have enough money to get my teeth fixed.

I'd like to hit the bestseller list but I don't jog or do aerobics, I hate cats and dogs, and I never knew John Lennon or Elvis.

A rare book is one which a friend borrows and remembers to return.

He sent a manuscript to the publisher with the note: "Please send a reply immediately as I have other irons in the fire."
The publisher returned the manuscript with a note: "We suggest you put this with the other irons."

An Eskimo in an igloo was reading to his youngster, "Little Jack Horner sat in a corner..."
The kid interrupted, "Daddy, what's a corner?"

This book should not be put aside. It should be thrown with force.

He got a book for his birthday, and he's still looking for a place to put the batteries.

He has such a short attention span that he needs a bookmark just to read a matchpack.

 **BOSS**

The boss is so cheap that he had a coin-operated time and temperature sign installed outside our office.

Office worker: "This is great weather we're having, isn't it?"
Boss: "We? Who made you a partner all of a sudden?"

Early in his business career, whenever things got tough, he just dug in, rolled up his sleeves and borrowed another $200,000 from his father.

The boss started out as a bootblack and ended up with a $10,000,000 business. I guess he didn't use much polish.

Our boss is always right--misinformed perhaps, sloppy, crude, bull-headed, fickle, and even stupid--but never wrong.

Be tolerant of the boss who disagrees with you--he has a right to his own ridiculous opinion.

The boss finally put it all together, however, he forgot where he put it.

The boss only does two things wrong--everything he says and everything he does.

The boss always says, "Nothing is impossible unless you have to do it by yourself."

"My company is one big, happy family. And that's because I hire all my relatives."

Until further notice, do not use the suggestion box. The handle is broken and it won't flush.

The boss said, "I don't know how we could get along without you around here. But starting tomorrow, we're going to try."

The boss said, "Listen, stupid..". He always calls me 'Listen'.

"This is my son, Frank. He's going to start at the bottom for a few days."

Employee: "I wasn't going to ask you for a raise, but somehow my children found out that American kids eat three meals a day."

The boss is very forthright. He's right about one-fourth of the time.

The boss fumed, "Don't tell me what I mean. Let me figure it out for myself!"

"It's too late to agree with me. I've already changed my mind!"

He's what you'd call a 20th Century Robin Hood. He steals from the rich, and he robs from the poor.

The boss just entrusted me with a special assignment. I wonder if he wants starch on his collars and cuffs?

The boss said of him, "He not only starts jobs he can't finish, he starts things he can't even begin!"

The boss told me, "Look, when I want your opinion, I'll give it to you!"

The boss screamed, "Wipe that opinion off your face!"

I know I'm one of the boss' favorites. Last week he promoted me to vice-slave.

An employee asked the boss for a recommendation for a new job. The boss wrote, "Bob Smith worked for us for ten years, and when he left we were very satisfied."

His relationship with the boss is based on more than respect and trust. It's based on fear.

There are a lot of people who believe in the boss' business acumen. But there are also a lot of people who believe in the Easter Bunny.

In business circles he has been called a Renaissance man. And that's because most of his ideas come from the 15th century.

Once the boss thought he was wrong, but he was mistaken.

Contrary to popular belief, he is not a 'yes man'. When the boss says "no", Bill says "no", too.

Making a mistake in front of the boss can be likened to cutting yourself in front of Dracula.

I've enjoyed working for the boss--representing him at functions, attending meetings for him. The only thing that really bothered me was going to the dentist for him.

I said to the boss, "You could promote a man like me."
The boss replied, "Yes--if he wasn't too much like you."

When the boss called to offer me the job, I was almost too excited to accept the charges.

The boss is tolerant of people who disagree with him. He once told me, "Everyone is entitled to his own stupid opinion."

One sure way for a joke to get a laugh--let the boss tell it.

I've asked the boss if he had any suggestions for me and he said, "Sure. Don't move to a larger house, and don't buy a piano!"

A fellow worker said to me, "I feel like telling the boss off again."
I said, "Again?"
He replied, "Yea, I felt like telling him off last week, too."

He has assembled a staff of talented, bright people. Good idea. If you're going to ignore advice, why not ignore the best?

The boss has a street downtown named after him. It's called "One Way".

The boss says, "I always quote myself. I like to add spice to my conversation."

"You look tired, dear. Did you have a bad day at the office?"
"I sure did. I took the employee aptitude test, and it's a good thing that I own the company!"

Employee: "Could I have the fourteenth off? It's our silver anniversary, and my wife and I would like to celebrate."
Boss: "Are we going to have to put up with this every 25 years?"

I gave the boss a milk of human kindness plant. It blossoms and blooms on love and attention. I'd show it to you tonight, but it died.

The boss is familiar with all the key business questions of the day. Unfortunately, he doesn't know any of the answers.

I asked the boss for a vacation, and he snapped, "I was away for two weeks! <u>That</u> was your vacation."

I get along alright with my boss. If he'd pay me a decent salary, I might even like him.

For years the boss has always called me his right-hand man. Then it occurred to me--he's left-handed.

If you think the boss never laughs, just ask him for a raise.

You've got to hand it to the boss. When he's right, he's the first to admit it.

The boss told me I was more like a son to him than an employee. So I asked him, "Well, how about an increase in my allowance?"

The boss came in in a bad mood this morning. Someone at home had already worked out the crossword puzzle on the Captain Crunch box.

My boss finally gave me that raise I was after. Only catch is that I have to mow his lawn every Saturday.

I rub elbows with the boss. He won't shake my hand.

The boss just returned from his vacation in South America where he opened a charm school for dictators.

Problem at the office this morning...the boss smiled and got a charley horse in the face.

I was going to ask him for a raise this morning, but it's not easy talking to someone on a rocking horse.

They say nothing's as cheap as it used to be. Obviously they've never met my boss.

The boss is really into exercise. If you ask him for a raise, he'll tell you to take a walk.

The boss had his suit made in Hong Kong. It looks like he swam back in it.

He's currently working on a new book. He's calling it The Joy Of Cheap.

A real boss is someone who puts a sign reading "suggestion box" on the paper shredder.

Somebody must be asking the boss for a raise. I'd know that laugh anywhere.

I knew right away that the boss was going to talk to me about my salary when he began, "It's the little things that count."

My boss is so generous. He heard you could feed a family of four in India for $10 a year, so he sent his whole family there.

Someone asked my boss, "How many people work here?" He said, "Oh, about five or six."

"Jones, how long have you been working here?"
"Ever since I heard you coming down the hall, sir."

"I notice that you get your hair cut during business hours."
"My hair grows during business hours."
"But it doesn't all grow during business hours."
"I didn't get it all cut."

This is America's traditional time for turkeys, fruitcakes and surprises. But enough about my boss. Let's talk about Christmas.

Every morning the boss pops his head in just to watch me work...so far he hasn't caught me at it.

The boss and I get along great. I laugh at all his jokes and he laughs at all my suggestions.

The boss said, "In a way, I'll hate to lose you. You've been just like a son to me...unappreciative, surly, insolent..."

He told me I was fired. I said, "Fired? I thought slaves had to be sold!"

The boss and I are friends pure and simple. I'm pure and he's...

Thanks to our boss, this Christmas was a learning experience. I never knew that the Salvation Army gave gift certificates.

The boss was looking over my expense account and said, "What's this?"
I said, "That's my hotel bill."
He said, "Make sure that you don't buy any more hotels."

The boss came back from the suggestion box complaining, "Why can't they be more specific? What lake? Which kite?"

The boss said, "This is just a suggestion, but remember who's making it."

The boss was invited to dinner, and he placed some lima beans on his plate. An excited youngster squealed, "Look, Daddy. He took some lima beans, and you said he didn't know beans!"

The boss says, "I will always stand by my convictions as long as necessary."

I think it's really nice how the boss says that my program should be given a fair and reasonable amount of time to work. And then he sets his egg timer.

I really love my job here. If this wasn't my job, I'd do it for nothing. And everytime I get my paycheck, I think I am.

My boss said to me, "How long have you been working here? Not counting tomorrow."

"Boss, will you like me as much if my plan doesn't work?"
"Oh, I'd like you as much. I'll just miss having you around."

My boss is so rich it takes his limo six minutes to go through the one minute car wash. It's even equipped with a power tissue dispenser.

Let's put this in perspective. All the boss wants from me is perfection-- although he'll settle for more.

The boss gave me a bonus that made it possible for my parents to work for the rest of their lives.

The boss just signed me to a multi-day contract.

The boss had the team yacht out the other day and it was a beautiful sight to see all 24 oars rowing in unison.

The boss told the guys, "I've got some good news and bad news for you. The good news is, take a 15-minute rest. The bad news is that after you rest I want to go water skiing."

Rich? He got a check back from the bank marked "Insufficient funds". The bank attached a note that said, "Not yours, ours."

The boss is really generous. Every fall, he treats the staff to flu shots!

The boss never loses his temper. He can always find it when he needs it.

Everybody is picking on the boss these days and it just isn't fair! After all, he hasn't done anything!

Before you have an argument with the boss, you better look at both sides--his side and the outside!

He said, "But, boss, if I get here on time it'll be such a long day!"

He has the perfect way of ending a meeting. He says, "All those opposed to my plan say, 'I resign'."

I told the boss to pay me what I'm worth, but he told me he's required by law to at least pay the minimum wage.

My boss told me that he was going to make a change in my department which didn't bother me until I remembered that I was the only one in my department.

I never agree with the boss, except during working hours.

The boss asked me how I managed to get to work exactly one hour late each day. I said, "I'm punctual."

The boss said to one of the guys in the office: "You're the most useless person I ever saw. You don't do an hour's work a month. Tell me one single way the firm benefits from employing you!"
The clerk responded, "When I go on vacation, there's no extra work thrown on the others."

Our boss is what you would call conservative. He still thinks an obscene gesture is reaching for your paycheck.

He's a very sensitive boss. You can tell that by the way he fires people. He takes them to lunch and orders theirs to go.

The boss said that he's going to write his autobiography as soon as he can figure out who the main character should be.

We're all congratulating him on his new book . . . The Fear Of Spending.

The boss is not as well off as you think. The telephone in his Mercedes is a party line.

This morning I had a long talk with my boss. Actually, he had a long talk. I had a long listen.

The boss always says that anything goes. And this morning he called me Anything.

The boss is so easy going. Just yesterday he told me, "Don't think of me as the boss...just think of me as a friend that's never wrong."

A sensitive, compassionate, caring man--he is best known as the creator of the company's motto: IF AT FIRST YOU DON'T SUCCEED--OUT!

The boss told me my work is improving. He said, "It doesn't take as long to redo it."

The boss is in his typical holiday mood. He has something that says DO NOT OPEN TILL CHRISTMAS. It's his wallet.

The boss just gave me his Cadillac. The ash trays were full.

The boss and I were discussing the definition of important with another office worker. The worker said, "Important is being invited into the Oval Office for a private conversation with the President."
I said, "I think important is being in the Oval Office with the President, you're talking to him, the hotline rings, and he puts them on hold."
The boss said, "No, important is being in the office with the President, the hotline rings, he answers it, hands the receiver to you and says, 'Here, it's for you'."

The boss was injured in an avalanche. His in-basket collapsed on him.

The boss just built himself a bigger office. His old office was so small, his paper planes kept smashing into the wall.

There is hope for the boss now that they've developed the artificial heart.

My boss is really generous. He's given me unlimited use of his Diners' Club card between five and seven o'clock in the morning.

The boss called a meeting to discuss employee absenteeism but was forced to cancel it when nobody showed up.

The boss is so conservative that people worship the eggs that he walks on.

The boss sent me on a business trip to the Thousand Islands and said, "Spend a week on each."

You can't help liking the boss. If you don't, he fires you.

The secretary came in my office while I was working at my desk. She asked, "What are you doing?"
I replied, "I'm writing my autobiography."
She said, "That's nice. What's it about?"

The boss is such a modest, unassuming man. He doesn't even demand that we call him sir. He says that kneeling and kissing his hand is sufficient.

My boss gave me a contract that has so many loopholes in it that the wind whistles right through it.

My boss made me take a vow of poverty and now he expects me to live up to it.

The boss suffers from a very rare disease--an ingrown money belt.

I owe a lot to the boss. He's made me realize that money isn't everything.

The boss just doubled my salary. I used to make $200 a week and now I make $200 every two weeks.

The boss is temperamental. He's 50 percent temper and 50 percent mental.

My boss sort of looks upon himself as being a pilot through clouds of confusion.

The boss has three stacking trays on his desk: IN, OUT, and OOPS.

Some people envy the boss with his gorgeous wife and beautiful yacht. It's not as leisurely a life as it appears. The other night I saw him out in a little rowboat. He had to take out the garbage.

My boss suffers from "Moon Syndrome". That's where you carry around only one-sixth of the weight you think you do.

My boss has a lot of confidence in me. The other day he said to me, "I've got a foolproof system and I'd like you to try it out."

The boss was examining the petty cash fund yesterday. He calls it the petty cash fund. The employees call it the payroll.

The boss doesn't really offer me any sense of security. Last week he gave me a desk nameplate lettered OCCUPANT.

The boss has his own version of F.D.R.'s fireside chats. If you don't take his side during a chat, you're fired.

The boss has a surefire way of getting support for his ideas. He says, "All in favor say 'Aye'; all opposed say 'Bye'."

Talk about neurotics. He's self-employed and hates the boss!

Our boss has taken this company from relative obscurity to anonymity.

I was surprised when the boss gave me a piece of his mind, considering the inventory is so low.

The boss gave me a sign for my desk. It reads: Like to Meet New People? Like a Change? Like Excitement? Like a New Job? Just Mess Up One More Time.

My first boss was eighty-years-old. He said, "I'm signing you to a lifetime contract."
I asked, "Yours or mine?"

I just bought the boss's Cadillac--the one that he only uses to drive back and forth to the bank. It had 173,000 miles on it.

The boss is too much of a workaholic. He invited me to his house last evening and showed me office movies.

The boss said, "I don't want to seem critical, but when was the last time you ever saw any of our workers wearing a sweat band?"

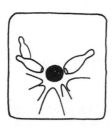

BOWLING

Interest your child in bowling. Get him off the streets and into the alleys.

One advantage of bowling over golf...you very seldom lose the ball.

BOXING

I ruined my hands in boxing...the referee kept walking on them.

One night at the Spectrum all the fans kept yelling for me. I sold 612 hot dogs that night!

Boxing trivia: Who was the last man to box Joe Louis?
                    The undertaker.

The boxer was so old that he wore orthopedic trunks, had Geritol in his water bucket, and put Poli-Grip on his mouthpiece.

He once had Joe Louis down on one knee. Louis bent down to see if he was still alive.

I was a colorful fighter--black and blue all over.

I used to feint with my nose and lash out with my chin.

I started off with a smashing left, then a right hook. Then the other fighter came out of his corner.

I began with a left cross, then a right cross, then Blue Cross.

I was bobbing and weaving, weaving and bobbing. And, before I got knocked out, I had finished two baskets and a braided rug.

I built my boxing career on natural talent and artificial respiration.

I swung with a crushing left hook, but I was backpeddling so fast that it never got there.

At the end of the second round, my corner told me, "Keep it up! You've got a no-hitter going!"

What a fight! When the bell rang I came right out and threw six straight punches in a row. Then the other guy came out of his corner.

My best punch was a rabbit punch but they wouldn't let me punch rabbits.

By the sixth round, I had my opponent covered with blood--mine!

If you wanted to see me fight, you had to get there early.

I was knocked out so many times that I sold advertising space on the soles of my shoes.

I was offered $500 to throw a fight in the third round. I had to say no. I told him I'd never gotten past the first.

The boxer's manager comforted him. "Don't be afraid. If he were any good, he wouldn't be fighting you."

As a boxer, he was on his back so often, he was mistaken for a civil service worker.

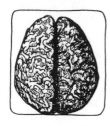

BRAINS

He's got more brains in his entire head than you have in your little finger.

The mind is a wonderful thing...everyone should have one.

If we're all so smart, why do people have to tell us to have a good day?

I'm about as nervous as a brain surgeon with the hiccups.

With his brain power and attention span, his computer doesn't need much of a memory.

BROADWAY

I won't say what the play was like, but the prompter got three curtain calls.

BROKEN ARM

He said, "I broke my arm playing pin-the-tail on the donkey."
I said, "How could you break your arm doing that?"
He replied, "We used a real donkey!"

BROTHER-IN-LAW

I asked my brother-in-law why he always wore my raincoat. He said, "You wouldn't want me to get your shirt wet, would you?"

The good news is that statistics show that we spend one-third of our lives in bed. The bad news is that as of next Wednesday, my brother-in-law will have completed his one-third.

You'll all be happy to know that my brother-in-law finally found a job. He didn't get it, he just found it.

I have a brother-in-law who has gotten thirty days so often that they're naming a month after him.

BUDGET

The economy is beginning to hurt. Our company is having a cash-flow problem. Flo is our cashier, and she hasn't been seen in days!

BUMPER STICKER

I am neither for or against apathy.

BUSINESS

At our last board meeting, a phone call interrupted the proceedings. The secretary announced, "The treasurer wants to give the financial report, and he's calling long distance."

A fellow applied for a job with our firm, but he told us his old job paid more. The personnel director said, "Yes, but did they offer insurance, rest periods and paid vacations?"
The man said, "Yes, and a $1,000 holiday bonus and all holidays off."
"Well then, why did you leave?"
"I had to. The company went bankrupt."

His business is really doing well. They've had two fires and only needed one of them.

Two partners were fishing and their boat tipped. One started swimming for shore, while the other floundered helplessly. The swimmer called, "Bob, can you float alone?"
Bob replied, "Here I am drowning, and you want to talk business!"

He's such a poor administrator, that if he were running a hospital, I'd invest in a mortuary.

I know that half of the money I spend on advertising is wasted, but I can't tell which half.

I don't know how he does it, but he's been with the company for four weeks and he's already three months behind in his work.

There are three things that I do at work each day. I get organized. I phone my wife. Then I get reorganized.

He received a notice: "Sorry, we cannot fill you order until your previous order is fully paid for."
He sent a reply: "Cancel my order. I can't wait that long."

A sporting goods dealer said that the recession was starting to ease for him a bit: bow and arrow sales are right on target, football equipment was gaining ground and even trampolines have rebounded.

He's a born executive. His father owns the business.

If the coffee breaks get much longer our employees might be late for quitting time.

The boss said, "I'm sorry, but if I let you take two hours for lunch today, I'll have to do the same for every man whose wife gives birth to quintuplets."

His going out of business sale was so successful he's now thinking of opening an entire chain of going out of business stores.

An executive looked a little discouraged and his wife asked why. He said, "You know those intelligence tests we're giving at the office? Well, today I took one and it's a good thing I own the company."

I made two mistakes last year. The first was starting a brand-new business. The second was starting it in a fire-proof building.

A management team came into my office to find out what our workers were best suited for. They found out that most of them are best suited for unemployment.

They talk about American efficiency, yet the secretary always answers the phone and nine times out of ten it's for her boss.

The boss is so proud because through the entire recession he's been able to keep his head above water. Of course! Wood floats!

My former business had nothing to do with football but it did wind up in the hands of a receiver.

Work is really important. If it wasn't for work, where would most people rest up from their vacations?

Our business is so bad, just to be safe we decided to have our Christmas party now.

The boss is all business. I saw him on the beach wearing a three-piece, pin-striped bathing suit.

Businesses are returning to simple toys...rubber balls are bouncing back; kite production has soared sky-high...even boomerangs are making a comeback.

An executive was interviewing a lady applicant. "I see your birthday is May 17th. What year?"
"Every year," she replied.

We'd make a change in management, but we can't figure out who's running the place now.

Creative writing is something that you occasionally find in magazines and invariably find in resumes.

How independent can you get? I know an exterminator who doesn't make house calls. Did you ever try to get 1,000 cockroaches in a cab?

I won't say how the company's doing but to give you an idea, they played "Taps" at our yearly business meeting.

He's a natural-born leader. His father is president of the company.

He had a kind of dull childhood. You know how most boys have sheets on their beds with pictures of spaceships and baseball players? His sheets had pictures of accountants and insurance salesmen.

How many persons does it take to screw in a lightbulb in the 76er office? None. We prefer to work in the dark.

Business was really thriving at that place. I walked in and asked for change for a twenty and they made me a partner.

Our sales department has set records hitting new highs in lows this year.

A business tycoon was working through a huge stack of papers while waiting in the maternity ward. A nurse came out and said, "Well, Mr. Wilson, it's a boy!"
Barely looking up from his papers, Wilson said, "Well, ask him what he wants."

A teacher asks the young son of a tycoon, "If you take 51% from 100%, what do you have?"
"That's easy," said the young businessman. "Control of the company!"

An efficiency expert is a guy who's smart enough to tell you how to run your company, but not smart enough to start his own.

My son's a born executive. He's only five, and already it takes him two-and-a-half hours to eat lunch.

Fresh out of college, he has what it takes to become a great business success. Rich parents.

We always try to cut corners around the office. Whereas some businesses have Apple computers, ours is a lemon.

Stealing his business secrets would be analagous to Sitting Bull stealing Custer's battle plans.

His parents envisioned him as a business tycoon in infancy. Who else do you know that ever wore pin-striped Pampers?

One of our employees is very bright. He starts thinking the moment he gets up in the morning and doesn't stop until he gets to his desk.

The company just installed the new boiler directly under his office. That way if it explodes between 10 a.m. and 4 p.m. no one will get hurt.

We have a new computer that can do the work of four executives--or one secretary.

Our chairman has written the annual report in terms that are easy for any stockholder to understand. It goes: "Look, Pat, look. See the earnings. The earnings are tiny. See the expenses. The expenses are huge. Run, Pat, run."

Our business is so bad that yesterday I went to my favorite lunch spot and they refused to serve me the businessman's lunch.

I'm very proud of the way I became general manager. I started out as president.

Our organization is really aggressive. Ours is the only office I know where Musak plays Sousa marches.

Our treasurer's idea of a fun prank is sending bankruptcy notices to our five biggest accounts.

We asked our business manager why he had spent 25 years in the finance department, and he said, "Because that's where they keep the money!"

His business aspirations are finally being realized. He's in the Fortune 500. That's right--he's one of the zeros.

He has marvelous letters of recommendation from his former employers--Curly, Moe and Larry.

Bob is one of the most highly suspected persons in the company.

Nobody knows exactly who he reports to. He says he has an unlisted boss.

Every piece of equipment in our office is covered by insurance...except the clock. And our employees are always watching that.

He goes to the airport, plunks down his airline credit card on the counter, and says, "Give me a ticket to anyplace. I've got business everywhere."

We have a great insurance policy at work. Have you read it? The benefit is that if we die, our families no longer have to pay the premiums.

Our company just found something that does the work of five men--a woman.

His business motto: "We'll use our hands and our hearts, and if we must, we'll use our heads."

Our competitors are equal opportunity employers. Last week they hired someone who was competent.

He is to our business what bumper stickers are to philosophy.

A fellow at work was complaining to me that his shoes were too tight. I asked, "Why don't you get a new pair?"
He said, "Let me put it this way. My wife is sick, my daughter married a bum, I lost all my savings in the stock market, and the only pleasure I'm getting from life these days is when I arrive home from work at night I can take off these shoes."

He's a mature thinker. All his ideas are over 30 years old.

Bill is proud that he is one of the few people in this company who can recite the twelve-times-table by memory.

BUTCHER

My butcher has a very interesting scale. Yesterday a fly landed on it...three and one-half pounds!

You know you're in trouble when the butcher puts wax paper on the scale and it weighs 88 cents.

The saddest story I ever heard was the one about the butcher who wanted to become a brain surgeon but didn't think he could afford to take the cut in pay.

Meat prices are so high these days that even plumbers and doctors are starting to notice.

I saw a new clerk being trained by a butcher like this: "If somebody comes in and asks the price of two pork chops you say, "Five dollars." Then watch them closely and if they don't grimace say, "And ninety-five cents." Then watch them even more carefully and if they still don't complain, you say, "Each."

The shoe maker was explaining to the dissatisfied customer why the soles were not of high quality. "All the good shoe leather is going into steaks."

In grammar, a redundancy is repeating yourself. Like saying "rich butcher."

DO-IT-YOURSELF
SPACE.

WRITE YOUR
OWN JOKE
HERE!

CALCULATOR

I just purchased a pocket calculator. Just press a button and it automatically tells me how many pockets I have in my suit.

I bought a calculator with a built-in memory, turned it on and it said, "What about yesterday when you tried to balance your checkbook and slammed me down on the table?"

I was using my new talking calculator in the super market. When I totaled up the money I had spent on junk food, my calculator said, "Have a great day, Lardo!"

CALIFORNIA

A thief robbed the First National Bank of Los Angeles today and vanished into thick air.

I was at the Los Angeles Hilton and looked out my window and saw a beautiful blue jay. Then I discovered that it was a cardinal holding its breath.

The air is so polluted in California that for the first time in history, tires are wearing out from the inside.

CAMP

Every summer we send our kids to the most reliable and inexpensive place we know of. It's called Camp Grandma.

This has been one of the most restful and relaxing summers we've ever had. I realized that when I said, "Tomorrow the kids come home from camp."
And my wife said, "Who?"

My kid had so much macaroni and mashed potatoes at camp that on a hot day he starched his own shirt.

My wife is so efficient. She saved countless hours of work by not sewing name tags into my son's clothing before sending him off to camp. She just had his name changed to "Machine Washable".

The walls at camp are so thin, I called the director and said, "Can you do something about my neighbor's TV set?"
He said, "Can you hear it?"
I said, "Hear it? I can see it!"

The swimming instructor was so sick one day that they sent the golf pro to take his place. I almost drowned. He kept telling me to keep my head down.

Summer camps are places that are staffed by 17-year-old counselors —which is amusing. You wouldn't trust them with your car — but with your kids, okay!

It's time that the kids go to summer camp. All day long my wife has been sewing names into their clothes — and you should see those names!

We're trying something new this summer by sending the dog to camp and the kids to obedience school.

Summer camp is where the parents spend a thousand dollars so their daughter can learn to make a fifty cent potholder.

It's a time of real adjustment when you send your kids to camp. The first morning he's away, you awaken and think, "Where's Billy?" By the third week you're wondering, "How's Billy?" Best of all is the fifth week when you wake up and think, "Who's Billy?"

Fear is zipping up your sleeping bag and that itch in your big toe start to move!

When his parents picked up little Sammy at camp they asked, "Were you homesick?"
Sammy said, "No, but some of the kids were. The ones who have dogs."

When their son returned from camp, they thought he had grown four inches. Then they washed his feet and he returned to his normal height.

Parents, carefully check out the place you send your kids to for the summer. Last summer, our neighbor kids told us that they had a camp director who was a short, little guy with a mustache who called his place Mein Kampf.

What a sight. Our son just brought all his dirty clothes home from summer camp and the washing machine turned green with nausea.

A child sent his parents a letter from camp. "Send food. All they serve here is breakfast, lunch, and dinner."

Post card from camp: "Dear Folks, I knew all along that something awful was going to happen here at camp. Well, last night it did. Love, John."

A camper was bothered by mosquitoes all day long. At night, as he looked out of his tent, he saw lightning bugs. "Oh, no!" he screamed. "Now they're coming after us with flashlights!"

Tenderfoot camper writing a card home to parents: "There are 50 boys here this week. I sure wish there were only 49."

The camp brochure said, "Running water in cabins," but I never expected a spring in my bed.

CARS

I once knew a woman who accomplished the unbelievable. Got seven miles to the gallon driving one of those sports cars. Nobody could figure it out until they watched her drive. When she got in the car, the first thing she did was pull the choke all the way out and hang her purse on it.

I won't say how I found out that this car has defective brakes, but we no longer have to back out of the garage.

In Detroit they've just developed a real winner! Windshield wipers that won't hold parking tickets.

I couldn't believe my car repair bill. Why the smallest thing on it was my telephone number!

These new, little cars are really something. Did you realize that they are so light-weight you can lower the rear end with a bumper sticker?

The service station charged my wife $53 yesterday for straightening her muffler, putting in a glove compartment filter and sharpening her aerial.

You can tell that there's something definitely wrong with my car. Oil was spurting out of the radio antenna. I have to wait for an explosion to get my hood opened. There's blue smoke coming out of my glove compartment and I have to hold my cigarette lighter out the window to drive at night.

I found a great way to beat inflation. When I get on the expressway, I turn off the ignition and let the other cars push me to work.

Some good news and some bad news for the auto industry. The good news is that Detroit has found the key to the automotive future. The bad news is that it fits the door of a Datsun.

"Pull over to the curb," the policeman ordered. "You don't have a taillight." The motorist stepped out, walked to the back of his car and started shaking. "Oh, it's not that bad," said the officer.

"It's not the taillight I'm worried about," said the motorist. "Where's my wife and trailer?"

Driver's tests should be more realistic. Like when women take their tests the examiner should have them pull down the mirror and put on lipstick at 60 m.p.h..

I took my car in for four new shocks and ended up with five.

Two men drove their cars toward each other on a narrow street. Neither could pass. One leaned out the window and shouted, "I never back up for a stupid idiot!"

"I always do," said the other, shifting the car in reverse.

Statistics reveal that a man gets hit by a car every twenty seconds. What a glutton for punishment that guy is!

I went for a ride with a friend of mine in his impressive new car with all those safety gadgets. When I got out of the car, I unbuckled the seat belt, unbuckled the shoulder strap, all the belts. I stepped out of the car and my pants fell down.

I won't say how far back the odometer was turned on that used car, but the mileage was in Roman numerals.

Ninety bucks just to have the car tuned up. Who did the tuning? Eugene Ormandy?

Everything is a ripoff these days. I went to the service station with a flat. The mechanic says, "Sure, we can fix it, but we'll have to go through the engine block to do it."

We call our car Flattery because it gets us nowhere.

My car breaks down so often, I bought the perfect second car. A tow-truck.

The government awarded the contracts for tanks to Chrysler. Do you think the Russians will be scared by 50,000 Dodge Omnis with cannons on the front? They should have given the contract to Ford and have them send Pintos in backwards!

One of our automakers had to recall 200,000 cars this week. They discovered that one of their assembly lines had accidentally installed some key engine parts that would last a lifetime.

How come they can make an aluminum soda can, which when discarded lasts forever, and a car, that when taken good care of, will rust out in two years?

He has a telephone in his car, but he says that it's a nuisance running to the garage everytime he wants to answer it.

My mechanic started me with the good news: "Your glove compartment and sunvisor are in great shape...Now about your transmission..."

My car has put two of Mr. Goodwrench's kids through college.

Everyone has forty-five miles of nerves in his body. More if he's a used car dealer.

A man shopping for a compact car complained to the car salesman: "That's almost the cost of a big car."
Said the salesman: "Well, if you want economy, you've got to pay for it."

That's a sharp looking car you're driving. How many miles do you get per gallon?
Six. My son gets the other twenty.

He just bought a motor home so that he would have a place to live while he looks for a place to park.

Service station washrooms are where it takes you fifteen minutes just to clean the soap.

This driving tip: When taking your driver's test, don't ask the examiner, "Which counts more, speed or accuracy?"

I hit a pothole that was so deep yesterday that I hit a miner on his way up.

My car is in such bad shape that the parking lot attendant offered me a tip if I'd park it.

Saw this great sign at a gas station: Courteous and efficient self-service.

"Mommy, what happens to a car when it's too old and banged up to run?"

"Somebody sells it to your father."

The mechanic advised, "My advice is to keep the oil and change the car."

Our garageman gets upset watching Mr. Goodwrench on TV. He can't understand why he uses a towel to clean his hands when he has perfectly good seat covers in front of him.

Parking lot supervisor to attendants: "Listen, boys, we haven't had one complaint about a dented fender all week. How do you expect me to make any money around here if you're leaving that much space?"

I baby my car. It doesn't go anywhere without a rattle.

My car is so old, well, it's even paid for!

My definition of a confident, secure individual is one who can hand the keys of his car to a parking lot attendant and never look back.

After four years I now have the self-service gas station procedure down to a science. I pump 15 gallons into the tank, splash a half gallon or so on my trousers, wipe my windshield with a dirty rag, pay the attendant the exact change, say 'thank you' to myself, and tell myself to 'have a nice day,' and then drive off leaving the gas cap on top of the pump.

I cured my kids from borrowing the car. I glued a rope starter to the trunk and I call it a lawn mower. Now they won't go near it!

I have a difficult decision to make concerning my car. I don't know whether to take it to the garage to have it overhauled, or to call the junk yard and have it hauled over.

Really, if Rolls Royces are that great, how come you don't see more people driving them?

When buying a used car, always check to see if the hood latch is worn out.

I play Toll Booth Bingo. Invariably, there are four lanes open, and the one I get in, the car in front of me is always asking the toll keeper for directions to Sascatchewan.

I just discovered why the department of transportation issues those Men At Work signs. If they didn't, how would you know what all those guys with hard hats drinking coffee were doing on the highway?

I also learned the salary structure of the highway workers. Those guys who hold shovels get $14 an hour, and the ones who carry flags get $18 an hour. After all, you can't lean on a red flag.

One of the true joys of life is walking to your car, finding the time expired on the parking meter, and not finding a ticket on your windshield.

My old car has two shock absorbers — my wife and me.

Someone asked me, "What model is your car?"
I replied, "It's no model. It's a horrible example."

This car will stop on a dime. It doesn't have the power to go over it.

If you travel less than 60 miles per hour on the expressway, they consider you double-parked.

I regret ever having put a phone in the car. I hate running out to the garage every time it rings.

My compact car is so small that the cigarette lighter doubles as a heater.

An unmarked car is one my wife has never driven.

My car has something that will last a lifetime — monthly payments.

One bit of advice: Never go to a mechanic who uses a Gucci wrench and car creeper.

Anyone who has watched a parking lot attendant park his car knows the reality of the statement, "What you don't know won't hurt you."

My car is so old that the insurance covers fire, theft and Indian raids.

The smart consumer buys a mini-compact. After all, they're so much easier to push.

CHARITY

It's just wonderful, the generous spirit of Americans. I know of one organization that's already collected $3,000,000 — and they don't even have a disease yet.

CHESS

Chess is a game that requires intense concentration and total silence. During one game an opponent sneezed and the other player said, "Gesundheit."
The rival countered, "Did you come here to play or talk?"

Chess is a game where people sit for hours, not moving a muscle, staring ahead. We have the same thing in the federal government. It's called Civil Service.

CHILDHOOD

His folks used to leave his baby carriage parked on the hill in neutral.

In little league I was the only kid ever traded to another family.

I loved music and played piano in the high school marching band.

When he was born there wasn't any name on his hospital wristband. It just said, "We will accept any reasonable offer."

No wonder he doesn't like his own appearance. On Halloween his parents used to send him out as is.

His parents were ashamed of him. They hired another kid to play him in home movies.

In school I wore my socks over my sneakers, in case the laces came untied I wouldn't trip over them.

My folks wanted twins when I was born. I tried to help out. I always dressed alike and went places together.

My parents wanted to name me Otto so that I would only have two letters to remember.

I had a rough childhood. Some kids have their pictures taken on a pony. I had mine taken on a bucking bronco.

I learned to swim the old-fashioned way. My father took me out in a boat when I was five years old. He threw me overboard. The swim wasn't so bad. It was getting out of that sack.

I was kidnapped as a kid. The ransom note said, "Pay us $5,000 or you'll see your kid again."

I had a pet turtle once. But I needed money so I sold his neck to a sweater company.

I was the studious, horn-rimmed glasses type. You know, the kind of kid who worries about the shortage of teachers.

He was the youngest of nine children. So he got nothing but hand-me-downs. And the other eight were sisters.

My parents didn't want me so they put a live teddy bear in my crib.

I was so skinny as a child that I had only one measle at a time.

He ran away from home as a child and his parents never found him. Of course they never looked for him.

His favorite pastime was stapling popcorn to the ground and watching pigeons go crazy.

My family never bought a pumpkin at Halloween. They made me stand in the window.

I told my mom I was running away from home. She said, "On your mark..."

When he was a kid his mother used to rock him, and she used big rocks!

I wasn't good-looking as a kid. I didn't acquire these looks until later in life.

When he was a kid, his mother sent his picture to Ripley. Ripley sent it back and wrote, "I don't believe it!"

As a kid, he stood in the corner so much in school that he developed a triangular forehead.

As a child, his parents moved a lot...but he always found them.

His parents used to take him for long walks in the woods, but he always found his way home.

Parents of bright children are always great believers in heredity.

The definition of genius is any child with grandparents.

I was so surprised at birth that I couldn't speak for 13 months.

His parents didn't exactly love him. They gave him his allowance in traveler's checks.

When I was kidnapped, my parents immediately snapped into action and rented out my room.

Our family was so large that mom made Jell-o in the bathtub.

There were nine kids, two dogs, and a cat. When Dad came home from work at night, he was afraid to ask, "What's new?"

My father was an electrician, so when I was born my appearance didn't shock him that much.

I was so skinny as a kid that I used to get backaches and stomachaches in the same place.

We couldn't afford shoes, so my mother painted my feet brown and laced up my toes.

I had a childhood accident when I banged my head on the kitchen sink. I was completely drained!

I only have four toes on my right foot. One little piggy went to market and never came back.

He was so ugly that his mother didn't push the baby carriage. She pulled it!

When he threatened to run away from home, his father made him put it in writing.

I was an ugly kid. You know how some parents put the senior pictures over the fireplace? My parents put mine in the fireplace.

I was so ugly that when I played little league baseball, the coach made me wear a catcher's mask--and I played right field!

His problem started in childhood. There wasn't a lot of money, and the kids had to swap clothes and wear hand-me-downs. It was tougher on Bob than it was on his four sisters.

He had a nasty disposition. As a kid, he had an imaginary friend that wouldn't even play with him.

One night I was studying by a roaring fire in the living room. My father came home and was really upset. You see, we didn't have a fireplace.

My parents were a little over-protective. I had the only tricycle on the block with training wheels.

I had a tough childhood. While some of the kids had sleds that were Flexible Flyers, mine was brittle.

I was a very timid child. I had a 200-Watt night light.

I was weak and puny as a kid. I was the only boy on the safety patrol who had to wear a yellow, corrective raincoat.

On Halloween his parents used to dress him as a speed bump.

He was a precocious child. At four months he was already eating solids...pencils, crayons, books...

When he was a baby his parents bought him a baby carriage with no brakes.

He played hide and seek and the kids would never look for him.

Once he had a fever and his father put a thermometer in his mouth and said, "Okay, now, bite hard!"

He asked his father if he could go ice skating and he said, "Wait until it gets warmer."

They took him to the beach and gave the lifeguard $5 saying, "Here, keep an eye off him."

When he was lost he said to the cop, "Do you think we'll find my parents?"
The cop replied, "I don't know. There are so many places they could hide."

He told his father, "Nobody likes me."
His dad said, "Don't say 'Nobody'. Everyone hasn't met you yet."

When he was a kid, his dad took him to the zoo. But they refused him.

I remember those cold winter mornings when I was a kid; Dad would take me hunting with him, and Mom would dress me warmly in my bunny suit.

As a little kid, he was somewhat backward, and rode a stickhorse to school until he was ten. Then one day it happened! Someone stole it and he was really upset because he had to walk all the way home that day.

His mother was smart. She kept him in a high crib so she could hear him when he fell out.

My great grandpa recalls his childhood: "In 1850, the bathtub was invented, and the telephone in 1875. I was able to sit in the bathtub for 25 years without the phone ringing once."

CHILDREN

Personally I don't mind having the children at home in the summer. I give them small chores to do around the home, although the three-year-old ran into a little trouble when he was putting on the new roof.

Dirty? Why after our kids are finished taking their baths, we don't know whether to drain the tub or dredge it!

How far apart should children be spaced?
Oh. I'd say about a mile and a half.

A six-year-old was asked by a friend, "What's new?"
"How should I know?" he replied. "They spell everything around here."

Two six-year-old boys were watching a little girl walk down the street. The one boy said to the other, "If I ever stop hating girls, she's the one I'm going to stop hating first."

Nurse to father waiting in maternity ward: "Well, did you want a boy or a girl?"
"A boy."
"Well, I'm afraid it's a girl."
"That's okay. That was my second choice."

Parents, raising kids is a lot like eating grapefruit. No matter how you do it, the little squirts get to you.

It's a little frustrating sometimes when you listen to your children saying their prayers. It costs thousands and thousands of dollars to raise them and you get mentioned ahead of the goldfish but after the gerbil.

Babies are nature's way of telling people what the world looks like at two o'clock in the morning.

Next year I think I'll send the kids to work and I'll go to summer camp!

As a child he once ran away with the circus, but the police caught him and made him give it back.

Personally, I never raise a finger against my children. I use the whole hand. It works a lot better.

I always wanted to spend more time with my kids. Then one day, I did!

You have to feel sorry for kids who wear braces. My daughter has so much tin in her mouth that we don't have to call her for dinner. All we do is hold up a magnet.

I won't say what my boy's room looks like but it's the first time I ever saw a roach running with one leg over its eye.

Kids today are so much more daring than we were. They have this new party game where they blindfold you. It's called "Pin the Blade on the Ceiling Fan".

You can always tell the difference between the first baby and the ones that come after. For your first baby you get a sterilizer, and a bottle is never used until it's been boiled for an hour. Now by the time the fourth child comes along, it's a little different with the bottle. He's sharing it with the dog.

I always wondered why babies spend so much time sucking their thumbs. Then one day I tasted the baby food!

CHINA

China plans to take a census of their one billion people in just ten days. No problem. All they'll have to do is count the chopsticks and divide by two.

When I was in China, I found the language very difficult. 100,000 words and none of them in English!

A single girl returned from a tour of China. "My two favorite things were Egg Foo Yung and Sum Yung Guy."

CHINESE

All Chinese names sound the same. I was in a Chinatown restaurant the other day and someone yelled, "Hey, you!" and half the people turned around. Then I said, "Who, me?" and the other half turned around.

CHINESE RESTAURANT

While in a Chinese restaurant, I saw an item on the menu, Pork Rice Almond Ding. I asked the waiter, "What's that?"
He said, "We take some pork, rice and almonds and put them in the microwave."
I said, "Well, what's the ding?"
He said, "That's the timer!"

At the Chinese restaurant there were three single waitresses whose names were, No Yen To, Too Yung To, Too Dumb To.

CHRISTMAS

My brother-in-law is a street corner Santa Claus. He isn't so bright, so they gave him a sheet of instructions. In fact, this morning I was watching him work. He went, "Ho, Ho, (look down as if reading instructions) Ho."

Every Christmas I undergo acupuncture. The family does the shopping and they stick me with the bills.

My son hasn't said much since Christmas. His new, electric toothbrush developed a short and welded his braces together.

The boss just gave us our Christmas bonus. Big deal. A dollar off any large pizza.

In honor of this festive season, our company cafeteria served a special red and green dish for lunch. Actually it was no big deal. That's the color their meat loaf always is.

What a break. Just in time for Christmas. Somebody just invented a battery-powered battery! Batteries not included.

My mother-in-law gives really exciting gifts for Christmas. Last year she gave me a gift certificate good for four hours of free advice.

Now today's consumer Christmas tip for kids, brought to you by the mall merchants' association. Remember, kids, if Santa brings everything you ask for, you're not asking for enough.

What a tie my mother-in-law got for me! What colors! You might say it's in a clash by itself!

She gave me a shirt with a neck size 14½. I take a size 16½. When I sent her a note I wrote, "Thanks for the present. I'd like to say more, only I'm all choked up."

I don't know whether we used good judgment in giving our seven-year-old one of those rockets that actually blasts off. As of 7 a.m. we've got the only cat in the neighborhood who knows what our house looks like from 400 feet up.

I never know what to get my wife for Christmas. It's next to impossible to buy for a person who has everything plus me!

This Christmas, go out and get your minister the finest—stained-glass contact lenses.

Have you been shopping in the malls, and downtown? It's incredible! You don't stroll—you get carried along with the crowd. I turned to one woman and said, "Have you ever seen such chaos?"
She said, "You ought to know. This is the ladies' room!"

I could tell the boss didn't go overboard this Christmas just by looking at the box he handed me. It said: Soap On A Rope (soap not included).

I wrote to the advice column: "Dear Sir: What would go well with the red, green and yellow argyles my wife gave me for Christmas?"
Answer: "Hip boots."

My wife still hasn't spoken to me since last Christmas. I asked her what she wanted for Christmas and she said, "Aw, just surprise me."
So at three o'clock Christmas morning, I leaned over and went, "Boo!"

This Christmas, give the teenage doll that's so realistic. It doesn't walk, it slouches.

Look at the price of Christmas trees. I paid $15 for one, took it home, and my wife's wearing it as a wrist corsage.

I had a terrible experience with the printer who printed my Christmas cards. He did the whole front cover backwards. Two hundred people I wished "Leon, Leon!"

Note on a Christmas package: Fragile, throw underhand.

Last Christmas I got my wife a gift certificate and she went right out and tried to exchange it for a larger size.

I bought a civil service doll for my daughter. It has no working parts.

Vinyl trees have become a tradition at our house. Every year I pack the kids in the car and we go over to DuPont and chop one down.

'Twas the night before Christmas and all through the house, not a creature was stirring...they had a food processor.

My mother-in-law came to visit last Christmas, and she's such a comic. Gave us a set of towels marked HERS and ITS.

This new ruling comes to us from the Health Department. If you have a history of heart trouble, you are absolutely forbidden from pricing Christmas trees.

Last Christmas I gave my wife a $20 gift certificate. She was so thrilled she said, "Oh, good, I'm going to use this to make a down payment on a $2,000 mink coat."

Batteries are very important. They make things work. That's why I'm giving a dozen to my brother-in-law.

I didn't realize how tight things were until I talked to Santa on the telephone. I inquired, "How's good, old Rudolph?"
He said, "Delicious."

Every Christmas I have this terrible decision to make. Whether to pay my son's tuition at the university or buy a Christmas tree.

Can my brother-in-law eat! For Christmas I gave him a battery-operated fork!

If you want to find yourself on the unemployment line, tell your boss that you wanted to thank him for his bonus by sending him a card but that would have used the bonus up.

Do you realize that on December 22nd summer begins in the Southern Hemisphere? Can you imagine that in some parts of the world at this very minute some people are singing, "I'm Dreaming of a Sweaty Christmas"?

I got my mother-in-law a nice gift but it keeps clawing its way through the gift wrapping.

Christmas cookies in my house last about as long as a cease-fire in Lebanon.

I'm proud to announce that I hold the land speed record for going through a Whitman's Sampler.

I can tell it's not long until Christmas. My son's building a new wing on his toy chest.

I got dozens of Christmas catalogs this year and it's so simple to decide what to give everyone for Christmas—a catalog!

My wife keeps in shape this time of year with a special exercise program—aerobic spending.

To me the three scariest words in the English language are Some Assembly Required.

My son didn't ask for much this Christmas—just a kickstand—with a Honda attached!

If anyone is thinking of sending me a Christmas gift this year, please don't bother. Just let me know where you live and I'll come over and pick it up myself.

My wife hates one of those Christmas songs. You know the one that goes, "You better not pout, you'd better not cry..." Those are two of her best weapons!

In December, it's jingle bells. In January, its juggle bills.

I get such delight watching my children hanging up their stockings Christmas Eve. It's not that it's Christmas Eve, it's just such a thrill to see them hang anything up!

There are lots of things that money can't buy. Unfortunately, none of them are on my kids' Christmas lists.

Announcement for basketball fans: John Ernest "Red" Kerr specifically asks that you do not send him any monogrammed shirts this Christmas.

If we look realistically, the Christmas presents of today are the garage sales of tomorrow.

For Christmas, his wife wanted a car of her own, but he bought her furs and jewels instead. He said he didn't know anyone who made imitation cars.

You can't win. Last Christmas, I gave my son a bowling ball and said, "Let's see you bust this..." And he lost it!

I spent fifteen dollars on a Christmas tree and had to bend over to put on the star!

We bought our daughter one of those home entertainment centers that features a color TV, stereo cassette player, video recorder, digital clock, and a 40-inch screen, and the best thing about it is that it never needs batteries. You just plug it in to the nearest nuclear power plant.

This is the time of year that I think a lot about large, year-end contributions, but I can never find anyone to give them to me.

I'm going to make a fortune this Christmas. I've developed a toy-operated battery.

I always take those Polaroid instant pictures on Christmas morning. That way I can have photos of my kids playing with their toys before they are broken.

Do you realize that if it wasn't for Christmas we would never get to know our wife's sizes?

Businesses say that this will be the greatest Christmas ever. I thought the first one was!

I don't mind getting money for Christmas. It's always just the right size.

My son is destined to become a genius in the business world. He just wrote a five-page letter to Santa and made five carbon copies for his grandparents and me.

My wife opened her Christmas gift and cooed, "Oh, you angel! Just what I need to exchange for what I really wanted."

At Christmastime our kids hang up their stockings, and then it's another year until they hang anything up again.

A department store Santa said to the youngster, "Ho, ho, ho! And what do you want for Christmas?"
The kid looked at Claus and said, "What's the matter. Didn't you get my letter?"

I gave my wife a mystery book for Christmas—a cookbook. You see, with her you never can tell how it's going to turn out.

A lady walked up to a toy counter and said, "Do you have electric trains for advanced children?"
The clerk said: "What age do you consider advanced?"
She said, "Fifty-two."

For Christmas, his father got a puppy for him and we all agreed that that was a pretty fair trade.

I'd like to remind you all that there are only nine shopping days left 'til Christmas, I take a size 15 shirt, 11 socks, I like club ties—and my hand grip fits the steering wheel of a Porsche.

Here's my favorite gift I got this Christmas—a chronometer watch. It gives you such information as the time, barometer readings, lunar cycles, wind velocity. In fact, ten seconds from now it will be low tide in Rangoon.

She doesn't sign her Christmas cards. Wants to send greetings, but doesn't want to become too involved.

I gave my wife an exchange certificate for Christmas so she could avoid the middleman.

CHURCH

After telling the story of Jonah and the whale to her Sunday school class, the teacher decided to quiz them. She asked, "Timmy, what is the moral of the story?"
Timmy thought for a minute, then said, "People make whales throw up."

I asked our six-year-old, "How did you like the service?"
She said, "I liked the music, but I thought the commercial was too long."

The worst gossip in the church came up to the pastor and said, "I'm ready to place my tongue on the altar."
To which the pastor replied, "I'd like to help you, but our altar is only fifteen feet long."

Wife: "Who was that at the door?"
Husband: "It was the new minister. That's the fourth time this week. I think his name is Pester Smith."

Pastor, I've got some terrible news. Someone broke into our church last night and stole ninety thousand dollars worth of pledges.

Does a good beginning and a good ending make a good sermon?
Yes, if they're close enough together.

A minister preached a very brief sermon and explained to the congregation, "My dog got into my office and ate all my notes."
On the way out the door, a visitor said to the pastor, "If your dog ever has pups, would you see that my minister gets one?"

A new pastor preached a stirring sermon on "Gossip" but then made a fatal error by closing the service by singing "I Love to Tell the Story".

The preacher was dickering with the salesman to lower the price on the new car. "Remember," he said, "I'm just a poor Baptist preacher."
"I know," said the salesman, "I've heard you preach!"

Sunday school teacher: "Cleanliness is next to what?"
Little boy answers, "Next to impossible!"

Sunday school teacher: "Lot was warned to take his wife and flee out of the city. But his wife turned around and turned into a pillar of salt."
A little girl raised her hand and said, "I was wondering what happened to the flea?"

He got up to leave during a long sermon. The minister said, "Where are you going?"
John replied, "To get a haircut."
The minister said, "You should have gotten one before you came."
John replied: "When I came in, I didn't need one!"

Bertha Belch was a missionary from Africa. The custodian was asked to fix the church sign. So he spelled: "Come hear Bertha Belch from Africa".

The Sunday school teacher told her class, "I want it so quiet that I'll be able to hear a pin drop."

After a few seconds of silence, a boy said, "Okay, teacher, let 'er drop."

A man goes to the doctor and says, "Doc, is there anything that you can do for my snoring?"

The doctor asks, "Why, does it disturb your wife?"

"It doesn't disturb her, just embarrasses her. It's the rest of the congregation it disturbs."

A lady said to her pastor, "Something that puzzles me. Exactly how old was Hezekiah?"

The pastor answered, "Well, he was different ages at different times."

"Oh," said the lady, "I never thought of it that way."

Noah to two snakes on the ark: "Go forth and multiply."

Snakes: "We can't. We're adders."

Remember Matthew the tax collector? They called him Levi for shorts.

CLEANLINESS

We try to bribe our son to take baths. We even bought him three toy boats to keep him company in the tub. I won't say what the water looked like when he was through bathing, but two of the boats went aground.

CLEVELAND

Why not put all future nuclear plants around Cleveland? Then if something happens, who cares?

CLOSING

I have to be going now. I placed an order for twenty dollars worth of groceries and I want to be home when they slide them under the door.

(convention closing) And as we head home with a bounce in our step, faith in our hearts, new ideas in our minds, bills in our pockets and towels in our suitcases...

Well, I've got to be closing. I have another show to give...in March.

If you liked the show tonight, tell your friends. If not, let's just make it our little secret.

In conclusion, let me end my program with these fitting words: WAKE UP!

I'd like to do something that very few speakers do...I'd like to ask for a ride home.

Due to the extreme complexity and the necessity for absolute accuracy in the discussion of this very difficult subject, will you please hold your questions until after I leave?

In closing...I just love that phrase. It's sort of like a wakeup call for the audience.

We're sorry that our guest, Father Raymond Adieu, couldn't make it tonight to pronounce the benediction. So without any Father Adieu, good night.

As Mason used to say to Dixon: "We've got to draw the line somewhere."

I'm going to close now, because I only have two minutes left on my allotted speaking time—and I usually need that for applause.

Before I close, I've been asked to make this announcement: Will the owner of the blue 1973 Chevy, license plate UQ 1837, please report to the parking lot? Your headlights are on. I dunno. Can you imagine the dumbell who's in such a hurry, he can't even remember to turn off his carlights? Boy, is that dumb? (Look at paper again). UQ 1837. (Reach into your pocket and pull out your car keys. Look at them a moment, look back at the paper, look up and say,) "Goodnight."

Our participants have proven tonight that the show must go on...and on...and on...

CLOTHING

Did you see his suit? The jacket fits fine, but the pants are a little tight across his chest.

His suits never go out of style. They look like that year after year.

I do hope he buys himself a new bathing suit this year. The one he has now has a big hole in the knee.

His clothes may seem loud to you, but I like them. They look as if they were designed by the fashion editor of a seed catalog.

He seems to keeps his clothes forever. The last time he bought a suit, the clerk said to him, "Do you want to throw it away at home, or should I burn it here?"

A charitable organization called and asked, "Do you have any old clothes?"
I replied, "Yes, but I'm still wearing them."

Look at that suit! This man has been a refugee from a steam iron for thirty years!

I don't know why, but suits just don't look good on me. Everytime I go into a clothing store, the salesman immediately knows my size: 42 baggy.

It seems everything you buy today is imported. Look at the shirt I'm wearing. Do you know what the washing instructions are? "Beat against flat rock!"

I told the clothing salesman I wanted to see something cheap. He said, "Go look in the mirror."

I love your outfit. Does a holster come with it?

I love that formal wear. I didn't know Fruit-of-the-Loom made tuxedos.

He has a tough time buying clothes. There aren't many stores that stock medium dumpy.

That's a great suit you have on, sir, although isn't it a bit alarming to think how many polyesters had to die to make it?

He has a suit of clothes for every day of the year, and I see that he is wearing it tonight.

What a great outfit you have on! It's not too often that you see two-toned bowling shirts!

I just noticed his outfit. I didn't know he had a blind tailor.

My daughter had a really embarrassing moment the other night. She went to a party and someone else was wearing the very same outfit she was—her date!

People are always picking on me. The other day I went into a clothing store and asked the clerk what I'd look best in and he said, "A ski mask!"

You can tell a lot about a person just by the way he dresses. For instance, just look at the outfit he's wearing tonight and you can tell four things about our guest: He's neat, tidy, affluent, and color blind.

His fashions are designed by Bob Blastoff. Look smashing in a Bob Blastoff suit, that makes you look like you just fell on a live grenade.

He's worn that suit so many years it's been in style five times.

He's not exactly a clothes horse—in fact it took him ten years just to learn how to work his belt loops!

When they issued the list for the 10 Best Dressed Men in America, it was _____ who typed it.

He said, "Whenever I'm down in the dumps I buy new clothes."
I was wondering where he got his clothes.

Doesn't that suit fit him like a glove? Now, he ought to get one that fits like a suit.

I like your suit. But what do you do when the horse gets cold?

He's a member of the jet set. As you can see he dressed in front of the propeller.

I like your outfit. Did the clown die?

A duck walked into a clothing store, tried on a hat, and started walking toward the door. The salesman said, "Are you going to pay cash for that, Mr. Duck?"
The duck replied, "No, just put it on my bill."

Look at his sartorial splendor! His clothes are a cross between Brooks Brothers and Ringling!

I can never look like those models in the clothing ads. They look so "spiffy" wearing ascots. I always look as if I'm treating strep throat.

I'll give you an idea of what my wardrobe is like. Goodwill pays me $500 a year not to clean out my closet.

My perma-press suit holds a crease. In fact, it holds thousands of them.

The bathing suit that she bought this year was so small that it came on an empty hanger.

I won't discuss his casual attire in detail. Let's just put it this way. He's always very careful to stay indoors on trash pickup days.

The clothing salesman said to him, "Would you like me to measure your chest or would you rather not know?"

"That's a beautiful coat you're wearing." "Thank you. My husband gave it to me for my 39th birthday." "My, it certainly has worn well!"

COACH

He doesn't know the meaning of the word fear. In fact, I just saw his grades and he doesn't know the meaning of a lot of words.

He's a neurotic coach. Everytime the team went into the huddle he wondered if they were talking about him.

The coach was asked what it was like to coach at the state prison. "Perfect!" he replied. "First, you always have the homecourt advantage. You play every game at home. Intimidation certainly means a lot. When you've got an arsonist and two murderers on the team, you're in pretty good shape. Third, the parents don't give a rip. And fourth, the alumni don't come back raising Cain with you!"

A rival coach said, "I don't see how anyone could flunk out of Texas Tech. Studying would be the high point of the day—being in out of the wind."

As a coach, I won half my games...the first half.

He summed up his coaching career. "I was desired, wired, hired, inspired, admired, tired, mired, and fired."

COFFEE

Sign in a restaurant window: "Don't make fun of our coffee. You may be old and weak yourself someday."

They call him Sanka because he has no active ingredient in the bean.

COLD

To keep a cold in your head from spreading to your chest, tie a knot in your neck.

My thermostat was so low this morning that I had to jump-start my electric razor.

Well, the flu season is upon us, so if you experience a feeling of tightness and you can't breathe, you may have the flu. It's either that or you're wearing designer jeans.

COLLEGE

One college is graduating so many functional illiterates it's putting their diplomas on cassettes.

As today's college graduates head into the real world they face enormous challenges. Two of them are reading and writing.

This is the time of year when college graduates move into the in-between stage of life—too old to go to summer camp and too young to retire.

June is when college graduates take their diplomas in hand and go out to conquer the world. July is when the world counterattacks.

I am a contributor to the Italian College Fund. Their motto is: "A fist is a terrible thing to waste."

We really had some tough teams at my alma mater. I'll never forget guys like Moose, Crusher, Bronco, and Tiger. And that was just the chess team!

Today's students have nothing about which to complain. Why 25 years ago, college kids really had problems—did you ever try to swallow 14 goldfish when at home you didn't even eat spinach?

There walks a college man. I'm sure you've heard of the ramblin' wreck from Georgia Tech? Well, he's a total loss from Holy Cross.

I know one football player who has been in college for twelve years. He can run and kick but he just can't pass.

My college just had another athletic scandal. Three of our basketball players were caught sneaking into the library.

He played hooky from correspondence school. He sent in empty envelopes.

He attended _____ University where he majored in registration.

I majored in education for a very good reason—I couldn't spell business administration.

She went to barber college and was head shearleader. She was kicked out for cutting classes.

I went to junior high, senior high, and college in the same community, which was a very convenient arrangement. That way I could use the same textbooks all the way through.

When I was a senior in college, I remember sitting at the dinner table and hearing my mother tell my father, "I'm really worried about Ken's grades. I sure hope he g-r-a-d-u-a-t-e-s."

I went to college in New Mexico on a basketball scholarship. My coach lined up a cinch course for me—basket weaving. The problem was that there were only three students, the professor graded on a curve, and the other two students were Navajo Indians.

My son has his academic future well-planned. He wants to go to the U. of M. for his B.A., U.C.L.A. for his M.B.A. and M.I.T. for his Ph.D.. Anyway by the time he's through I'll be B.R.O.K.E..

He studied hard in college and majored in journalism. Now he has his own paper route.

The owner of a restaurant was saying to a new employee, "Wash these dishes."
The fella said, "But, sir, I'm a college graduate."
The owner replied, "You are?" Well, in that case, I'll show you how."

How can they admit kids to college when they don't even know how to write? For instance, they admitted one girl because she made straight A's. The B's she made were a little crooked.

It kind of startles you a little bit when you ask a college senior what time it is and he says, "Wait a minute. I'll look at my tick-tock."

It is reassuring, however, to see that colleges are putting the emphasis on the basics again. One school has gotten so strict it won't even give a football player his letter unless he can tell which one it is.

Many people haven't heard of my alma mater, but let me assure you, it's one of the goodest colleges in the United States.

There is only one way to cope with the rising costs of putting a kid through college. When they're very young, start an education fund for them and every year add to it. Then, just when they're ready to enter college, rob a bank.

I played football in college...'62, '63, '64, '65, '66, '67, '68, '69...

The team nicknamed me "Judge" when I was in college. I sat on the bench for four years.

When he was in college, he kept the women running in circles. He was the women's track coach.

Statistics show that 90 percent of people who actually listen to commencement speeches are parents who are making one last attempt to get something for their money.

College did a lot for him. He can now fill out his unemployment form in Latin and French!

He's educated beyond his intelligence. He went to public school on a scholarship.

A recent survey at my alma mater revealed that most of the students preferred wearing sandals to shoes because it made it easier for them to count to twenty.

His alma mater sells bumper stickers that say: IF YOU CAN READ THIS, YOU'RE COLLEGE MATERIAL.

I went to a little known, small college. Whereas some colleges have marching bands, we had a marching quartet.

He graduated with a B.A., and that stood for "barely adequate".

He took an aptitude test his senior year in college. The examiner told him, "You have a bright future in any field where a close relative holds a senior management position."

He's got more degrees than a thermometer.

He's a three-letter man from the University of Texas. He sat on a branding iron.

I was a half back in college. I'd tear the tickets in two at the gate, and give half back.

The college athletic offices all sport signs on their doors. For instance: "If you're too tall for this door, report to the basketball coach." Or, "If you're too wide for this door, please report to the football coach." And my personal favorite, "If you took a bite out of this door, report to the hockey coach."

A wealthy graduate, talking to a college president, said, "Well, now that I've made a lot of money, I'd like to do something for the good old alma mater and donate a building. Let's see, in what subject did I excel?"
After looking over his transcript, the president told the philanthropist, "I suggest you build a dormitory. Judging from your records it looks like you slept most of the time."

I asked a college grad what he was doing, and he informed me, "I'm on the cutting edge of technology." I later learned that he mows the lawn at Apple Computers.

My son just made his first money since he graduated from college six months ago. He sold the watch I gave him for graduation.

Vocabulary teacher: "Say a word five times and it will be yours for life."
Coed: "Robert, Robert, Robert, Robert, Robert."

A college grad handed his diploma to his father and said, "Well, I finished medical school like you and mom wanted. Now I'm going to be a fireman like I've been telling you since I was six."

I was so skinny, I had to go to college at Illinois. It was the only letter that would fit on my chest.

At our school, they burned the coach in effigy and everything else in the cafeteria.

"What does your son plan to do after he graduates?"
"Well, judging from the letters and collect calls we get, I think he wants to be a professional fund raiser."

 # COLUMBUS

If Christopher Columbus had had a wife at home, could he have discovered America? "You're going where? With whom? To find what? Coming back when? And I suppose she's giving you those three ships for nothing?"

 # COMMERCIALS

Popcorn for tonight's program was supplied by Orville Whopperpopper, maker of the world's finest nuclear popcorn. Next time your family nags you for popcorn, pop 'em some Whopperpopper. They'll get a real bang out of it.

Soft drinks for tonight's program were supplied by Wow Free the exciting all-new cola that contains no caffeine. And honestly, you don't miss the caffeine at all—because they replaced it with horse radish.

If not completely satisfied, just return the unused portion of the jar, and we'll return the unused portion of your money.

The exciting new Arm and Hammer arm and hammer. Perfect for hanging pictures, adding a roof, and hundreds of other odd jobs. Look for the Arm and Hammer arm and hammer wherever arms and hammers are sold.

Haircuts for today's show were supplied by Ernie's Barber College. Ernie's—where there's never an extra charge for band-aids.

Kiddies, try a big bowl of those great new Crunchy Monsters. They contain more iron than a Schwinn bicycle.

My appearance here tonight is being underwritten by Harvey Schlock's Income Tax Service and Travel Agency. Remember Harvey's slogan: "If I make a mistake on your income tax, you can be in South America the same day."

Remember, Colonel Sanders' Tanning Oil is available in two formulas: regular and crispy.

Try new Liquid Plumber Facial Cream. Remember, if it'll unclog your sink, it'll certainly unclog your pores!

Tonight's jokes are provided through the courtesy of Flipper's Fast Fish, the fantastic fast fish franchise featuring fabulous french-fried flounder fins. Sunday's special: Save 70 cents on super sardine sticks sauteed in sweet and sour sauce.

Our corn liniment will not remove corns, but it will cause them to relocate to the bottom of your toes so that only you personally can step on them.

Try one box and if you don't like it, don't complain. After all, we've got millions of them.

Friend, are you nervous? When you play basketball, do you find yourself dribbling when you don't have the ball?

Some cereals are shot out of a cannon. We kick ours into the box.

Remember, we make no claims. We make no guarantees. We just make $3.50 a book.

Remember, kids, Choco-Crisp is the only candy bar that comes without a wrapper, and it's handled by dealers everywhere.

One customer put too much of our hair restorer on and smothered to death before he could get to the barber.

We're not the Breakfast of Champions. We're the breakfast for kids who just want to reach the semi-finals or get the "good sportsmanship" award.

Remember, Schlegelmich's Soap, the brand name that you can't spell backwards or forwards.

The phone number is Hudson 8-9927. Let me repeat that. Central 6-5512.

With every order of our vitamins we'll include our new book on how to remove tonsils in your free time.

Our show is being brought to you by Barkees Dog Biscuits—the biscuit that tastes just like the mailman's leg.

Remember, by offering inferior merchandise, we're able to pass the savings along to you.

Yes, folks, our product contains no preservatives, no artificial color or flavor. In fact, when you open the box, you'll find that it's empty.

All I ask is to have as much fun as the people that they show in the soft drink commercials.

If the label says, "New" or "Improved", that means the price has gone up.

Today's show is brought to you by Bow-Wow Po Lite, the only diet dog food. Just the thing for your fat Fido.

Today's program is being sponsored by the Elephant Transfer Company. We may be slow, but we never forget an address.

CONTEST

Our new contest. Just send us $25,000 and we'll send you 25 words or less.

CONTRADICTIONS

Just came across a new phrase to add to my list of expressions that contradict each other, like "honest politician" and "military intelligence". How about "postal service"?

The government uses some misleading terms. They call a nuclear missile a "Peacekeeper", new taxes "revenue enhancers", but what will they call unemployment, "a vacation extender?"

CONVENTION SITES

I attended the Plumbers' Convention in Flushing, New York...the Hot Dog Manufacturers' Association in Frankfort, Kentucky...Parents of Twins in Minneapolis/St. Paul... Weight Watchers' Convention in Gainsville, Florida, and the National Contortionists' Convention in South Bend, Indiana.

COWS

I started milking cows in the sixth grade and I milked them until I finished high school...not continuously...

I crossed a cow with an octopus and developed a do-it-yourself milker...

We had a buck-tooth cow and everywhere she went she said, "Moof."

A tragic thing happened to one of our cows. She was bitten on the udder by an adder.

Some great cow songs: "If Heifer I Would Leave You"; "Catch a Falling Steer and Put it in Your Pocket"; "The Bullfight Crowd Shouted 'Ole' As the Bull Tore Hernando's Hide Away".

Did you hear about the absent-minded cow that only gave milk of amnesia?

It's really easy to milk a cow. Any jerk can do it.

Our cow got the hiccoughs and churned her own butter.

It was so hot yesterday that the cows gave evaporated milk.

Do you know how long cows should be milked?
The same as the short ones!

This milk is so fresh that an hour ago it was grass!

The cow chewed Kentucky bluegrass and mooed indigo.

CREDIT

Credit card companies don't fool around. I had a cousin who took a vacation, ran up $3,000 on his credit cards and died on the way back. Beat the credit card companies, right? No way! First time I ever saw lillies repossessed.

If you really want to drive your creditors crazy, fill out one of those change of address cards at the post office—and then don't move!

CRIME

You can spot a crime if you walk into your bank and everybody's doing business face down...or if you come home from vacation and the neighbors say that the guy in the moving van said, "Thanks."

A guy was sent to Leavenworth because he was making big money. About a third of an inch too big.

A woman held up a department store with a pricing gun. She said, "Give me all the money in the safe or I'll mark down everything in this place!"

Crime is so bad in the United States that the Statue of Liberty is holding both arms in the air!

The trouble with opportunity knocking on the door in these days of high crime rates is that by the time you unhook the chain, push back the bolt, turn two locks and shut off the burglar alarm, it's gone.

DO-IT-YOURSELF
SPACE.

WRITE YOUR
OWN JOKE
HERE!

DAFFYNITION

Windshield scraper: That's that fine implement that falls out of your glove compartment all summer long, hides under the seat in the winter, and breaks the first time you try to use it.

DATING

"Young man, did I hear the clock strike four when you brought my daughter in?"
"Yes, you did sir. It was going to strike eleven, but I held the gong so it wouldn't awaken you."

"Why won't you marry me? Is there someone else?"
"There must be!"

"Please whisper those three little words that will make me walk on air."
"Go hang yourself!"

I know a girl who wears her heart on her sleeve.
I told you those transplants weren't perfected.

"I guess you've been out with worse looking fellows than I am, haven't you?" (repeat)
(girl) "I heard you the first time. I was just trying to think."

"I'd like to marry you."
"Well, leave your name and address and if nothing better turns up, I'll call you."

"I want to be honest. You're the first girl I've ever kissed."
"I want to be honest. You've got a lot to learn."

"If you give me your phone number I'll give you a call."
"It's in the book."
"Good, what's your name?"
"It's in the book, too."

"If I tried to kiss you, would you call for help?"
"Do you need help?"

"I can tell just by looking in a girl's eyes exactly how she feels about me."
"Gee, that must be embarrassing for you."

My first girlfriend and I both wore braces. I'll never forget the first time we kissed during a thunderstorm, we short-circuited four city blocks and her earrings lit up.

Her date was really terrible. Not only did he lie about the size of his yacht, he made her help with the rowing!

When I took her out to eat, she ordered the most expensive thing on the menu—a Big Mac with double cheese.

He heard that it was always proper to flatter his date. One night he went out with a girl who was rather plump. When he took her to the door, he was stumped for something nice to say. Finally, he sputtered, "You know, for a fat girl you don't sweat much."

I wouldn't marry you if you were the last man on earth.
I know, honey, because you'd be killed in the rush.

I took her to a restaurant and asked her, "How do you like your rice—baked or fried?"
She said, "Thrown!"

He took her to an amusement park and I asked, "Did you take her through the Tunnel of Love?"
He said, "Yeah, but I didn't like it. It was dark, and damp, and we got all wet."
I said, "Was there a leak in your boat?"
He replied, "There's a boat?"

He took a girl horseback riding and when they stopped to rest the horses rubbed their necks against each other affectionately. The guy said to the girl, "Ah, me, that's what I'd like to do."
His girl responded, "Well, go ahead, it's your horse."

When I said to my future wife: "I'm not much to look at," she said, "That's okay, you'll be at the office most of the day anyway."

"Excuse me for bothering you by coming to the door for your daughter, sir, but my car horn's not working."

"Has anyone ever told you how wonderful you are?"
"No."
"Then where did you get the idea?"

"What would you say if I asked you to be my wife?"
"Nothing. I can't talk and laugh at the same time."

His friend fixed him up with a blind date. After seeing her, he said, "What are you trying to do to me? Look at her. She's ugly, she's old, she squints, she has buck teeth."
His friend said, "Why are you whispering? She's deaf, too."

When I first saw her, lights flashed, there was a buzzing in my ears, bells sounded—we were in a video arcade.

As they were driving down the road, he said, "You're beautiful. That golden hair."
"Thank you!"
"And your big, blue eyes. They're beautiful, too!"
"Thank you!"
"And your lips and pearly teeth."
"Can you drive with one hand?" she asked softly.
"Sure," he hopefully replied.
"Well, wipe your nose. It's running."

Last night I took my girl out for a royal feast. First we went to Burger King and then we went to Dairy Queen for dessert.

My daughter is searching for the perfect guy. I keep telling her, "You might as well give up the search. Your mother got the last one."

My girl dropped me when she discovered that the two carat diamond that I gave her had the faint smell of Crackerjacks about it.

The couple was strolling along the beach, lost in love. The young beau looked out to the sea and eloquently said, "Roll on, thou deep, dark, blue ocean--roll."
His girl looked at him with admiring eyes and spoke, "Oh, Herman. You're wonderful. It's doing it!"

When I dated her, I knew she was a real lady. She only dunked her doughnuts up to her knuckles.

We went for a walk one evening. I looked at the stars and said, "Do you like astronomy?"
She said, "No, I don't go for that kosher food."

She had a face that only a mother could love--a near-sighted mother.

She threw out subtle hints. On hot summer days she used to fan me with a marriage license.

The older gentleman approached the young lovely and asked, "Where have you been all my life?"
She answered, "Well, for the first forty years, I wasn't even born!"

At the restaurant she said, "I'll have the oysters Rockefeller, the pressed duck, and baked Alaska, unless, of course, you're saving for a ring or something..."

Boy: "Frankly, you're not the first girl I've ever kissed."
Girl: "Frankly, you've still got a lot to learn."

I went to a party where I was to meet a blind date. I walked up to the girl and said, "Hi, are you Mary Beth?"
She asked, "Are you Ken?"
I said, "Yes."
She said, "I'm not Mary Beth!"

He told her he'd die if she turned him down, but she did. And sure enough, 62 years later, he did.

I took her out in my car and she insisted that I put the top down. I did and it took me three hours. I don't have a convertible.

Harold was bragging to a friend about the intelligence of his girl friend. "Why, Mary has brains enough for two!"
"Well then, she's just the girl for you," replied his friend.

Everytime I found a girl who could cook like my mother, she looked like my father.

He purchased a little black book as a teenager and confidently wrote on the inside cover, "Volume One."

DAUGHTERS

Ability is what you need to have if the boss doesn't have any daughters.

My daughter has no luck at all. Last year a fella asked if he could change her name to his and she said yes. And ever since he's been calling her Bruce.

DAYLIGHT SAVING TIME

We move our clocks ahead an hour Saturday night but I don't mind losing an hour's sleep. I get it back Sunday morning during the minister's sermon.

Okay, for Daylight Saving Time we just set our clocks up an hour, that's easy. But what about folks who live on farms? How do you reset a rooster?

I could never figure out that when we set our clocks back an hour, the sun goes down an hour earlier. How does the sun know to do that?

DEEJAY LINES

I had a terrible thing happen to me this morning. I heard a mother say to her six-year-old, "Do you want to hear the _____ Show?"
He said, "No!"
She said, "Then behave yourself."

The time is now twenty after twelve. And for those of you attending (local college) that means the short hand is on the twelve and the big hand is on the four.

DENTIST

If you want to keep your teeth in good condition, brush your teeth after every meal and mind your own business.

My dentist is so cheap that he makes you spit the Lavoris back into the bottle.

"Doc, you still haven't pulled the right tooth."
"I know," said the dentist, "but I'm getting to it."

Never trust a dentist who mixes his fillings from a recipe in a Betty Crocker cookbook.

"How much will it cost to have this tooth pulled?"
"Twenty dollars," said the dentist.
"Twenty dollars for thirty seconds work?"
"Well, if you like," said the dentist, "I can work more slowly."

I went to a discount dentist. He's the first one I ever went to that uses a Black and Decker drill.

My dentist is poor. He doesn't have a chair that goes back and forth. He has to climb on the patient's knee and bob up and down.

There's so much in the world that doesn't make sense. Have you ever wondered why it costs $30 to have your entire house cleaned—and $40 to have your teeth cleaned?

Today a dentist removed a five pound molar from an ailing elephant. The trick was to get it to spit into that little sink.

My dentist is cheap, mainly because he doesn't go in for a lot of fancy equipment...like a sink. When he's finished working on you he says, "O.K., rinse and swallow."

The dentist told me, I have some good news and bad news for you. The bad news is you have seven teeth that must come out, you need a lot of root canal work, and your gums are all diseased."
I asked, "What's the good news?"
He said, "I broke 80 on the golf course yesterday."

My dentist just introduced a new toothpaste called Partico. It's the only kind on the market that comes with food particles already in it for people who are too busy to eat between brushings.

My dentist married a manicurist. Now they fight tooth and nail.

He pioneered the orthodontic technique whereby an entire savings account can be removed through a child's mouth.

He goes to the dentist twice a year. Once for each tooth.

 # DIET

The second day of a diet is always easier than the first—by the second day you're off of it.

The trouble with square meals is that they make you round.

My doctor told me that if I were three inches taller, I'd be at my perfect weight. So, I went right out and joined Height Watchers.

I embarked on the long, painful road to thinness last weekend, and I ran into a problem right away. I can't travel on an empty stomach.

I tried dieting once, but it didn't work. Cottage cheese makes lousy hot fudge sundaes.

My doctor put me on a no-starch diet. However, I can eat all the soap and bleach I want.

Just a reminder: What's on the table soon becomes what's on the chair.

I'm on the new wonder diet. I eat what I want tonight and wonder if my clothes will fit tomorrow.

I went on the toothpick and after-dinner mint diet. I pretend that I've already eaten.

I'm on the Shakespeare diet. Tubby or not Tubby.

I'm on the army diet. Everything I eat goes to the front.

Cottage cheese must be the most fattening food around. Everywhere I go, I see fat people eating it.

My doctor told me that if I take six of these little pills (reach into your pocket and pull out a ping-pong ball) before each meal, that it would definitely curb my appetite.

I'm on a new diet. I don't eat anything but food.

I finally solved my weight problem. I purchased a new metric scale and now I have no idea what I weigh.

Dieting: Tightening the belt on your birthday suit.

I got tired of watching my weight, so I hired a sitter to watch it while I go out for pizza.

My doctor says the new fiber diet he put me on should help me lose lots of weight. And I guess he's right. Have you ever seen a fat moth?

He's on a new diet. He's given up eating M&M's because they got too hard to peel.

He's on a seafood diet. He sees food and he eats it.

He's on a new diet. He eats garlic, onions and limburger cheese. He hasn't lost any weight, but from a distance he looks thin.

He eats nothing but bananas and drinks coconut milk. Hasn't lost any weight, but you ought to see him climb trees.

I tried the rice diet, but between meals I got an awful urge to fold shirts.

When he says he diets religiously, that means he doesn't eat in church.

He stepped on one of those new computerized talking scales. The scale went clang, bang, and a voice in the machine said, "One at a time, please."

Desperation is a fellow shaving himself before he steps on the scale.

I just went on the Cleveland diet. You can eat only what can live in Lake Erie.

It's time to go on a diet when you have to let out the shower curtain.

She's a light eater. As soon as it's light, she starts to eat.

He eats low-fat food. The fat keeps going lower and lower. He now has 48-inch ankles.

He's on a sure-fire diet. He never eats while his wife is talking.

I just joined an organization that couldn't care less. Their motto is: A WAIST IS A TERRIBLE THING TO MIND.

You know you should diet when you get caught in a thunderstorm and nothing below your waist gets wet.

It's time to cut back if you wear out a fork every week.

You should diet if you have nightmares that someone named Captain Ahab is following you with a harpoon.

You're overweight if the couch gets up when you do.

You know that it's time to diet if in order to use the seesaw in the park, you have to invite the entire neighborhood.

I'm on the acupuncture diet. I eat anything I want and lose weight through leakage.

He knew he should diet when his mouth developed stretch marks.

Lose a few pounds when the drugstore scale fortune tells you, "No group discounts."

He became serious about dieting when the local stockyard named him "Man of the Year".

You've got a real diet problem when Weight Watchers revokes your membership.

It's time to lose weight if the bus driver asks you to sit on the right side because he wants to turn that way.

Lose some weight if someone calls you fat and all you can do is turn the other chin.

You're starting to get desperate if you get on the bathroom scale, deduct five pounds for your underwear and jewelry, and you're still overweight.

It's time to diet if they ban you on the Super Mountain roller coaster ride, because the last time you were on, you flattened the dips.

It's time to diet if you have to bend your knees in order to touch your necktie.

I just couldn't keep on my diet. So I did the next best thing. I became jolly.

You should start on a diet immediately if your car leaves deep tire prints in the concrete driveway.

You know it's time to shed a few pounds if you must dig a hole between two trees so your hammock clears the ground.

I'm on the decorator's diet. It's curtains for my bay window.

I found a candy that I can eat while dieting--chocolate-covered lettuce.

Another great way to lose weight. Send it through the mail.

A diet is what you keep putting off while your keep putting on.

 # DOCTOR

He told me that he'd have me on my feet in less than a month, and he was right. When I got his bill, I had to sell my car.

He went to the doctor, and the doctor told him he had six months to live. He went to another doctor who told him the same thing. So now he has a year...

Depression is when your doctor dies of the same thing for which he was treating you.

My doctor examined me at my annual physical and said, "Well, you're as sound as a dollar, but there is a chance you might recover."

I've got to admit, I'm a big sissy when it comes to going to the doctor. I even take a local anesthetic when I get my glasses adjusted.

A recent survey shows that of all jobs, caddies live the longest. They get plenty of fresh air and exercise, and if there's ever a medical emergency, a doctor is always nearby.

I was born on a Wednesday, and the way that I remember is that the doctor slapped me with a putter.

This May, my son will fulfill his life-long dream to associate himself with the great doctors, surgeons, and medical researchers of our time, when he graduates from Harvard. He's going to be a caddy.

My opthamologist doesn't exactly inspire confidence. He sends out his bills in Braille.

The doctor told me, "I don't care how you feel. I'll release you from the hospital when I think you're ready to be released and not a dollar sooner."

"You're coughing more easily this morning," the doctor said.
"I should be," replied the patient. "I've been practicing all night."

"Don't forget," the lady told the doctor, "When my Melvin made lots of money for you by giving measles to the entire fifth grade."

Nurse: "That man to whom you just gave a clean bill of health just dropped over dead in the office as he was leaving, doctor. What should I do?"
"Turn him around," said the doctor, "so it looks as if he was walking in."

An inept surgeon was finally discharged from the hospital. It wasn't because of all the patients he lost. It was because of all the deep gashes he left in the operating table.

Never trust a doctor whose tongue depressor tastes like the Baskin and Robbins flavor of the month.

Never trust a doctor who stores his hypodermic needles on a dartboard.

Nurse to patient: "You have an appointment in two weeks."
Patient: "But I could be dead in two weeks!"
Nurse: "Well, in that case, you can cancel your appointment."

After the doctor operated, he discovered he left a sponge in me. I don't have any pain, but I really get thirsty.

I asked the doctor, "What kind of shape am I in?"
"Let's put it this way," said the doc, "from now on I want you to pay me in advance."

What's the difference between an allergy and an itch?
About $25 a visit.

"Did your father die a natural death?"
"Oh, no, he had a doctor."

The doctor gave me something to raise my low blood pressure. His bill!

"Doc, I have this ringing in my ears."
"Okay, don't answer it."

I just left my doctor. I'm okay, but my savings died.

My doctor said, "Let me start with your medical history. Do you pay your doctor bills promptly?"

"Well, how did the appendectomy go?" the veteran surgeon asked the intern.
"Appendectomy?" replied the intern. "I thought it was an autopsy!"

A medical school professor asked a nervous freshman, "How do you feel about euthanasia?"
"I think they have the same problems kids over here do," replied the student.

Forget about doctors' fees. Have you priced "get-well" cards lately?

My doctor gave me a prescription: "Take one pill as often as you can afford it."

My doc just discovered a cure for amnesia, but forgot what it was.

An apple a day keeps the doctor away. Sure, but so do golf and European vacations.

The doctor told me I needed an operation. I said, "I want a second opinion."
He said, "Okay, you're also overweight."

My eye doctor said, "Close one eye and tell me what you see."
I said, "Half of a bad suit."

I asked the doctor, "Doc, for $50, what can you do for me?"
He said, "I'll send you a get-well card."

Doesn't it always bug you how people talk about doctors "practicing medicine"? What--do they practice it until they get it right?

I went to my doctor for my annual physical and told him, "I feel great!"
The doctor said, "Well, I have a cure for that..."

I have a great doctor. When you're at death's door, he'll pull you through.

Never trust a doctor who tells you you're dead. Get a second opinion.

Never trust a doctor who attaches a pacemaker with Krazy Glue.

A doctor is someone who acts like a humanitarian and charges like a plumber.

I told my doctor I wanted a second opinion. He said, "Okay, see me tomorrow."

My doctor asked me if I ever had a stress test. I said, "Yeah, when I got your last bill."

It made me nervous when I was about to have an operation, and I overhead the doctor say to his nurse, "I'll take all calls."

I said to the doctor, "When I stand on my head all the blood rushes to it. Yet when I stand on my feet the blood doesn't rush to them. Why?" The doctor answered, "Your feet aren't empty."

He had an injury and the doctor told him, "Take a pill every day and walk a mile each day. Call me at the end of the month."
At the end of the month, the patient called and said, "Doc, what do I do now? I'm thirty miles from home and out of pills."

Hear about the doctor who went on a ski trip and was lost in the snow for a week? He stamped out H-E-L-P in the snow but nobody could read his writing.

My doctor says he just returned from an African safari and didn't kill a thing. He said he would have been better off staying at the hospital.

"No doubt about it. You're crazy."
"I want a second opinion."
"Okay, you're ugly, too."

"Doc, I have a cold or something in my head."
"I'll bet it's a cold."

My doctor says, "I'm well aware that the cost of medical care is outrageous--but so is the price of yachts."

I could tell that my doctor was in a hurry to finish the operation by his instructions to the nurse: "Clamp, sutures, putter..."

I've learned one thing about doctors. If he examines you and gives you a long, confident nod it means, "Your guess is as good as mine."

I wonder about my doctor. I mean it's okay to take out my appendix and my tonsils, but through the same incision?

He was an honest doctor. On the death certificate where it said "Cause of Death", he signed his name.

Doctor leaving his office to move his car: "I'll be back in a minute. Now don't anyone get well."

My doctor told me, "You have six months to live."
I said, "I'll never be able to pay your bill in that time."
He said, "Okay, I'll give you another six months."

A guy said to his doctor, "My foot hurts. What should I do?"
The doctor replied, "Limp!"

My doctor told me to take a hot bath before retiring. That's ridiculous. It'll be years before I retire.

Tonight we salute Dr. Nemo, developer of the brain by-pass...

I asked the doctor, "Is it anything serious?"
He said, "Only if you have plans for next year."

"I'm well aware that the cost of medical insurance is soaring," said the doctor, "but so is the cost of my malpractice insurance!"

The very first words that Rip Van Winkle heard after awaking from his twenty year sleep, "The doctor will see you now."

I always wanted to be a doctor but it didn't work. I could never stand the sight of golf balls.

My doctor says I shouldn't smoke, drink, overeat, dissipate or do anything else that could interfere with paying his bill.

I asked the doctor, "How do I stand?"
He answered, "That's what puzzles me."

If you are a doctor, you can always expect to face constant challenges, frustration, adversity, and yes, even heartbreak. So much for golf, now let's talk about medicine.

He didn't believe in doctors. He bought medical books and successfully treated himself for 25 years. Then one day he died of a misprint.

He treated a guy for jaundice for three years and then found out he was Chinese.

The doctor took out his stethoscope and carefully listened to my wallet.

He's earned so much money as a doctor that he can occasionally tell a patient that there's nothing wrong with him.

After waiting three hours in a doctor's waiting room, an old man stood up wearily and remarked on his way out the door, "Well, I guess I'll go home and die a natural death."

(doctor in an operating room) Phew, that was a close one! An inch either way and it would have been out of my speciality.

The doctor told me he'd have me walking in three weeks, and he was right. When I got his bill, I had to sell my car to pay him.

A doctor examining a patient complaining of an earache noticed a string hanging from her ear. The physician tugged and tugged on the string, and with great effort, extracted a bouquet of flowers from her left ear. "Now where did this come from?" queried the doctor. "How should I know?" snapped the lady. "Read the card!"

My doctor is unique. I open my wallet and he goes, "Ah."
Doctors are really specialists these days. I met one the other day who specializes in diseases of the nose--left nostril.

He went for his annual physical. After the examination, the doctor said to his wife, "I don't like the looks of him."
His wife said, "But he's so good to the kids."

Doctors' Convention: "You've all heard the motion. All those in favor, open your mouths, stick out your tongues, and say, "Ah."

"Doctor, I'm so grateful. How can I repay you?"
"Simply by cash, check, or money order!"

I just know that my son is going to grow up to be a doctor. He is already collecting old magazines.

There is one thing my doctor can do better than anyone else. Read his own handwriting.

He's a surgeon who moonlights as a chef at a Japanese restaurant.

My doctor gave me a four-way cold tablet, but it couldn't figure out which way to go.

A western doctor came across a poor pioneer who had been brutally attacked by Indians. The vicitim had been scalped, wounded, and an arrow was sticking from his back. As the doctor started to remove the arrow, he asked, "Does it hurt much?"
"Only when I laugh," said the settler.

"Doctor, I'm suffering from kleptomania."
"Have you taken anything for it?"
"Yeah, anything I can lay my hands on."

The average American goes to the doctor five times a year--and the average doctor goes to Europe six times a year.

My doctor says he'll give me a clean bill of health as soon as my check clears.

I have a really tremendous doctor but I have trouble getting sick between his vacations.

We need all the doctors we can get. After all, what would we do with all the old magazines?

He went to his doctor this morning, complaining of amnesia, and his doctor said, "Hmm...have you ever had this before?"

I saw a sign in the doctor's office that said, "10 to 1". So I went home. I want better odds than that.

(at a doctors' convention) It's such a pleasure to be talking to a group of doctors without having to take my clothes off.

I've been seeing spots in front of my eyes.
Have you seen a doctor?
No, just spots.

I don't have much faith in my doctor. All of his patients are sick.

The doctor had to get a new adding machine. The old one only went up to millions.

(to patient) "Let me know if that medicine works...I'm having the same problem myself."

We've decided to postpone your operation until you're stronger-- financially.

I called the doctor the other morning at 3 a.m. and said, "I hate to bother you, but I have a bad case of insomnia."
He replied, "What are you trying to do...start an epidemic?"

I told my doctor, "I'm temporarily broke, but I'll remember you in my will."
The doctor replied, "Oh, would you let me have that prescription back I just wrote for you? There's one small change I'd like to make."

Doctors' creed: Always write your prescriptions illegibly and your bills plainly.

I have a doctor who doesn't really inspire confidence. I asked him, "How long do you plan to practice medicine?"
He answered, "Until I get it right."

The doctor looked at the patient and said, "You have acute appendicitis."
The patient looked at the doctor and said, "Look, doc, I came here to be examined, not flattered."
My doctor told me: "First the good news. You're going to have a disease named after you."

Doesn't it give you a weird feeling when your doctor turns to his nurse and asks her to phone disease control in Atlanta?

I always wanted to be a surgeon but one thing stopped me. I just couldn't stand the sight of money.

I won't say that he's a clumsy doctor, but vultures are constantly making lazy circles over his office.

"I can do nothing for your sickness. It's hereditary."
"Well, then send the bill to my father."

A minor operation is one performed on someone else.

I told the doctor, "I'm not fat. I've just got big bones."
He said, "Sure you do. And you need those big bones. Why they're the only things that can hold up all that fat."

I just heard the saddest story. A doctor lost all his money on the horses. In an act of desperation, he tried to rob a bank. But nobody could read the holdup note.

A suffering patient looked at his doctor and asked, "Are you certain I'll pull through? I heard of a man who was treated for jaundice and died of diptheria."
"Don't be silly," said the doctor, "when I treat you for jaundice you die of jaundice."

My doctor advised me that I could avoid a sharp pain in my eye while drinking coffee by taking the spoon out of the cup.

Things you hate to hear a doctor say..."Scalpel...Suture...see if there's a mop in the closet..." or, "Maybe someday Blue Cross will cover that."

This reminder just for doctors. It's April and time to take the snow tires off your golf cart.

My brother wanted to be a doctor, but my parents just couldn't afford the golf lessons.

According to a recent study, 20,000 surgeons in the U.S. are incompetent. It's hard to believe, but many of these doctors didn't know the difference between such basic medical terms as bogie and birdie.

Did you ever read the bottom line on the optometrist's chart? It says, "If you can read this, you've just wasted $35."

I asked, "Is this operation necessary?"
The surgeon said, "Of course. I have a mortgage payment next week."

I went to the doctor and said, "Doc, I don't know what's wrong with me, but everytime I look in the mirror, I want to throw up."
He checked me over and said, "Well, I don't know what's wrong with you either, but your eyesight's perfect."

He's a meticulous doctor. One time I had the German measles, and he gave me two shots--East and West!

The doctor has just slashed prices on his annual two-for-one appendectomy sale. Have your appendix removed at the regular price and get another organ of your choice taken out absolutely free!

My doctor was amazed to discover that I had a disease that hadn't been around for almost a century. Turned out that I caught it from one of the magazines in his waiting room.

He was suspended from medical school for having excessively legible handwriting.

Does it make you nervous when you tell your doctor your symptoms, and he starts backing away?

My doctor is very hygenic. Always washes his hands before he touches your wallet.

Does it make you nervous when your doctor says, "We'll videotape the operation so that we can see what we did wrong."?

My doctor told me that I was suffering from insomnia but that I shouldn't lose any sleep over it.

He took over the practice of a doctor who was forced to retire when he performed an appendectomy on a Toyota.

DOG

We sent our dog to obedience school, and in just two weeks we've noticed the difference! Now he says grace and puts on a napkin before he bites the mailman's leg.

I went to a movie and saw a dog seated next to his master. At the end of the film, the dog applauded enthusiastically. I said to the owner, "Wow, that's really amazing!"
"It sure is," he replied, "he hated the book!"

Our dog is like one of the family, but it's hard to tell which one.

His dog has a flat nose. He got it from chasing parked cars.

I go to a veterinarian who is also a taxidermist. His motto is: "Either way you get your dog back."

"Is it true that Pat's dog plays poker?"
"Yeah, but he's not very good, though. Everytime he gets a good hand, he starts to wag his tail."

I made a bad mistake by buying a dog from a waiter. It never comes when I call him.

DOUBLE CROSS

I crossed an ape with a computer and got a Hairy Reasoner.

I crossed a hermit with a seal and got a guy that was hermetically sealed.

I crossed a shark with a penguin and got an animal dressed to kill.

I crossed a turkey with a kangaroo so that next Thanksgiving the ladies will be able to stuff him from the outside.

I crossed a canary with the roller derby and got a cheep skate.

He crossed a hen with a banjo and got a chicken that plucked itself.

I crossed my hen with a parrot. Now when she lays an egg she can come over and tell me about it.

I crossed a kangaroo with a horse for cowboys who want to ride inside on cold winter days.

I crossed a turkey with a porcupine. Now I can eat and pick my teeth at the same time.

He crossed an electric blanket with a toaster to help people pop out of bed in the morning.

A beekeeper crossed his bees with lightning bugs so that he could develop a night shift at his hives.

 # DRAMA

When I was in college I played the role of a man who had been married for 30 years. When I wrote and told my father, he wrote back and said, "Good, son. And I hope that the next role you get is a speaking part."

 # DRIVER EDUCATION

The school board in the rural community voted to discontinue driver education. The mule died.

 # DRIVING

I saw one lady go through three straight red lights. Unfortunately, two of them were on the back of a truck.

I just saw a scary thing. My wife teaching my mother-in-law how to drive.

EASTER

Honesty is the best policy...unless, of course, your wife asks your opinion of her new Easter outfit.

Times are pretty tough. We gave our neighbors an Easter bunny and on Easter Sunday I called them and asked, "How is it?"
They said, "Very Tasty!"

ECONOMY

Do you think there's any significance to the fact that a group photo of our economic advisors has just been published? It shows them all lined up in punt formation.

Put your money where your mouth is--lick a stamp.

To get the economy going again, we need a government handout-- the government's got to take its hand out of our pockets.

When it comes to changing the lives of millions of people, nothing beats the government's economic program. But the plague came pretty close.

At least during the great depression we didn't have to hold three jobs just to stay broke.

This year I quit spending my money foolishly and invested it prudently. That's my excuse for being broke, what's yours?

Remember when people used to keep their valuables in a sock? For a lot of people today, a sock is valuable.

The Federal Reserve says there's been a drop in the money supply. I guess the economy went on vacation, too.

You can tell it's a recession. Last night my wife turned to me and said,"Take in the garbage."

There would be no economic problems today if the poor would just spend more.

I spent the weekend reading the economists forecasts for the next few months. I also read some non-fiction.

One economist said that the economy would pick up by the last quarter. Well, I'm down to my last quarter.

An economist's business experience really pays off. It helps them spot a recession the minute it's over.

The trouble with inflation is it makes you think small. Like yesterday I found myself thinking why our parakeet eats so much.

Doesn't it get to you when you walk past a pet store and hear the whimpering, and you look at the pleading eyes, and you see the nose pressed against the window? And this is just the owner!

If the electricity rates rise much higher, a porch light will be a status symbol.

There's really no need for us to worry about the Federal budget deficit. Look, it's big enough to take care of itself.

Economists are certainly busy people. They spend half their time predicting economic turns, and the other half explaining why the economy didn't turn out that way.

In today's world of inflation a big spender is anyone who supports a wife and kids.

Someone asked, "How do you get along on so little these days?"
The guy answered, "Oh, I make out okay. It's the wife and kids that have a struggle."

If things keep getting worse, there'll only be two major businesses left --breaking and entering.

The ten cent stamp is gone...the ten cent cup of coffee is gone...but look at the bright side...we still have the ten cent quarter.

Our new budget is $14 billion...not too bad when you consider that that's in U.S. dollars.

We are having what the experts call "remote control" economy. The chances of it being controlled are remote.

You know things are getting bad when the children start fighting over who's going to lick the broccoli pan!

There are a lot of things that money can't buy. Like what it did ten years ago.

They say that teenagers don't know the value of a dollar. They certainly do! That's why they always ask for ten!

It's simple economics. America is the richest nation on earth because we own more Toyotas and Sonys.

Some people have to moonlight in order to see the daylight.

Our national flower is the cost of living rose.

Is there any sense to teenagers studying economics. After all, what could a high school teacher possibly know about money?

I'm not hungry for wealth. All I want is as much money as my wife thinks I have.

Say what you want to about the American economy. It's the only country in the world where poor people have trouble finding a parking place.

Our economic forecast: We're beginning to see the light at the end of the gang plank.

The economists say that Christmas shopping is at an all-time low. Business in one department store is so slow that the clerks stayed in practice by taking turns being rude to each other.

EDISON (THOMAS)

On this day in history, Thomas Edison invented the phonograph. It was either that or sell his record collection.

Edison was working late one night on his invention, the incandescent light bulb. He finally got it to work and he went to wake his wife to tell her the good news, "I've done it," he yelled. "I got it to work!" "That's nice, dear," Mrs. Edison said. "Now turn out the light and get some sleep."

It was Edison who said that genius is one percent inspiration and 99 percent perspiration. I don't know about that. I hate to think of anyone with hands that sweaty handling electricity!

We can be thankful that Edison invented the light bulb. Why if it wasn't for him, we'd all be watching TV in the dark!

On this date in American history, Alexander Graham Bell said to Thomas Edison, "Tom, how come there's no light in this phone booth?"

EDUCATION

My kid's going to be afraid to go back to school in September. He got the summer job his teacher was after.

Teachers will tell you that for every student with a spark of genius, there are nine with ignition trouble.

We're lucky that the teachers' strike is over. There were too many kids hanging around with no place to drop out of.

Never be proud about how much you know. After all, even a piece of lettuce knows more than you do. It knows if that little light really does go out after the refrigerator door is shut.

This morning I phoned a school and said, "I'd like to speak to Bertram W. Eagleton, dean of the Perfect Diction College." He said, "Thspeaking."

One thing about today's education has me worried. Most of the tests given are multiple choice. For the first time in history, some kids are graduating magna cum lucky.

A. B. Dick died on this day in 1934. In 1887, A. B. made history by inventing the mimeograph machine, thereby guaranteeing from then on that he would be rich, famous, and that teachers all over the world would smell weird.

My old third grade teacher retired last week. She said that in the good old days kids used to bring her apples but now all they did was drive her bananas.

What's all this noise about silent prayer in schools? What do they think happens everytime a teacher gives a test or passes out report cards?

 **ELECTIONS**

Did you ever reflect that (losing candidate) and the earth have a lot in common? You see, the earth is flattened at the poles and so was (name).

I never realized how bad my eyes were until election day. I went to the polling place, closed the curtain, pulled the lever, and then I heard a sound such as I never heard in a voting booth--flushing!

I'll never forget the first time I voted in a presidential election. It was 1948 in Chicago. I'll never forget the second, third, and fourth times I voted in a presidential election. It was 1948 in Chicago.

I was hurt on election day by the white backlash. The elastic in my jockey shorts broke.

No one is sure what the election in Pennsylvania means, but the new state flower is hemlock.

Standing behind every President of the United States is a proud wife--and a flabbergasted mother-in-law.

It is only fitting that he won in all the outlying districts. After all, he was out lying in all of them.

ELEPHANTS

How do you find elephants?
They're so big, how could you miss them?

How do you stop an elephant from smelling?
Tie a knot in his trunk.

Why is an elephant big, gray, and wrinkled?
Because if he was small, white and round, he'd be an aspirin.

How do you know if there's an elephant under your bed?
Your nose is touching the ceiling!

A male elephant watching a female elephant going by..."Wow a perfect 250 by 210 by 400!"

Why did the elephants picket?
They were tired of working for peanuts!

They say that an elephant never forgets. What has he got to remember?

Teacher: "Bobby, where are elephants found?"
Bobby: "The elephant, teacher, is such a large animal, it scarcely ever gets lost."

EMCEE LINES

Next we have a little girl who was named after Joan of Arc. And not too long after her either.

Why are you so grim? You people are looking at me as if I were your daughter's first date.

Although it is usually difficult to speak to a small audience your unwavering torpidity and warm-hearted obfuscation this evening has made up for what you lack in numbers.

Good ladies, evening and gentlemen. That's it! Next time I'll write everything down!

Ladies and Gentlemen--well, I guess that takes care of most of you.

(to man writing) He steals jokes faster than anyone I know. One year, he was unable to steal any of my material. He had to cancel all his after-dinner speeches, and nearly starved to death.

EMPLOYEES

We had some trouble with our storeroom clerk. Now we didn't realize we had a problem until our last inventory, which we took in his garage!

I asked the boss for an extra day off to make up for all the coffee breaks I missed while I was away on vacation.

ETHNICVILLE

There's an Ethnic who thinks Gatorade is welfare for crocodiles.

The Ethnics put Astroturf in their stadium because they wanted to keep their homecoming queen from grazing.

It cost an additional $250,000 to have the Astroturf job completed because they had a sprinkling system installed.

An Ethnic won a gold medal in the Olympics and was so proud of it that he took it right to a shop in Ethnicville and had it bronzed.

How can you spot an Ethnicville plane in a snowstorm?
It's the one with chains on the propeller.

An Ethnic meteorologist gets confused every time it rains. He can't figure out how the rain gets through those dark clouds.

There was an Ethnic who smelled good only on the right side because he didn't know where he could buy Left Guard.

An Ethnic was stranded on an escalator during a power outage.

An Ethnic had a hard time telling the difference between his two horses. He finally decided to measure them and sure enough the white horse was five inches taller than the black horse.

Two Ethnics were fishing and they were so successful they decided to mark the spot so they could return the next day.
The one asked, "How did you mark the spot?"
The other said, "I put an 'X' in the bottom of the boat."
The other said, "That was dumb. What if we don't get the same boat tomorrow?"

Did you hear about the Ethnicville car pool? They all meet at work.

What do they print on the soles of Ethnic shoes?
This side down.

Did you hear about the Ethnic that broke his arm raking leaves?
He fell out of a tree.

Did you hear about the Ethnic who bought only one snow boot for winter? He heard that there was only going to be one foot of snow.

Did you hear about the two Ethnics who got their luggage mixed up at the airport? They both had brown paper bags.

Some Ethnics were trying to raise chickens on a chicken farm. First they tried to bury them head first. No results. Then they planted them feet first. No results. They decided to write the Ethnic Farm Bureau explaining the problem. The Ethnic Farm Bureau wrote back, "Please send us a soil sample."

What's green, purple, chartreuse and red?
An Ethnic housewife going to church on Sunday.

Did you hear about the Ethnics who were pushing their house down the street trying to jump start the furnace?

An intellectual Ethnic is one who can hear the "William Tell Overture" without thinking of the Lone Ranger.

I want to tell this joke. Are there any Ethnics in the audience? (Pause). Oh, there are? In that case, I'll tell it very slowly.

How do you make an Ethnic laugh on Monday? Tell him a joke on Friday.

An Ethnic construction foreman to worker: "No wonder those nails won't go into the wood. You're hammering head first and those are the nails for the other side of the wall."

Do you know that we only use one-third of our brain?
Ethnic: Wonder what we do with the other third.

Why do Ethnic dogs have flat noses?
From chasing parked cars.

He was going to see the Ethnics' favorite movie: "Escape to Alcatraz."

How do you sink an Ethnic submarine?
Knock on the hatch.

An Ethnic and his wife won a trip around the world for two, but they turned it down because they wanted to go somewhere else.

Flash! After two years of extensive development and research, three Ethnics have finally succeeded in creating a pencil with an eraser at both ends.

Why did 19 Ethnics go to the movies together? Because the sign outside the theater said "18 and Under Not Admitted."

An Ethnic counts his cattle by counting their hooves and dividing by four.

How does an Ethnic spell "farm"?
E-I-E-I-O

Why don't Ethnics get ten-minute coffee breaks?
It takes too long to retrain them.

Did you hear about the Ethnic who decided he didn't want to go to the rock concert because tickets were $5 in advance and $6 at the door? He thought $11 was too much to pay for a ticket.

Definition of an Ethnic intellectual: One who reads to himself without moving his lips.

Did you hear about the Ethnic who was stabbed 40 times in the head? He was learning to eat with a fork.

Why are Ethnic airline stewardesses always so tired?
From running alongside the planes holding up pictures of clouds.

Did you read about the new Ethnicville Hilton?
They have a revolving restaurant in the basement.

Did you hear about the Ethnic that went ice fishing and brought back a 200-pound block of ice? He and his wife both drowned when they tried to fry it.

They don't let Ethnics join the army because they don't make square helmets.

An Ethnic terrorist tried to blow up a school bus and burned his lips on the exhaust pipe.

An Ethnic went on an elephant hunt and got a hernia carrying the decoys.

An Ethnic was fired from the banana factory. He kept throwing the crooked ones away.

An Ethnic backed off the bus because he overheard someone say, "Let's grab his seat when he leaves."

Why don't they have ice cubes in Ethnicville?
Because the lady who had the recipe left town.

An Ethnic was in the Indy 500 and made 70 pit stops--two for gas, two for tires, and 66 to ask directions.

Ethnics are never hired as elevator operators because it's too hard for them to remember the route.

An Ethnicville father told his sons that he wanted to be buried at sea. All three of them drowned trying to dig the grave.

Why do football fields in Iowa have astroturf?
So the cheerleaders won't graze after the games.

Why don't they use Kool-Aid in Moorestown, New Jersey?
Because no one in town can figure out how to get two quarts of water into that little envelope.

In America they say, "It's ten o'clock. Do you know where your children are?"
In Ethnicville they say, "It's ten o'clock. Do you know what time it is?"

I asked the Ethnic, "How do you like your new refrigerator?"
He said, "Fine, but my wife hasn't gotten the knack yet of chopping up the ice so it'll fit into those little, square trays."

How do Ethnics count money?
"One, two, three, four, five, another, another, another..."

What do you call an Ethnic submarine captain?
Chicken of the Sea.

Newsflash: Two Ethnics died this morning trying to dig a cellar in their houseboat.

What's the first thing an Ethnic father buys his son?
Booties with cleats.

Ethnicville cheerleader at Ethnicville Stadium: "Give me an F; give me an I; give me a G; give me an H; give me a T. What does that spell?" (Complete silence.)

An Ethnic was asked by the teacher, "How many degrees are in a circle?"
"Well, that all depends on how big the circle is."

There's a new product on the market: a one-piece jigsaw puzzle for Ethnics.

There's a new Ethnic parachute. It opens on impact.

Did you hear about the Ethnic who spent two weeks in a revolving door looking for a doorknob?

Did you hear about the Ethnic girl who couldn't guess in which direction the elevator was going after she had been given <u>two</u> guesses?

That Ethnic needs two hands to drink his soup. He needs one hand to catch the drippings under his fork.

Two Ethnics were at the zoo when the lion let out a deafening roar. One Ethnic started to run, but the other said, "You go if you want to. But I'm going to stay for the whole movie."

Haircuts cost four dollars in Ethnicville because their charge is one dollar per corner.

An Ethnic had his car demolished when he was racing to beat the train and hit the 23rd boxcar.

"How long does it take to fly to Rome?" asked the Ethnic.
"Just a minute." said the travel agent.
"Thank you very much," said the Ethnic.

"I don't understand why this match doesn't work," said the Ethnic. "It worked before."

The Ethnic economist stated: "As more and more people are thrown out of their jobs, the result is unemployment."

The first tactical instruction given to Ethnic army recruits--how to retreat.

"We don't have to move to a more expensive apartment after all," the Ethnic told his wife. "The landlord just raised the rent on our apartment!"

The Ethnicville Water Polo team had to disband when three of their horses drowned.

Did you hear about the intelligent Ethnic? It was just a rumor.

One Ethnic thought that high cholesterol was a religious holiday.

An Ethnic was asked why he dragged a chain all over town.
"Did you ever try to push one?" he replied.

What do 1776 and 1492 have in common?
They are adjoining rooms at the Ethnic Hilton.

What does it say on the top step of Ethnic ladders?
<u>Stop!</u>

Two Ethnics at a funeral, "He looks good, doesn't he?"
"Well, he should. He just got out of the hospital."

Did you hear about the Ethnic who dug three holes to bury his dog?
The first two weren't deep enough.

The most difficult decision that an Ethnic has to make before going to a formal party is whether to wear his green socks or his red socks.

To an Ethnic, A Saturday Night Special is a bath.

In Ethnicville, if you don't pay your garbage bill they stop delivery.

An Ethnicville counterfeiter made bogus $2 bills ingeniously. He rubbed the zeros off the $20 bills.

In Ethnicville matched crystal is three peanut butter jars with the same label.

There was an Ethnic who bought a bottle of Mennen's Skin Bracer, and he was found dead on the bathroom floor the next morning. The autopsy revealed that he was slapped to death.

An Ethnic once said, "I'd give my right arm to be ambidexterous."

The Ethnic Factory Workers Union goes on strike during their lunch hour so they won't lose any money.

An Ethnic called a locksmith. "I locked my keys in the car and I'd like you to come over right away. It's starting to rain and my convertible top's down."

Turtleneck sweaters are very popular in Ethnicville. That's because they keep their flea collars hidden.

An Ethnic kept going back to the ticket window to buy tickets for a movie. The cashier said, "But I've already sold you five tickets!" "I know," said the Ethnic, "but some guy in there keeps ripping up my ticket!"

Did you hear about the Ethnic housewife who had an accident while ironing her curtains? She fell out the window.

The Ethnic Sunday News ran a $1000 Crossword Puzzle Contest with these directions: "If you want to play just for fun and don't want to wait until next week for the answers, you'll find the solutions on the back page."

Why are there only twenty hours in an Ethnic day?
Have you ever seen an Ethnic with 24 fingers and toes?

Why did the Ethnic spend three hours in the car wash?
He thought it was raining too hard to drive.

There was an Ethnic who wore white bowling shoes so that when he mugged people they wouldn't be able to find his footprints in the snow.

Did you ever read about the Ethnic Olympian who was lapped in the 100-yard dash?

In case of rain, this year's Ethnic 'Round the World Yacht Race will be held indoors.

The Ethnic couple had twins, a boy and a girl.
"What did you name the girl?" a friend asked.
"We named the girl Denise."
"Oh, that's pretty. And what did you name the boy?"
"Oh, we named the boy Denephew."

How can you tell an Ethnic mother-in-law at a wedding?
She's the one on her hands and knees picking up the rice.

Did you hear about the Ethnic coyote who chewed off three legs and was still caught in the trap?

Did you read about the Ethnic kamikaze pilot who returned safely from 40 missions?

An Ethnic shot an arrow in the air--and missed!

What does it say on the bottom of Coke bottles in Ethnicville?
"Open other end!"

Why is the average age of an Ethnic soldier 57?
They get them right out of high school.

An Ethnic walked into a discount store and bought four boxes of mothballs.
"Those tiny moths are hard to hit," he explained.

Did you hear about the Ethnic father in the waiting room of the maternity ward who said, "Here, have a cigar. I'm a father."
"Congratulations. What is it--a boy or a girl?"
"I don't know," said the Ethnic. "All cigars look alike to me."

Then there was the Ethnic who lost a fortune investing in frozen radio dinners.

An Ethnic was offered a job driving a snow plow.
"What, in this weather?" he yelled.

An Ethnic loan shark lent out all his money and then skipped town.

An Ethnic used car dealer was caught turning back all the fuel gauges.

An Ethnic walks into a restaurant and yells, "I'm in a big hurry, waiter. Just bring me the bill."

An Ethnic bought a Country Squire wagon. When he got it home he began ripping all the wood paneling off the side with a crow bar. When he finished he said, "You know, I liked it a lot better when it was in the crate."

How can you tell an Ethnic pirate?
He's the one with eyepatches over both eyes.

Did you see the Ethnic calling his dog? He put two fingers in his mouth and shouted, "Here, Fido."

The Ethnic space program keeps running into difficulties. The astronauts keep falling off the kite.

"Could you back up about a half mile?" the Ethnic asked the taxi driver. "I'm about 80 cents short."

Ethnics make the best secret agents because even under torture they can't remember what they were assigned to do.

A girl fell overboard on a cruise and yelled to the Ethnic, "Drop me a line, will ya?" "Sure," said the Ethnic, "what's your address?"

It takes two Ethnics to wash a car. One to hold the sponge and one to drive back and forth.

An Ethnic was told to go to the end of the line but soon returned.
"Why did you come back here? I thought I told you to go to the end of the line!" barked the officer.
"I did," said the Ethnic, "but there was someone already there."

The Ethnics were pitted against their arch rivals from another town. When the five o'clock factory whistle blew, the rivals walked off the field, thinking it was the end of the game. Three plays later, the Ethnic Turkeys scored.

"Hey, Joe, an alligator just bit off my leg!"
"Which one?"
"How should I know? All alligators look alike to me!"

An Ethnic fell out a five-story window and landed on the pavement below. A friend rushed up and said, "What happened?"
The Ethnic replied, "How should I know? I just got here!"

Two Ethnics were observing a telephone lineman stretching a new line in Ethnicville. "Those dummies!" said one to the other. "They're putting it so high the cows can walk right under it!"

Two groups of Ethnics were told by their foreman to install telephone poles. He said he would return to check on their progress. Upon his return, he found that one group had put twelve poles in place. "That's excellent!" he remarked.
When he checked on the second group, he found that they had placed only two. "Two?" the foreman questioned. "The other crew completed twelve!"
"Yeah," said one of the workers, "but look how far they left them sticking out of the ground!"

Why did they outlaw lynching in Ethnicville? Because the guy who knew how to tie knots left town.

What is written at the top of post cards in Ethnicville? "Private and confidential."

Why did the Ethnic have his house moved five feet off the orginal foundation? Because there was slack in the clothesline.

An Ethnicville pickup truck plummeted from a bridge into the river below. The two in the front were saved, but the two in the back drowned because the tailgate was stuck.

The Ethnic always carried a turkey with him, just in case he needed spare parts.

Two Ethnics were hunting and found some tracks which they followed for over two hours. Then tragedy struck! A train hit them!

Residents of Ethnicville are having a border dispute with the neighboring town. The Ethnicites are lobbing dynamite across the border, and their enemies are lighting the sticks and throwing them back.

A mind reader moved to Ethnicville and died a week later. He starved to death.

How many Ethnics does it take to pave a driveway? Ten if you smooth them out evenly.

An Ethnic arriving at a train station looked awfully sick after his trip. When his friend met him, he asked, "What's the matter with you? You look awful."

The rider said, "I always become nauseous when I have to ride backwards on the train."

"Well, why didn't you ask to trade seats with the person across from you?"

"I thought about that, but there wasn't anybody there."

The Ethnic Labor Union agreed to a five percent cut in wages. "But the good news," said the union boss, " is that we got it backdated six months."

EVOLUTION

If there's anything to the theory of evolution, I figure that 500 years from now every American will have crooked toes and black and blue hands from hitting vending machines.

EXCLUSIVE NEIGHBORHOODS

Their neighborhood is so ritzy that they have an unlisted zip code.

His town is so exclusive that the Salvation Army band has a string section.

His neighbor is so rich that he has a bird bath in his backyard. Now that might not sound unusual, but his has a salad bar!

EXERCISE

The only exercise he ever gets is jogging his memory.

I'm not geared right for exercise. I've got a ten-speed bike and one-speed legs.

I just joined Exercise Anonymous. You call them when you're tempted to exercise, and they send over a guy to eat a chocolate sundae with you until the urge passes.

It's a good thing he likes to read so much. Moving his lips is about the only exercise he gets.

I was going to start on my weight lifting program yesterday, but I wasn't able to lift the barbells out of the trunk of my car.

His whole family believes in exercise and conditioning. If you think he's in great shape, you should see his Aunt Rocky.

I exercised on one of those flesh-reducing rollers morning, noon, and night for six months, and it worked! You should see how little that roller is!

The only exercise I've been getting lately is acting as a pall bearer for my friends who exercise.

Exercise? If my body was a city it would be up for urban renewal!

Everybody else is doing it, so I sent away for some weights to go into training. I was really embarrassed. I couldn't pick them up down at the freight office, so this young, smart kid had to show off and throw them in the back of the pickup for me. I hate kids like her!

I started exercising and I'm here to report that in just three months I can touch my knees without bending the floor.

I do my exercises every morning without fail. After waking, I tell myself, "Ready now. Up. Down." After two strenuous minutes, I'm ready to try the other eyelid.

This afternoon I phoned to sign up for a fitness class and the instructor told me to wear loose clothing. I said, "Look, if I had any loose-fitting clothing, I wouldn't need the class."

It's important to remember when exercising, start slowly and then gradually taper off.

It's just not right to say the man doesn't get any exercise--he happens to be a very brisk eater!

My wife said that Richard Simmons recommends swimming for a good physique. I asked, "Has he checked to see what ducks look like?"

I've hit middle age and I'm very sensible about my exercising. Each weekend our group goes out and plays a sensible kind of tennis--mixed triples.

One good thing about being in rotten physical shape--at least you don't have to exercise to keep it up.

If exercise can help you lose weight, then how come you don't lose weight automatically just by carrying all that extra weight around?

I can't win! For five months now I've been pumping iron to lose weight. I haven't lost a single pound, but my arms are six inches longer.

If it wasn't for coughing, I wouldn't get any exercise at all.

I've got a great exercise to keep men physically fit. I'm going to put treadmills in women's clothing stores for husbands to use while they wait for their wives.

I have a couch at work that I named Nautilus. That way I can honestly tell people that this afternoon I put in two hours on the Nautilus.

My idea of exercise is pulling apart socks that have static cling.

He uses a routine he calls his gardener's exercise. He starts out fresh as a daisy and winds up bushed.

FAMILY

Father: "I don't care if the basement wall is cracked. Please stop telling everyone that you come from a broken home!"

"Our son always wanted to be a magician and saw people in half."
"Is he an only child?"
"No, he has several half brothers and sisters."

"When I die, I'm going to leave my brain to science."
"Good, every little bit helps."

FARMING

"These apples are awfully small and they're not very flavorful are they?"
Farmer: "Yup, lucky that they're small."

Uncle Horace wanted to raise chickens, so he bought 5,000 of them. They all died. He figured that he planted them too close together.

I visited a pig farm and observed a farmer in the orchard, holding his pigs up one by one to graze on apples in the trees. I asked, "Doesn't that take a lot of time?"
He said, "What's time to a pig?"

Things grow so fast in our area, that you drop in the seeds and jump back.

His hens lay eggs so big that seven of 'em make a dozen.

A farmer invited four friends into his house. The visitors found only two chairs and were too embarrassed to sit down. Finally, one said, "I don't believe you have enough chairs."
The farmer said, "Oh, I've got plenty of chairs. Just too much company."

He's in farming--sort of an entremanure.

FASHION

Do you remember when you used to dress up in a ridiculous outfit and go to a masquerade party? Now you go to work!

FAT

Fat? Who else has a driver's license that says Photo Continued On Other Side?

You know that you're overweight if you get out of a metal chair and have to fluff it.

You can see he's gaining weight. His appendix scar is 14 inches long.

He's a man with everything. The only trouble is that it all settled in one place!

He does have a slight weight problem. Slight? Twenty more pounds and there'd be a total eclipse of his feet.

I went to one of those fat farms and they really work. The first day I went, I was $750 lighter.

They say, "Feed a cold and starve a fever." I often wonder why Orson Welles has so many colds.

You know you're overweight when you try to loosen your belt and can't find it.

He's so happy with the new electric door opener he bought last week--not for the garage, for the refrigerator!

He's so fat that if he gets on an elevator, it better be going down.

They say that for every pound you are overweight, your blood has to travel four extra miles. From the looks of this guy, his blood must be on a trip around the world.

He was so fat as a kid that when he ran away from home he had to take the truck route.

There was a lot of confusion during the snowstorm. I went over to help a fat lady get into a taxi cab. After pushing and shoving and slipping on the ice I told her I didn't think I could help her get in.
She said, "In? I was trying to get out!"

My wife's arms are getting shorter. I know they're getting shorter because when we were first married, she could reach around me.

He's so fat that they had to give him his own zip code.

He had a big weekend. He led a 'Save the Whales' rally outside a Weight Watchers meeting.

As a kid he was too fat to play little league baseball, so the coach used him to draw the on-deck circle.

He's always been fat. As a kid, when he played cowboys and Indians, he always got to be the posse.

He's so fat that the last time he weighed himself the needle spun around so many times it screwed the scale to the bathroom floor.

Talk about fat kids! He had a tricycle built for two.

187

He's so fat that he looks like the original mold for the hula hoop.

I was really fat as a kid. One day I was standing in the middle of the street and a cop came up to me and told me to break it up.

I was so fat that when I had my shoes shined I had to take the guy's word for it.

He was so fat as a kid that he could only play seek.

My neighbor is so fat that she has to wear stretch jewelry.

She's so fat that her yearbook picture said, "Continued next page..."

She's so fat that her senior picture was taken by satellite.

It's people like him who have made the world what it is today ...crowded!

He's so fat he has to clip his toenails by memory.

He's so fat that when he goes horseback riding the horse can't get its front feet down.

One thing I like about hot fudge sundaes is that they never leave you with that funny diet after-taste.

She doesn't have any trouble watching her weight. Wherever she looks, there it is!

She's so fat her passport is a fold-out. The light of her life is the light in the refrigerator.

Here's a little known fact. On this date in 1968, Orson Welles turned down seconds.

I know he's a little concerned about his weight. To_____, designer jeans is a toga.

An appetite? I once heard him call out for pizza during the middle of our Thanksgiving dinner!

I don't look upon it as a pot belly but rather as an awning for my knees.

You're overweight if you step on a dog's tail and it dies.

He's so chubby that he has more chins than a Chinese phone book.

He really has a great body. The only trouble is that it's inside the one that you see. In India, they'd worship him.

I bring my lunch in a paper bag. He brings his in a U-Haul.

Fat? When she goes into the bakery she takes all the numbers.

No man is an island. But Orson Welles comes pretty close.

I always thought he drank so much water because it was good for his cardio-vascular system. Now I've learned he does it to keep his tongue and teeth from overheating.

He's so fat he has wide ties that look narrow.

What an appetite! They gave him a pair of wooden chopsticks at a Chinese restaurant, and he ate so fast with them that he started two fires!

He knew that it was time to go on a diet when he discovered that he had the world's only form-fitting bathtub.

I did some heavy reading this morning. I read the bathroom scale.

My main problem is that everything I eat turns to me.

He's so fat that when he's invited to a costume party, all he has to do is stick a pine cone in each ear and he can go as the state of Maine.

How would you describe him? What's the next size after obese?

He's not really fat. He's just built up a natural immunity to thinness.

He doesn't get angry if someone calls him fat. He just turns the other chin.

Fat? He looks like a kangaroo with all the kids home.

He knew he was overweight when his rowing machine sank.

His doctor told him to cut back on food. That can be compared with telling baby clothing manufacturers to cut back on using blue and pink.

Two tonsils lived in a fat guy's throat. "Where are we?" one asked the other.

"We must be in Capistrano," the other replied, "cause here comes another swallow."

When they took a picture of that fat kid on the bearskin rug, the bear's tongue was hanging out.

He's always been overweight. Who have you ever known that complained about a hula hoop being too tight?

He's so fat that he shows up on the weather satellite photo map.

You know that it's time to diet if you're dining alone and the waitress asks you if you want separate checks.

He's so fat that when you buy him a pizza you don't have to cut it.

He's got a skin condition...too much of it.

When he was a kid, all the other kids had a hula hoop to play with. He had to use his for a belt.

He'd like to watch what he eats but his eyes aren't quick enough.

His idea of a balanced meal is a hoagie in each hand.

He was so fat that when they tried to bury him in the sand they had to run out for more beach.

I shouldn't make fun of him. He's attached to a machine that keeps him alive--a refrigerator.

He suffers from Dunlaps disease. His stomach dun-laps over his belt.

He's the only man who's ever eaten all the varieties at Dunkin Donuts and tasted all the flavors at Baskin Robbins.

When he went to Ocean City no one else could swim while he was in the ocean.

I'm not really fat. I was just blowing up a balloon and the air went the wrong way.

Heavy? He's so big his shorts fill up the washing machine!

He's always nibbling on something. Why last month, the electric bill for the refrigerator light alone was eight dollars.

A recent poll showed that 62% of American people think they are overweight. The other 38% didn't answer, which is easy to understand. It's hard to talk when your mouth's full.

What an appetite! Last week he caught a cold from standing in front of the open refrigerator.

Obesity runs in his family. Well, actually it doesn't run--it waddles.

When you see a fat woman, be diplomatic. Don't tell her she's overweight. Tell her she has a whale of a figure.

I never saw any advantage in being fat until the health club offered me the group rate. They let me use the exercycle built for two!

Obesity is noticeable because it's centrally located.

You know you're too fat when you think that, "We fly wide bodies to New York" is an insult.

You know you're overweight when the mirror on your bathroom door gets too narrow.

You're fat if your weight chart indicates you should be eight feet four inches.

It's time to diet when a tilt steering wheel and six-way power seats are no longer an option...

It's time to reduce when "One Size Fits All" doesn't include you.

You know you're fat if your fingers get stuck in the holes of the desk phone.

You know that you have a serious weight problem if you can't get you and the water into the tub at the same time.

He whipped through a five-course dinner and had a chocolate sundae and a huge piece of pie for dessert. I asked, "How do you do it?"
He replied, "Eating makes me hungry!"

You know you're overweight when the All-You-Can Eat restaurant doesn't let you in anymore.

He stepped on one of those talking scales and it said, "Come back in fifteen minutes when you're alone."

He asked his broker, "What should I do about pork bellies?" His broker replied, "Exercise, man exercise!"

He's so fat it takes two pennies to weigh him.

Fat? Ten more pounds and he could be admitted to the Union as a new state.

She always takes a calorie book with her when she goes to a restaurant so she'll have something to read while she's eating dessert.

He's so fat that it takes him two trips just to go through a revolving door.

He's the only guy I know who uses a fork as a letter opener.

He never met a meal he didn't like.

If any man could make sparks fly with a plastic fork, this is the man!

An indignant fat lady standing on a bus said, "Well, isn't one of you gentlemen going to get up so that I can sit?" A slightly built man stood and said, "I can't do the full job, but I'll be happy to make a small contribution."

He really watches his weight. He has it right out there in front where he can.

I was walking down the street and bumped into him. I was on the other side of the street at the time.

In the first place, he's put on a few pounds. And come to think of it, he's put on a few pounds in the second place, too.

He is on a diet where he goes horseback riding every morning. It's been partially successful. So far his horse has lost 25 pounds.

You are really not overweight until you have to buy a larger mirror.

I've seen him order everything on the menu except, "Thank you for dining with us."

Before coming here he had a job where he tied a cord around his neck and worked parades as a balloon.

He's got to lose a few pounds. Yesterday, he had to let out his toga.

He has a sign outside his house: Home of the Whopper.

A fat man took his family to the beach. The little boy asked, "Mommy, can I go swimming?"
"Not now, dear," the mother answered. "Daddy's using the ocean."

He wore a blue suit to work yesterday, and when he yawned at the bus stop, two people dropped letters in his mouth.

He was hospitalized and placed on a strict diet. The office staff sent flowers. He sent them a reply, "Thanks, they were delicious."

The doctor gave him some pills and said, "You don't swallow these. You spill them on the floor each morning and pick them up one at a time."

For years scientists have told us, "you cannot put more into a container than it can hold." They have obviously never seen him in a bathing suit.

A fat lady stepped on the drug store scale and sent the needle flying to the other side. A little girl watching nearby squealed, "Wow, look at all you get for a nickel!"

Fat? His favorite food is seconds.

He doesn't have big bones. He just suffers from an overactive fork.

He walked into a clothing store and said, "I'd like to see a bathing suit in my size."
"The clerk said, "So would I."

Hey, but what I lack in muscles, I more than make up for in flab.

Since he started to date her, she has gained twenty pounds and his love has turned into in_fat_uation.

FATHER/SON

I have two recurring dreams about my son. The first has him stretching forth his hand saying, "I am honored to accept the Nobel Prize." The other dream has him saying, "Ya want fries with this, sir?"

I don't mind my 20-year-old son living at home. He doesn't take up that much room. Just a few square feet in front of the refrigerator.

FATHER'S DAY

I don't wish to brag, but in my family I get absolute obedience. For instance, every Father's Day I tell my family not to spend a lot of money on me--and they don't!

Father's Day presents a new challenge: What do you give to the man who has absolutely nothing?

Father's Day is much like Mother's Day, only you get much cheaper gifts.

You know what I got for Father's Day this year? The bills from Mother's Day.

FILE

Do you file your fingernails?
No, I just throw them away after I cut them.

FIRE

A woman called the fire department and said, "My house is on fire. Can you come right over here?"
The fire chief said, "Sure, how do we get there?"
The woman replied, "Don't you guys still have that big, red truck?"

He had a fire in his house and lost all three of his books. The thing that made him mad was that he hadn't finished coloring two of them.

FISHING

I discovered that the fish were on vacation the same week I was.

Fishing is simply a matter of timing. All you have to do is get here yesterday when the fish were biting.

I was fishing ten yards away from a guy who was catching fish after fish, while I was catching nothing. I walked over and whispered, "What's your secret?" He mumbled something inaudible. I asked again. He spit a wad out of his mouth and said, "You gotta keep the worms warm."

Did you ever wonder if a fish swims home and lies about the size of the bait he stole?

There are a lot of fish in the sea. I'm the man who left them there.

One river in Canada has so many trout that they have to swim standing up.

A friend told me, "I spent four hours catching a tuna. One hour to land him, and three to shove him into that tiny can."

He caught a marlin and dislocated two shoulders trying to describe it.

Two fishermen made a ten dollar bet as to who could catch the first fish. One got a bite and became so excited that he fell into the lake. The other said, "Hey, the bet's off if you're going to dive in after them."

Scientists tell us that a trout in the water grows one inch per year. However, once it is caught, it grows one inch a day.

"Did you catch anything?"
"No," said the young fisherman. "I don't think my worm is really trying."

 **FLIES**

"I don't like the flies in here."
"Well, come around tomorrow, we'll have some new ones."

"I don't like all these flies."
"Well, pick out the ones you like and I'll kill the rest."

FOOD

I love seafood. My favorite is salt water taffy.

No one will ever starve in America, just as long as there's a Welcome Wagon and he can move every day.

No matter how you slice it, pizza is too hot when you start eating it and too cold when you finish it.

The best way to keep your food bill down is to use a heavy paperweight.

If you're wondering what your wife does with all the grocery money, just stand sideways and look in the mirror.

I don't mind spending $82 in the supermarket, but in the express line?

I've been having such stomach pains and I can't figure out why. I could hardly finish the pizza that I had for breakfast this morning.

FOOD PRICES

The food additives don't bother me nearly as much as the price additives.

A woman asked a clerk why he put the eggs at the bottom of the bag. He answered, "We put the eggs at the bottom of the bag so that when they break, they won't run all over the rest of your groceries."

We know that we can't take it with us. In fact, at today's food prices, most of us are already in the hole before we get there.

It seems that all my money goes for food, but the kids just won't eat anything else.

Grocery bags have gotten a lot stronger. The bag that could hold five dollars worth of food ten years ago now easily holds $50 worth.

It's a fact that grocery shopping carts are just the right size to hold exactly one paycheck.

I have to go now. You see, I ordered $20 worth of groceries to be delivered, and I want to be home when they slide them in under the door.

Someone asked the grocer, "How much are these tomatoes?"
He said, "Eighty cents a pound."
"Do you raise them yourself?"
"Yes," said the grocer, "they were just sixty cents a pound yesterday."

I went into the supermarket and bought a two-week supply of butter, milk, and eggs. I said to the cashier, "I'm sorry, but all I have is this $100 bill."
The cashier replied, "That's alright. I know you. You can pay us the rest tomorrow."

 # FOOTBALL

Old quarterbacks never die--they just pass away.

Wives, you know you're married to a real football addict if he refers to you as his "first-round draft choice."

Our clever defensive coordinator was responsible for devising his famous 'Doughnut Defense'. That's the defense with the big hole in the middle.

The med school football team had cheerleaders that yelled, "Hypodermic! Hypodermic!"
I said, "What does that cheer mean?"
A friend replied, "It means, 'Stick it to 'em.' "

Our football team was so bad, our homecoming was scheduled as an away game.

The team finally found a way to gain yardage. They run their game films backwards.

We played in a domed-stadium. We wouldn't quick kick unless we had the air-conditioning at our backs.

The football coach begged the college math prof to give his star player a makeup test. The professor agreed. The coach anxiously asked, "How did Jones do?"
"I'm sorry," said the prof. "It's hopeless. Look, he wrote 7 times 5 equals 33."
"Give him a break," said the coach, "he only missed by one."

I thought one of the lineman had a tattoo on his leg but it turned out to be a government meat inspection stamp. Instead of a number, he should have a license plate.

Our tackle is so big that the coach put a white shirt on him and used him as a movie screen when he ran the game films.

Due to injuries, the coach was forced to use a little-used sub who was also quite dense. He gave him the play, and just to make sure, he said, "Now, Sam, what do you do on this play?"
"I do my best, coach," Sam answered.

The coach was marching on the field alongside the band. A majorette threw her baton in the air and then dropped it. A fan yelled, "Hey, I see you coach the band, too."

He went to medical school and played on the football team. They stressed academics rather than athletics. In fact, their team mascot was a cadaver.

Did you read where that quarterback is being paid $40 million? Why, for just $2 million, I'd be the ball!

"Hey, Helen," said a husband with his hand on the TV knob, "do you have anything to say before football season starts?"

We were tipping off our plays. Whenever we broke from the huddle, three backs were laughing and the other was white as a ghost.

Football is a game when 22 big, strong, healthy players run around like crazy for two hours while 50,000 people who really need the exercise sit in the stands and watch them.

Did you hear about the world's dumbest center? They had to stencil on his football pants: This End Up. On his shoes they put T.G.I.F. Toes go in first.

He left his coaching job because of illness and fatigue. The fans were sick and tired of him.

We played the barber college football team. They didn't win a game all season. Seems like every time they got rolling, one of the players would be penalized for clipping.

One college has gotten so strict academically that it won't even give a football player his letter unless he can tell which one it is.

They recently televised a football game without announcers. Now my wife wants them to do that on radio, too.

I say let's make football more entertaining and give the quarterback something else to think about. Let's arm each middle linebacker with two lemon meringue pies!

Our team had such a slow-moving attack that all our game films were shown on a slide projector!

The fullback said, "My goal this season is to rush for 1,500 or 2,000 yards...whichever comes first."

When it appeared that the football team would beat the other team to escape the Big Ten cellar, the students began chanting, "We're number nine! We're number nine!"

In a lop-sided contest, one man was heard to mumble to the quarterback as he moved toward the exit, "Hit the lights and lock up when you leave, Bert."

A good football coach needs a patient wife, a loyal dog, and a great quarterback. Not necessarily in that order.

Referring to a phenomonal running back: "He may not be in a class by himself, but whatever class he's in, it doesn't take long to call the roll."

Our only problems this season are offense, defense, and teamwork.

I got really good seats to see the Eagles this year. To see the game you need prescription binoculars.

Where did they ever get that new end? He's so bad he has to use both hands to keep from dropping his Gatorade cup.

A bunch of chickens was in a yard when a football flew over the fence. A rooster walked by and said, "I'm not complaining, girls, but look at the work they're doing next door."

NFL cheerleaders are the girl-next-door types. That is if next door happens to be Caesar's Palace.

One coach is really tough on his team. If they don't win this week's game they get the ultimate punishment--they have to attend classes!

Our high school cheerleaders were really ugly. One game our team got a face mask penalty--because the cheerleaders weren't wearing any.

He had two ambitions in life: to be a coach or join the circus. So he signed with the Philadelphia Eagles, and now he has both!

My wife hates football. Everytime I sit down to watch a game she starts to vacuum and I have to get up and move to another part of the stadium.

The annual football game was held between the big animals and the little animals. The big animals led 75-0 at halftime. At the start of the second half, a centipede made three consecutive sacks on an elephant. Time out! In the huddle they asked the centipede, "Where were you in the first half?"
He said, "Oh, I was in the locker room getting my ankles taped!"

Our football team was so bad that one Saturday we tore down the goal posts hoping that would keep our team from playing next week.

Husband: "Why do you weep and sniffle over the imaginary woes of the people in soap operas?"
Wife: "For the same reason you scream and yell when a man you don't even know scores a touchdown."

One of our neighbors is making interesting plans for the future. She says when her husband dies, she's not going to have him buried. I said, "What are you going to do?"
She said, "I'm going to have him stuffed and mounted and put on the living room couch. Then I'll turn on the TV to a football game, talk to him, and he won't answer. It'll be just like he never left."

The coach's favorite play: "It's the one where one of our players pitches the ball back to the official after he has scored a touchdown."

The coach was always ahead of the other coaches. When they started the two-platoon system, he had a three-platoon system--one on offense, one on defense, and one to go to classes.

One of our quarterbacks can do anything with a football except autograph it.

I tried out for halfback, but gave up the second day of practice, when one tackle grabbed my right leg and a linebacker grabbed my left leg, and the tackle looked at me and yelled, "Make a wish!"

The football captain gave his teammates a pep talk. "Today, Coach Schmidt is 56. Let's go out on that field and give him something to remember on his birthday!" And they did. They went out on that field and were beaten 56 to nothing.

The difference between pro football and college football is that pro football players get paid by check.

Our team had to turn down an invitation to the Sugar Bowl because our quarterback had diabetes.

Our college was very ethical. All they'd give the players was room, board, tuition, and $900 a week for textbooks and laundry.

An incensed coach ran out on the field and yelled at the referee, "You stink." Whereupon the referee paced off an additional 15 yards, looked back at the coach and said, "Okay, how do I smell from here?"

A quarterback was walloped by a blind-side tackle. After the mean hit, the coach rushed to his side to check on his fallen player's mental condition.
Coach: "What's your name?"
Quarterback: "Who wants to know?"

A Czech place kicker was asked to read the bottom line of an eye chart. "Read it?" said he. "I know him!"

A football fan fell asleep in his chair while watching "Monday Night Football."
The next morning, his wife nudged him and said, "Wake up. It's twenty to seven." "In whose favor?" said the husband, not missing a beat.

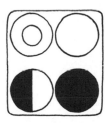 # FORECAST

Next year I predict...the stock market will go up, then down, then up, then down...there will be babies born in India...a jet liner with 300 aboard will arrive late at Kennedy Airport...no cure will be discovered for high doctor's fees...during dry weather, some farm states will have dust...things will be expensive...

He has the unique ability to foretell what will happen tomorrow, next month, and next year--and to explain afterward why it did not happen.

 # FOURTH OF JULY

Independence Day is really a fabulous experience. It gives you the opportunity to spend hours sitting on hot, crowded highways--so you can spend hours on hot, crowded beaches.

FRANKENSTEIN

One Frankenstein monster never spoke, he just went like this (roar). Fortunately, I can understand this because I'm married.

Everytime I hear the monster go like that, I get up and take out the trash.

FRIENDSHIP WEEK

It's Jewish-Italian Friendship Week, so take a rabbi named Vito to lunch.

FUNERALS

The gravestone said, "Here lies a politician and an honest man."
A passerby said, "Can you imagine? Two people in the same grave!"

Overheard: "It's really too bad. I hope he didn't die of anything serious."

Did you ever imagine that your obituary might read something like this? "In place of flowers, the family requests that all donations be sent to Visa, Mastercard, and American Express."

Have you noticed that people who work in funeral homes resemble each other?
You have to nudge them just to make sure that they're not one of the customers.

Remember, you can always count on an undertaker. He's the last one to let you down.

When you're in sales, you have to adjust to special circumstances. For instance, if you work for a funeral home--don't expect repeat business.

Remember, if you don't go to your friends' funerals, don't expect them to come to yours!

Is this man patriotic? At his funeral, they'd be afraid to play the Star Spangled Banner.

He's so cheap he's been out pricing generic funerals.

 # FURNITURE DISEASE

He's suffering from furniture disease. His chest keeps dropping into his drawers.

DO-IT-YOURSELF
SPACE.

WRITE YOUR
OWN JOKE
HERE!

GARDEN

I'm not very successful with growing house plants. I bought a hanging house plant, and the rope died.

I love to work to develop new types of flowers. I crossed a pansy with a rambling rose. Well, the rose still rambles, but it takes very small steps.

Some things in life just naturally go together. Like having the best garden and the worst back in town.

You should see the bill we got from our landscaper for lawn care. Would you believe $55 to feed the lawn? They must be feeding it mulch wellington.

Due to gardening I now have calluses in places I didn't even know I had places.

He tried out his new lawn mower today and found out that toes are very good for mulch.

A sign in the window said, "Say It with Flowers". A man walked up to the florist and ordered one rose.
"Just one?" the florist inquired.
"Yes," the man replied, "I'm a man of few words."

She's so sadistic that she planted onions next to the weeping willow.

I don't exactly have a green thumb. For instance, we have a rock garden, and last week, three of them died.

It's not that I'm too lazy to do yard work. I just don't want to disturb the ecology.

I'm not bragging, but my garden looks like a picture postcard--from the Sahara Desert!

When it comes to his lawn, he's a perfectionist. Every blade of grass is exactly two feet high.

My wife goes wild buying plant food. I mean our lawn has the fattest grass on the block!

I know she's been letting the neighbor borrow the power mower again. There's strange blood on it.

This winter I discovered something that will make my front lawn look as good as my neighbor's; a huge snowfall!

My wife has been talking to her flowers for years, and not once have I heard one of them answer. I suppose they must all be mums.

This year I'm trying a new strategy with my lawn. I'm planting the weeds first in hopes that the grass will take over.

I took that tip from Better Homes and Gardens magazine and put coffee grounds in the soil. It worked beautifully. However, now the morning glories are up all night!

Nothing discourages an amateur gardener like watching the family eat his entire garden at one meal.

Here's a garden tip: Don't throw away those seed packets for your vegetable garden. They are often just the right size to store your crop.

Give dandelions an inch, and they'll take a yard.

Gardening--man's effort to improve his lot.

 # GETTYSBURG ADDRESS

I just met a truly unique individual. He writes the Gettysburg Address on the head of a pin. What makes it incredible is that he uses a crayon!

GIRLS

The girls in town are just as attractive as they were 30 years ago. In fact, under all those cosmetics, they might be the very same girls.

She was so fat that her senior class picture was taken by Rand McNally.

She was also very ugly. Once she was robbed by the kissing bandit, and he shook hands with her.

She knew that it was time to go on a diet when the service station attendant asked her if she wanted her shoes rotated every 4,000 miles.

One Christmas she stood under the mistletoe, and it died.

She's so fat, she uses Crisco for lip gloss.

I took her to McDonald's, and she got stuck in the arch.

She's so ugly, she looks like a professional blind date.

She's not very good looking. She's the only girl I know who looks better in curlers.

I saw her go into the dry cleaners with dresses and drapes, and she had to tell them which was which.

She's bow-legged and he's knock-kneed. When they stand together in bathing suits they spell "ox".

She had such affectionate eyes, they kept looking at each other.

She was fat, but I didn't mind because anywhere I sat in English class I was near her. And the teacher didn't mind either because everytime she got up and turned around she erased the blackboard.

I took her downtown, and she was wearing a red, white, and blue dress and three people tried to mail a letter.

One time when we were downtown, she was wearing a yellow dress and some wise guy yelled, "Taxi!"

I once went out with a girl who looked like the girl next door--that is if you live in a horrible neighborhood!

She was so ugly that when I took her to the beach the tide refused to come in.

She had such buck teeth that she could eat an apple through my catcher's mask.

She had the longest tongue I've ever seen. She could drop a letter in a mailbox and then seal it!

She was so fat that she got a job sitting in the front seat of trucks while they changed the back tire.

She was so fat that the computer dating service matched her with Cleveland.

She's the only woman I know who can wear a form-fitting poncho.

She was on the heavy side. The only girl I know who wore stretch jewelry.

She's so ugly that her driver's license had a picture of her car.

She's so fat that her bathtub has stretch marks.

She had funny eyes. She could check her earrings without looking in the mirror.

She wasn't much to look at. I took her to the beach. Boy, could she catch a Frisbee in her mouth!

Her name was Essie McVey Tyler Crump. Our romance didn't last long. I carved her name on a tree, and it fell on her!

My mother used to try to fix me up with blind dates. She'd say, "She's pretty in her own way."
To which I would reply, "Well, then put her with her own kind."

Fat? When she wears high heels she strikes oil!

Ugly? When I took her to the beach, they asked me what I used for bait.

Fat? She was jumping up and down on the Richard Simmons Show, and the TV fell off the stand.

If exercise eliminates fat, how come she has that double chin?

She had a coming out party--but they made her go back in again!

People look at her and say, "Ah, those eyes, those lips, those chins..."

She lost five pounds the easy way. She weighed herself before she put on her makeup.

She was so ugly that guys used to ask her for her phone number so they wouldn't dial it by mistake.

She was so ugly that she once entered a beauty contest. Not only did she come in last, but she was hit in the mouth by Miss Congeniality.

She was so ugly that she used to rent herself out to cure hiccups.

Her eyes intrigued me. Especially the middle one.

She had a million dollar figure, only when she walked it looked like it was all in loose change.

When her eyes came to the bridge of her nose, they crossed.

She was so near-sighted that she had to count elephants to get to sleep.

She was heavy. She wasn't voted "the most likely to succeed" or "the most popular". Just "the most girl".

She ate her lunch out of a satellite dish.

She wasn't a vision, but she certainly was a sight.

Not only could she wiggle her ears, but she could swat flies with them.

In spite of all her problems, she still kept a stiff upper lip. She had to. She had buck teeth.

I won't say what kind of figure she has, but in India she'd be sacred.

She was so fat that one time she had the mumps for two weeks before anyone knew it.

She was so skinny that she could stand on a bag of potato chips without breaking any.

She's got such a big mouth that when she smiles she gets lipstick on her ears.

I was at the Department of Motor Vehicles and saw a guy with the ugliest girl I had ever seen. So ugly that they made him take the eye test three times!

She was at Harvard Medical School for three years as an exhibit.

She was so fat that she made her living selling shade.

She had hazel eyes, chestnut hair, almond skin...she was nuts.

She was the kind of girl who could cure men of whistling.

She's so ugly, she has bags over her eyes.

She had a cute little nose. It turned up, then down, then sideways.

She was so fat that when she put on a pair of heels, they became slippers.

When she wore corduroys, the ridges went flat.

What a mouth. The dentist can put both hands in at the same time.

Her mouth is so big she can whisper in her own ear.

She had the face of a professional lemon-taster.

She has the kind of lips I like. One on the top and one on the bottom.

In her high school class picture, she was the front row.

For her birthday I got her a stretch couch.

She had more chins than the Chinese phone directory.

She got an offer to model cello cases.

She put on a wedding gown, and ten people went snow blind.

She was so fat that she forced clothing manufacturers to change the label to read, "One size fits most".

She had the complexion of a peach--yellow and fuzzy.

When I looked into those eyes, time stood still. Her face could stop a clock.

She had so much bridgework that I had to pay a toll when I wanted to kiss her.

She had pedestrian eyes. They looked both ways before crossing.

She had a school-girl complexion with big diplomas under her eyes.

She would have been five-feet-ten, if they could have straightened her bow legs.

She's so skinny that I grabbed her by the elbow and cut my finger.

She was really heavy. She had old license plates dangling on her charm bracelet.

Her bikini was so skimpy that it looked as if it had been turned out by two silkworms on their coffee break.

She has nice even teeth. One, three, five, and seven are missing.

She was so fat that when she had her picture taken they charged her group rates.

 **GOLF**

You must be creative when playing golf with your boss. You find yourself saying things like: "Wow, you really smacked that one. Did you see how high the water splashed?"

Golf gives you great exercise, improves your health, and increases your stamina, so you're strong enough to play again next week.

Golf is such an aggravating, frustrating game. I sure am glad I don't have to play again until tomorrow.

A partner showed up fifteen minutes late for tee time. His friend asked, "Why are you late?"
"I had to toss a coin to decide whether I should mow the lawn or play a round of golf."
"And that took you twenty minutes?"
"Yeah, I had to toss the coin twenty times."

"How come you're playing so poorly today?"
"Well, I got a haircut yesterday, and I'm having a hard time keeping my head down."

He hits into sandtraps so often, that he had to trade in his golf cart for a dune buggy.

In high school, I was captain of the junior varsity miniature golf team until I was injured. Windmills.

A golfer sliced a ball onto the highway, then hooked another into the woods, followed by a drive that landed in a lake.
"Why don't you use an old ball?" his partner asked.
"I never had an old ball," the duffer replied.

He doesn't cheat at golf. He just plays for his health. And, of course, a low score makes him feel much better.

Show me a good loser and I'll show you a man who is playing golf with his boss.

My wife said, "You're so wrapped up in golf you don't even remember our wedding day!"
"Sure I do," I said. "That's the day I sank that 30-foot putt!"

I had a tough round yesterday. I lost four balls. Three in the ball washer.

"I've got good news and bad news," the caddy told the golfer. "The good news is that you got a birdie on the sixth hole. The bad news is you're playing the fifth!"

I worked as a caddy at a country club and they had a great employee health plan. Every Wednesday you'd get to see the doctor.

A golfer hit a terrible shot into the lake. He said, "I can't go after that. If I jump in the lake I might drown."
"No chance of that," replied his caddy. "You don't keep your head down long enough."

When he goes golfing with the boss, he goes a little too far. This morning they were playing and the boss hit into a sandtrap 200 feet from the green and he conceded the putt.

I can tell this is a golf banquet. Everyone coming to the mike has held it with an interlocking grip.

"Why don't you play golf with George anymore?"
"Would you play with someone who puts down the wrong score and moves the ball when you're not watching?"
"No."
"Neither will George."

He's really frustrated. He got a hole-in-one the other day and found that he couldn't get it stuffed or mounted.

He bought one of those golf instruction books that told him to keep his head down. While he was keeping his head down, someone stole his golf cart.

What a golfer! The other day, he missed a hole-in-one by just four strokes!

He lost only two golf balls last year. He was putting at the time.

Want to know his handicap? His irons, his driver, and his putter.

A golf course is a site to be holed.

The golfer, whacking his way through some terribly high weeds complained, "This is a terrible course."
The caddy replied, "No, it isn't. We left the course two or three miles back."

My wife ran over my golf clubs with the car, although she did tell me not to leave them on the front porch.

He has a beautiful short game. Unfortunately it's off the tee.

Miniature golf is tougher than real golf. You never turn on the TV and hear, "Jack Nicklaus is putting. Oh, he hit the windmill!"

The course I play is getting tougher--they've increased the speed of the windmill and narrowed the clown's mouth!

What a swing! I've got more ways to slice than a food processor!

Jack Nicklaus is doing Geritol commercials for people who are feeling under par.

I shoot in the low seventies, because if it gets any colder, I won't play!

If golf is a rich man's game, how come there are so many poor players?

Never go golfing with an undertaker. He's always on top at the last hole.

When he goes golfing he always wears two pairs of socks, just in case he gets a hole-in-one.

I played golf yesterday and shot a birdie. I was putting and the dumb thing kept chirping!

His doctor told him to play thirty-six holes a day, so he went out and bought a harmonica.

My trouble is that I stand too close to the ball...after I've hit it!

He's wearing his golfing socks. You know, the ones with eighteen holes.

"My wife says if I don't quit playing golf she'll leave me."
"That's too bad."
"Yeah, I'll miss her."

I used to watch golf on TV until my doctor told me I needed more exercise. So now I watch tennis.

Today I was one under...one under a tree, one under a rock, one under a bush...

Yeah, I play golf. But only on days ending in the letter "y".

"I'd move heaven and earth to break 100," a golf duffer said.
"You better concentrate on heaven," said the caddy. "You've moved enough earth already."

Last summer I discovered something that took ten strokes off my game. It's called an eraser.

Sure I know how to address the ball. I just don't put enough stamps on it.

The world's worst golfer hit a ball into a monstrous trap. "What club shall I use?" he asked the caddy.
"Never mind what club," the caddy answered, "just take along plenty of food and water."

I asked the caddy, "What do you think of my game?"
He said, "It's okay, but I like golf better."

A doctor who golfs has one great advantage over the rest of us. Nobody can read his scorecard.

One sure way to stay employed: Have the boss make a hole-in-one and you're the only witness.

A golfer sliced his ball into a thicket, then into a sand trap, and smacked one across the highway into heavy woods. But, he went after it in a seemingly impossible search. "Why don't you forget about it and drop another one?"
"I can't," said the duffer. "This is my lucky ball!"

A golfer drove an errant shot off the course and into a pig pen, killing one of the pigs. An irate farmer blasted the golfer up and down until the golfer said, "Okay, I'll replace your pig."
"You ain't fat enough!" screamed the farmer.

"May I play through? I just received word that my wife was in a serious accident."

He drove the ball into the rough, flushing out a quail. His partner mused, "That's the first time I've ever seen a partridge on a par three."

He's so fat he has trouble playing golf. If he puts the ball where he can hit it, he can't see it, and if he puts the ball where he can see it, he can't hit it.

An inept golfer drove his tee shot into an ant hill. After many swings, he succeeded in smashing the anthill, but still hadn't hit the ball. One ant said to another, "If we're going to survive, we'd better get on the ball!"

Golfer to partner: "I'm anxious to make this shot. That's my mother-in-law up there on the clubhouse porch."
Partner: "It's no use. You're 200 yards away. You couldn't possibly hit her from here."

At the first tee, a golfer took four mighty swings, missing the ball each time. He shook his head and moaned, "This is the toughest course I've ever played."

A girl dressed in a white wedding gown rushed toward the first tee, confronting a guy ready to tee off. The golfer turned toward her angrily and said, "I told you--if it rains!"

Golf partners were playing the 16th hole when a funeral procession passed. One took off his cap, placed it over his heart for thirty seconds, and resumed his putting stance. "We'd have been married 25 years today," he said.

When he golfs, he always takes along two caddies because he always has to send one back for laughing too loudly.

Golfer: "You must be the worst caddy in the world!"
Caddy: "No, sir. That would be too much of a coincidence!"

A player hit a tee shot that was picked up by a strong gale, travelled 465 yards, up onto the green, and rolled into the cup.
"Not bad," said his partner. "I'll take my practice shot and then we can get started."

A novice slammed the ball down the fairway and the ball rolled three inches from the cup. The caddy jumped up and down excitedly.
"What do I now?" the beginner asked.
"Tap the ball into the cup, sir."
"Now you tell me!"

He said to his caddy, "I bet there are people who are a lot worse at golf than I am."
The caddy said, "Sure, but they don't play."

A beginner hit his first tee shot and it dropped into the hole for a hole-in-one. His second shot bounced onto the green, rolled slowly, and teetered into the cup.

"Thank goodness," said the beginner. "I thought I missed."

To caddy: "Why do you keep looking at your watch?"
Caddy: "It's not my watch, sir. It's my compass."

I play with a golfer who is so accustomed to shaving his score, that once he got a hole-in-one and carded a zero.

Today I played golf and shot a 68. Tomorrow I'm going to go back and try the second hole.

He's such a poor golfer that even his tee shots are unplayable lies.

I didn't win playing golf today, but at least I got to hit the ball more times than anyone else.

Remember, golf is flog spelled backwards.

The way some people play golf, the green flags at the hole should always be at half mast.

Teacher: Remember what happens to boys who use bad language when they play marbles.
Boy: Yep, teacher, they grow up to play golf.

Today he's using two caddies because his wife says he doesn't spend enough time with the kids.

He does everything first class. I played golf with him Tuesday, and he used suede golf balls!

His opponent placed the ball on the tee and took a wild swing, missing the ball badly.
The flustered guy said, "Wow, it's a good thing I discovered early in the game that this course is at least two inches lower than the one I normally play."

"How should I play this putt, caddy?"
"Try to keep it low, sir."

GOOD DAY

I knew this was going to be a good day when I walked into the supermarket and found a shopping cart with all the wheels going in the same direction.

Being here tonight is the perfect climax to an already dull day.

GOOF AROUND DAY

Here's an exciting way to celebrate goof around day...
* Go jogging in swim fins...
* Damp mop the ceiling...
* Establish the world's record for yawning while clicking a ball-point pen...
* Count the raisins in a box of Raisin Bran while whistling "The Flight of the Bumble Bee"...
* Take a challenging self-improvement course--like learning to eat potato chips silently...
* Paint a big oil puddle on the driveway under your neighbor's new car...
* Train your Frisbee to catch a dog...
* Get pictures of Arthur Godfrey, Doris Day, and Howdy Doody. Put them together, get a pencil and play connect the freckles...
* Write a ten thousand word essay on why Vincent Van Gogh wouldn't have enjoyed stereo...
* Develop an automatic warning device for your car that buzzes one day before the payment is due...

GOOFS

(after a garbled sentence, push up on your teeth) You just can't buy these things at a garage sale.

I suppose you think it's easy trying to talk with a broken tongue.

(after an interruption) I love these little pauses. It gives me a chance to catch my breath and plan my escape.

GOVERNMENT

I won't say where all the money is going that we send to Washington each April, but they just sent out for eight more drains.

The latest statistics show that 3,500,000 Americans are idle. Unfortunately, most of them work for the government.

GRADUATION

Three essentials for graduation are: (1) a cap, (2) a gown, and (3) ear plugs so you don't have to listen to the commencement speech.

I had a recent conversation with a college graduate. I asked him, "What was your major?"
He said, "English Grammar, Communications Skills and Advanced Oratory and Diction."
I said, "Really?"
He said, "Yeah."

The graduate who has the best future is the one who knows four languages, has mastered computer programming and accounting, has a working knowledge of nuclear physics and advanced genetics--and isn't averse to heavy lifting.

During the graduation ceremony I helped five handicapped students by reading the commencement program to them. Two were blind and three were football players.

Doesn't it make you a little nervous when the commencement speaker is saying, "The future is in your hands," and one of the kids to whom he is speaking is the one who throws your newspaper in the rose bushes every day?

I don't know what to give my cousin for graduation. Should I give him a digital watch or reading lessons?

GRANDCHILDREN

We don't make a big deal about our grandchildren. They're only two and four-years-old. The surgeon is two and the Most Valuable Player is four.

Our grandchildren are so much fun we should have had them first.

We know why they're called grandchildren. It's grand to see them come and grand to see them go.

How is it that the boy who wasn't good enough to marry your daughter is the father of the brightest grandchild in the whole world?

HAIR

My kid has so much hair, we had to let out his beanie four times!

HALLOWEEN

This year at Halloween I'm going to go over to my sister's house and frighten my brother-in-law. I'm going to dress up like a job.

Halloween is always a special celebration. It's the only time of the year when Rodney Dangerfield looks normal.

My ten-year-old wanted to dress up like a bum, so he asked if he could wear one of my old, worn-out suits for Halloween--so I took it off.

Last Halloween a five-year-old knocked on the door and my wife opened it wearing a mud pack, a chin strap, curlers and her rubber reducing pants--and the kid gave her candy.

HANDYMAN

I'm not handy. People know that when I ask the question, "How do you get blood off a saw?"

HEALTH

My doctor just informed me that I'm as sound as a dollar, but he thinks I'll recover.

Girls call me 'the strong, silent type'. That's because I can't hold my stomach in and talk at the same time.

Life is all mixed up. How many people in the audience went to bed last night and you weren't sleepy? Then you had to get up the next morning and you were dead tired. This makes sense?

The doctor gave me so many shots of penicillin that every time I sneeze, I cure someone.

There's absolutely nothing the matter with my health except the body that it's found in.

He's so anemic that when a mosquito lands on him all he gets is practice.

He just got a disease that is so rare that they haven't even had a telethon for it.

To prevent a head cold from moving to your chest, tie a knot in your neck.

Tonight we ask you to give generously to wipe out the greatest killer of them all--natural causes.

I'm in such poor shape that the health club makes me use the rear entrance.

If I had known that I was going to live this long, I would have taken better care of myself.

You know you're out of shape when you get winded on an escalator.

HEALTH FOODS

I don't eat health foods. I need all the preservatives I can get.

I insist that my kids eat something every day from the four basic food groups: fresh, frozen, fast and junk.

I went to a friend's house and saw him eat a dinner of wheat germ and brown rice. I was relieved the next morning when I saw him eat his typical breakfast of a Dr. Pepper, Hostess Twinkie and a bag of taco chips.

I stopped buying natural foods when I kept reading that people keep dying of natural causes.

He ate so many pumpkin seeds that one day he got caught in a rain storm and he sprouted.

When a health food salesman comes to your door, go ahead and vitamin.

HECKLERS

(put-down) He saw Guess Who's Coming to Dinner? twice and guessed wrong both times!

Sir, if I had wanted criticism I would have stayed home. You see, I have a wife and two teenagers.

Isn't she sweet? She has all the charm of a meter maid with a quota.

HECTIC LIFE

Times are so hectic that there's no longer the chance to enjoy culture in life. If it wasn't for being put on hold, I wouldn't hear any good music at all.

HISTORY

My son failed history so I told him, "When I was your age, history was my best subject."
He said, "Big deal. When you were my age, what had happened?"

Let's just keep things in balance. Forty years from now, kids in history classes will be yawning over what troubles us today.

HOCKEY

I took my kid to the fights the other night. It was the first time he had ever seen ice hockey.

I went to the fights the other night and a hockey game broke out.

HOMES

I just got some great news. My real estate agent called to tell me he found land on my property.

I called a real estate agent from a phone booth and asked, "What can I get for $500 a month?"
He replied, "You're standing in it."

Our dining room table goes back to Louis the Fourteenth. And our living room couch goes back to Sears on the fifteenth.

Sign on a neighbor's front lawn: "Beware of vicious dog--formerly 'Keep Off the Grass'."

One thing you learn when moving is that the word "fragile" to moving lines is a code word meaning "slam dunk."

A yawning host looked at his watch and said to a visiting couple, "Who pays attention to time when good friends get together? Why it's only twelve-fourteen and-a-half."

We must improve the insulation in our house. We have the only vacuum cleaner on the block with snow tires.

My wife decorated the home around the color of one object--the telephone. And it was yellow. No matter what time of day it is, it is light in our house.

My realtor told me, "This basement is dryer than the Sahara."
Two weeks later I walked into his office and declared, "Some Sahara! I put two mouse traps in my basement and caught a flounder and a haddock!"

Be careful when the real estate ad reads, "This home has a certain air about it..." That translates to: "It's located right next to a pig farm."

Do you really care that the average home costs so much today? Fifty percent of us can't afford one. The statisticians say the average American is born in a hospital, married in a church, and dies in a car, so what do you need a home for anyway?

I wanted to buy a house in the suburbs and my realtor found one in my price range--only it was in Beirut.

They used terrific lumber in my house. We've got 3,000 termites dying of anemia.

The first place I lived burned down. The fireman said he had never seen a car burn so fast.

We have really big bugs in our home. The other night I stepped outside to get the paper, and when I came back in the bugs had changed the channel on the television!

Buying a home is one investment that will show appreciation. We bought a home three months ago and already the electrician appreciates it, the plumber appreciates it, the fuel company appreciates it, and the bank that holds the giant mortgage simply adores it!

My house is really cold. They say that M&M's don't melt in your hand. Big deal. In my house, neither do ice cubes!

I'm not saying our builder made a mistake, but did you ever hear of going downstairs to the attic?

I once owned a home that was on the median strip of an expressway. I liked it a lot. The only trouble with it was when I'd leave the driveway I had to be going 60 m.p.h..

You know that your home is a bit drafty when you flip a pancake into the air in your kitchen and it comes down in your den.

An army family of eight was temporarily headquartered in a hotel room. An officer remarked to one of the children, "Isn't it too bad that you don't have a home?"
The child replied, "Oh, we have a home. We just don't have a house to put it in."

My family is real energy conscious. We don't use any more energy than your typical domed-stadium.

Here's some sage advice for those of you who are about to buy a home; don't worry that it be near a shopping center, or a school, or public transportation. Just make sure it's near a hardware store.

I won't say how messy the home is, but yesterday the phone rang and we couldn't find it.

We lost our canary. I just can't understand it. It was there this morning when I was vacuuming its cage.

Today I spent two hours just making crazy faces at the goldfish. I know it sounds dumb, but they started it!

Our home is so cold that we open the refrigerator door just to warm up.

Our home is very patriotic in the winter. Our noses turn red, our hands turn white, and our lips turn blue.

One problem that we have at home is that Rex spends all his time barking at my wife and me, he begs for food, and is always crawling up on the couch to sleep. The big problem is that Rex is our son.

HORSE RACING

One horse kept turning around to check where his plow was.

The horse that he bet on was so slow that after the race they sold him to the post office.

I went and bet $10 on the first race. Hey, if Paul Revere had the horse I bet on, we'd still be under British rule.

Two bookies were coming out of church and one said to the other, "How many times have I told you it's 'hallelujah' and not 'Hialeah'!"

The horse I bet on was so slow that he kept a diary of the trip.

He bet on a horse that was so slow that the next time it ran it was from a bottle of glue.

HOSPITAL

I had surgery at Perpetual Payments Hospital. They closed their recovery room there because nobody ever used it.

The hospital has four different room rates. For $400 a day you're in a room that has a waterbed filled with chicken soup; for $200 a day you're in a semi-private room; for $100 a day you're in a ward, and for $30 you're the top person in a wheelchair.

The food in the hospital was so bad I asked to be put back on the intravenous feeding.

You know what happens when you don't pay your hospital bill? Did you ever have an appendix put back in?

Here's the world's most honest doctor. The nurse asks, "What are you operating for?"
The doctor says, "$950."
The nurse says, "No, I mean what does the patient have?"
The doctor replies, "$950."

I was a patient at the Mary Baker Eddy Memorial Hospital.

My surgeon just came out of retirement. He's brushing up on the latest medical techniques through trial and error.

A guy with a white gown examined me every day. He wasn't even a doctor. He was just the Good Humor man on his lunch hour.

Hospital visitors are necessary. What makes visitors important is they bring the candy, fruit and ice cream that are necessary to feed the ones that bring the magazines and books.

Have you ever noticed that hospital visitors never talk to the patients they are visiting? They spend 90% of their time talking to each other, to the other patients down the hall and to the other patient in the room. My wife had such a good time in the hospital I was home two weeks before she found out!

He just got out of the hospital. He's recuperating from a speed-reading accident.

Dr. Scalpel told his patient, "I've got some good news and bad news for you. The bad news is that I cut off your good leg by mistake. And the good news is that your bad leg is getting better."

"You operated just in time," the veteran surgeon told the young doctor. "In another two days the patient would have recovered without surgery."

"The operation was a complete success," the surgeon told the wife, "until your husband fell off the operating table."

"Is this operation very dangerous?" asked the patient.
"That, my good man," responded the doctor, "is what we are going to find out."

"Of course you'll get well," said the doctor, "even if it takes every cent you've got."

I was in the hospital for an operation. The students (office staff) sent me a get-well card that read: "Our class (staff) voted 13-12 to wish you a speedy recovery."

Patient to doc: "What do you mean, this operation is going to cost me an arm and a leg?"

Our local hospital reported a deficit for the past fiscal year of $300,000. The director said, "There is no cause for alarm, however. After all, it's only a matter of one or two more patients."

A patient said, "My feet are freezing. How about a hot-water bottle for my feet?"
The nurse stared coldly and said, "I'm the head nurse."
"Well, get me a foot nurse then!" screamed the patient.

After the operation they put me in the expensive care unit.

HOTEL

"What do you have in your mattresses?"
"Only the finest straw."
"Now I know where the expression comes from, 'The straw that broke the camel's back.' "

My suite was so small that the refrigerator opens in.

I remember my first apartment. I got married and carried my wife over the threshold. She saw my apartment and said, "Don't put me down!"

I was at a hotel last week where the chambermaid knocked on the door at seven in the morning to remind me that my "Do Not Disturb" sign was still on the doorknob.

My hotel room was so small that every time I bent over I rearranged the furniture.

I stayed in such an exclusive hotel that room service had an unlisted number.

I called room service to ask for a towel and they told me that someone else was using it.

At the hotel, my room wasn't bugged, but the bed was!

My hotel room was so small that I could only brush my teeth in one direction.

That hotel is really something. Every twenty minutes they change the rates. It's the only place in the world where you can go broke sleeping.

The first law of travel is: The guy who sets his alarm for 4 a.m., takes a shower, and has trouble starting his car at 5 a.m., is going to be in the room right next to you.

I love this hotel and the room and bath that I have. A little inconvenient though. They're in two different buildings.

I called room service and asked, "Is this room service? Please send up a room!"

My hotel room was so small the venetian blinds had only one slat.

My hotel room was so small that the closet had space for only one hanger.

My hotel room was so small that I didn't even have room to complain.

My hotel had a sign on the wall that read: "Please don't slam the door. It's holding up the walls."

What a fantastic hotel! It even has an air-conditioned steam room!

They advertised "Three Seasons Bed". It came without a spring.

I spent the night at a hotel called The Z. It was directly behind the Y.

Talk about your classy hotels! I know lots of hotels have music in the elevators--but live?

Their service is so slow that when you order breakfast you have to leave a forwarding address.

He left the hotel without paying his bill and received a notice: "Please send amount of the bill."
His reply, "Sirs, the amount of the bill is $155."

The clerk asked, "Would you like a room with a tub or a shower?"
He said, "What's the difference?"
"Well," said the clerk, "with a tub, you sit down."

A tip-weary tourist heard a knock at his door. "Telegram, sir."
Not wanting to have to tip again, the hotel guest said, "Please slip it under the door."
"I can't," was the reply.
"Why not?" asked the guest.
"Because it's on a tray."

That hotel was so posh they had wall-to-wall carpeting-- on the ceiling.

There wasn't a single roach in the hotel where we stayed. They were all married and had large families.

A chess convention met in the lobby of a downtown hotel. They spent the first hour bragging to each other about recent chess victories. The manager suddenly rushed in and threw them all out of the lobby, instructing them to go to their rooms. The manager explained, "If there's one thing I can't stand, it's chess nuts boasting by an open foyer."

Hotels should change those signs in the rooms that read, "Have you left anything?" to "Have you anything left?"

The room was so small that they used a bath mat for wall-to-wall carpeting.

Everytime a truck went by the termites would hold hands to keep the place from falling down.

My bed was so hard that I had to get up twice during the night just to get some rest.

I'll never forget that hotel. My checkbook won't let me!

The walls were so thin I got sunburned without ever leaving my room. And who wants to leave a room at $150 a day?

The hotel was so large that you had to dial long distance just to reach the front desk.

I had a small room overlooking a waste basket.

Hilton purchased The Leaning Tower of Pisa and they're going to call it the Tiltin' Hilton.

In Russia they call it "The Comrade Hilton."

The coffee shop charged $1.75 for a cup of coffee. But I got back at them by using 400 packs of Sweet and Low.

The hotel was really ready for this convention. This is the first time that I have ever seen a Gideon Bible on a chain.

HOUSEHOLD HINTS

To save hours of work cleaning the oven, unscrew the light bulb.

The best way to get ants out of the kitchen is to pour sugar all over your living room rug.

Unsightly scratches on the kitchen counter can be easily removed with a pail of water, a hard brush, and eleven sticks of dynamite.

Never hire an electrician with no eyebrows.

Don't hire a carpenter with more than three fingers missing from one hand.

An ordinary garden rake makes an excellent device for drying homemade doughnuts.

Today is an excellent day for revenge. Pay the paper boy with a wet check.

Remember, ladies, two goldfish placed in a punch bowl will keep the sugar stirred up.

Ladies, buy the new cellophane newspaper so that you will be able to see your husband while you are talking to him at the breakfast table.

HOUSEWORK

My wife is so fastidious, twice a week she files her nails---under N.

HOW YOU KNOW IT'S GOING TO BE A ROTTEN DAY

You see a "60 Minutes" news team waiting in your office...

Your birthday cake collapses from the weight of the candles...

You turn on the news and they're showing emergency routes out of the city...

Your twin sister forgets your birthday...

Your car horn accidentally sticks when you are following a motorcycle gang on the freeway...

Your boss tells you not to bother taking off your coat...

The bird singing outside your window is a buzzard...

You wake up and your braces are locked together...

You call your answering service and they tell you it's none of your business...

Your income tax check bounces...

You put both contact lenses in the same eye...

Your artificial flower dies...

The Good Humor Man yells at you...

Your swimming pool burns down...

Your mother-in-law shows up at your house with six suitcases and a burial deed...

Your sun dial is slow...

You lose the life-preserver on your rowing machine...

Your wife cleans your false teeth in the blender...

The car breaks down going to work. You have an argument with the boss. You lose your biggest account. The mechanic charges you $143 to fix the car. You get home, drop into your favorite easy chair and locate the egg that you couldn't find at Easter.

You're in an airplane and the B. F. Goodrich blimp is gaining on you...

You compliment the boss's wife on the perfume she's wearing and she isn't wearing any...

You spray spot remover under your arms...

The restaurant check has been sitting on the table for ten minutes and no one has touched it...

You know that it's going to be a bad day when you get a nasty paper cut from a get-well card...

You ask about your blind date and are told, "She has a great personality and beautiful posture."

You come out of your memory class and forget where you parked your car...

Your water bed catches fire...

You know it's going to be a rotten day when you wreck your car while driving home from the bank after making the final payment.

 # HUNTING

A hunter bragging about his South African trip said, "I looked in my tent and saw a ferocious ape. Then guess what I did."
"Took down the mirror?" his listener asked.

He's a deer hunter but none of them ever became aware of it.

A guy was out hunting, came to a fork in the road and read a sign which said, "Bear left." So he went home.

A schoolboy was an avid hunter. When his teacher asked if he knew the four seasons he said, "Sure. Rabbit, squirrel, deer and bear."

The last time I went hunting ducks even the decoy got away.

A razorback hog charged right at me. It didn't get me, but it was a close shave.

I was surrounded by a bull and a panther. I shot the panther first because I figured I could always shoot the bull anytime.

I won't say what kind of hunter he is, but he subscribes to Field and Stream, large-print edition.

An Indian ruler was such an avid hunter that he forbade all subjects in the kingdom from hunting. His angered patrons rebelled and overthrew him, making this the first time in history that a reign was called on account of the game.

A sign on a country road read: "No hunting."
Underneath someone scrawled, "You're telling me!"

A man trailed into the hunting camp looking pale as a ghost. "Are all the others out of the woods yet?
"Yep," came the answer.
"Well," he sighed in relief, "I shot a deer then."

"While I was hunting, I was confronted by a ferocious grizzly. I leaped to catch a limb twenty feet above my head."
"Did you catch it?"
"I missed it on the way up, but luckily I grabbed it on the way down."

"Did I tell you about the time I was face-to-face with a ferocious lion and he kept creeping closer and closer to me?"
"No, what did you do?"
"I calmly moved on to the next cage."

"I shot many ferocious tigers in Africa."
"There aren't any tigers in Africa!"
"I know. I shot them all!"

A hunter and his friend spied the footprints of a giant bear. One said, "You go see where he went. I'll go back to see where he came from."

DO-IT-YOURSELF
SPACE.

WRITE YOUR
OWN JOKE
HERE!

IDEAS

The reason some ideas die so quickly in a person's head is that they can't stand solitary confinement.

As a kid, he had the idea that he wanted to become a professional after-dinner speaker, but he had to give up his dream when it was discovered that he was allergic to stuffed chicken breast and cold mashed potatoes.

IMPOSSIBLE

The next time someone tells you that nothing is impossible, get them to try eating an ice cream cone from the bottom up!

The person who said, "Nothing is impossible" never tried to barbecue pancakes.

The next time someone tries to tell you that nothing is impossible, try to get him to put his skis over his shoulder and go through a revolving door.

The next time someone says to you, "Nothing's impossible..." tell him, "Go dribble a football."

Those who say nothing is impossible have never tried to get bubble gum out of an angora sweater, tried to slam a revolving door, or tried to get off a book club's mailing list.

INDIAN

We can blame all the crime we have today on Indians. They should have had stricter immigration laws.

An Indian was sitting next to a woman in a movie theater. Following the movie, the woman inquired, "You're an Indian, aren't you? Tell me, how do you like our city?"
The Indian answered, "Fine, madam. How do you like our country?"

I went into the hospital last week to donate blood. On the couch directly across from me was an Apache Indian. I looked over and inquired, " Are you a full-blooded Apache?"
He answered, "I was. Now I pint short."

Great Indian Chief Running Deer told his braves, "On a long journey of many suns, you must have the eye of the hawk, the instincts of the elk, the direction of a crow. It also helps to follow the interstates."

When they were finished looking at a series of distant smoke signals, one chief said to the brave, "We're going to have to do something about Little Big Horse. His spelling is something awful."

A tourist asked an Indian how large a fire he made when sending smoke signals. The chief replied, "It all depends on whether it's local or long distance."

I've an Indian lawyer--Sioux, of course.

In Tucson, a tourist introduced to an Indian, was told that the chief had a perfect memory. Skeptical, the traveler asked, "What did you have for breakfast on September 6, 1936?"
The Indian answered, "Eggs."
The tourist said, "That's nothing. Everyone eats eggs for breakfast."
Eight years later, the tourist's train again stopped in Tucson, and he saw the same Indian sitting at the station. He went up to him and

jovially said, "How!"
The Indian said, "Scrambled!"

At the time of the atom bomb tests in New Mexico, an Indian was sending love messages by smoke signal to his girl friend. Suddenly, a mushroom cloud filled the sky. The amazed brave said, "Wow, I wish I'd said that!"

An Indian sending smoke signals had a fire extinguisher at his side. A traveller asked why. The redskin said, "If me mispellum word, me erasum."

INSURANCE

An insurance salesman was trying to close a deal with a reluctant prospect. He boasted, "One month ago, a man took out a policy with us. The other day he had an accident and we paid him $15,000. Now think: tomorrow you may be the lucky one!"

"You say your business collected $500,000 from flood insurance. How in the world do you start a flood?"

Here's why insurance companies are mostly indestructible:
The cost of damages most times is less than the deductible.

Life insurance is something that keeps a man poor all his life so he can die rich.

You've got to be crazy to buy life insurance. Here's a guy betting that you're going to live, and you're betting him you're going to die, and you hope he wins, and they charge you for thinking that.

The insurance salesman said to me, "Don't let me frighten you into a hasty decision. Sleep on it tonight. If you wake up tomorrow morning, let me know."

I just signed up for group insurance. I get $5000 if I die in a group.

My fire and theft insurance only pays me if I'm robbed while my house is burning.

I thought my group insurance was okay until I discovered that I could only collect if the whole group is sick.

I just got a great new insurance policy. You pay premiums for 40 years and then if you're hit by a train and killed, you get income for life.

My insurance company has a catchy slogan: "After you're gone, we'll still be here."

INTRODUCTIONS

Our guest tonight is a sophisticate. I know that by observing him at the dinner table. He said, "Waiter, I'll have the vichyssoise. And this time try to keep it from getting cold."

When he came into the room someone told him to go to the end of the line.
"I can't," he said, "Someone is already there."

On the way to the program tonight I was stopped for speeding. I begged the officer to give me a warning. So he fired three shots over my head.

That introduction was truly mediocre.

I saw a sad thing on the way to the banquet. A man locked his keys in the car and was working like crazy with a coat hanger trying to get his family out.

I'm _____, the Picasso of comedy. Which means when these jokes are dead they'll be worth a fortune!

We have a strange and wonderful relationship. I'm wonderful and he's strange.

People often ask me what being on the road a lot does to our marriage. My wife and I have an understanding that before I go on a trip we write down what we're arguing about so we can pick up where we left off when I get home.

Hi, I've got some good news and bad news. The good news is that I'm going to have a great show! The bad news is that it's not tonight.

I just want you folks to know that I gave up jury duty to be here.

Here I am, _____, the doctor of comedy. Unfortunately, the patient always dies.

Look at it this way. While you're listening to me perform, the value of your house is going UP.

Our speaker is really excited tonight, and for good reason. His Ginsu knives and Pocket Fisherman arrived in the mail on the same day!

Our next speaker is one you'll remember the rest of your life. That is if you have a good memory, and not much on your mind. And you get hit by a truck tonight.

And now, I'd like to introduce the world's greatest speaker, a speaker whose humor is legend...a speaker who chooses words perfectly...a speaker who writes his own introductions.

I'm grateful to be invited to speak here tonight. You see, I'm married, and what I'm usually invited to do is listen.

And now here he is, the Three Mile Island of Comedy...

As you know, our program director is always on the lookout for speakers who can capture the imagination, stimulate the intellect, captivate your fancy, and rivet your attention. And so, while his search continues, tonight we've settled for...

Am I going too fast for those of you who are taking notes?

Here's a man who really has his hands full. Sort of like Orson Welles' masseur.

His worst experience was when he spoke to a convention of waiters and waitresses and couldn't get anyone's attention.

I'd like to say hello to all you beautiful people out there---and to all you ugly people, too.

You seem to be in a great mood tonight, but I'll fix that.

(quieting an audience) Could you be a little quieter in the back please? There are people up here trying to sleep.

That was the second best introduction I've ever had. The other one came when the fellow who was supposed to introduce me didn't show up and I had to introduce myself.

The program director wasn't exactly sure how I'd do tonight. When I asked him the size of the room he said, "It sleeps 500."

Would Mr. and Mrs. _____ please go to the lobby and call the babysitter? She says not to be alarmed. She just wants to know where the fire extinguisher is.

I'm glad to be here. I followed the toastmaster's instructions but I got here anyway.

I've been to so many chicken dinners that when I go home, I don't sit, I roost!

Our speaker tonight doesn't have a middle name. He comes from a very poor family.

Our efficiency expert is here tonight. In fact, he's in the lobby right now making up foursomes to go through the revolving door.

Our next speaker is with the city. His brother doesn't work either.

Our speaker tonight is world famous. He's been written up in magazines, trade journals, and this evening he was mentioned on the TV weather report. They said a mass of hot air was coming up from the South.

Our next speaker has spent a lifetime boning up on his specialty and today he is one of the head men in his field. And so, without further delay, I would like to introduce one of the industry's foremost boneheads...

He's got the type of act that just underwhelms you.

He comes to us from his most recent appearance where he did a telethon for hiccups.

And now, a man who is ahead of his time and behind in his mortgage payments...

Flattering introductions are like berths in the N.B.A. playoffs. Everybody gets one.

Our next speaker needs no introduction, because nobody cares who he is anyway.

He's the image of good will. His shirt, his tie, his suit, they're all from Goodwill!

He's accomplished so much in such a short time that when he dies, he's considering having himself bronzed.

Ladies and gentlemen and honored guests, and good old what's your name...

And now, here he is, Lawrence Welk's lost son, the human dynamo himself, who yawns in the face of danger, and in everyone else's face, for that matter...

Once or twice in a career you get a chance to introduce somebody who's at the top of his trade. A person whose name is synonymous with competence, integrity, enthusiasm. Unfortunately, this is not one of those times.

He was nervous when I told him he had to speak tonight.
He said, "What if they boo me?"
I said, "Don't be silly! People can't boo and yawn at the same time."

Thank you for that warm introduction. Beautifully restrained, I might add.

Let me thank you for that generous applause. Many emcees introduce a speaker by saying, "Without any further ado..." Well, I need all the ado I can get!

(answering questions) Let's answer some questions. And we'll start with the smokers because they don't have as much time as the rest of us.

Surely, I could stand here and be charming, funny, and witty, but I don't want to change the format of my show.

I almost didn't make it to the banquet on time tonight. My wife just got a bunch of new clothes, so she pushed all her old ones to one side of the closet and the house tipped.

Our speaker tonight requires no introduction. He failed to show up.

He's done so many wonderful things in such a brief time, it's hard to exaggerate his accomplishments...but I'll do my best.

Ladies and gentlemen...I guess that takes in most of you.

He's been voted one of the finest minds in_____, which is a lot like being named to the ten best-dressed list in Russia.

Our next speaker is very active in church...he squirms and fidgets, and wiggles.

He's an outstanding athlete and the proud possessor of a black belt. He also has a brown belt, a white belt and red suspenders.

Here's a man who's world famous in certain parts of the country.

I was standing around prior to the show and signed about thirty autographs. If anyone would like one, I still have them here in my pocket.

I just returned from a pleasure trip. I took my mother-in-law to the airport.

Coming up next is a man who needs no introduction. However, he insists upon it.

Talk about cheap equipment. The last place I performed the microphone had a rope starter!

Someone asked me after a show, "Why do you act so crazy?"
I told him, "I got news for you, friend. I can't act!"

First of all, we'll have the reading of the minutes of our last meeting. "Twenty minutes after seven; nine minutes until eight; twenty-four minutes until ten."

This program is the result of months of intensive neglect.

My subject this evening is, "How Come If I'm So Important I'm Not Too Busy To Be Here?"

Before coming here this evening, I couldn't find my socks. So I called information and the operator said, "They're behind the couch!"

If I can make just one person laugh tonight, I'm in trouble.

Your job is to make believe your applause is sincere and I'm to make believe I deserve it.

(after receiving an award) It hasn't been easy getting to where I am tonight. Your program committee gave me the wrong address.

(when the microphone doesn't work) Aren't you glad this outfit doesn't make pacemakers?

Our next guest has been called a self-made man. This, of course, was in the days before quality control.

Thanks for that fine introduction, but it sure confused my wife. Halfway through the introduction she nudged me and asked, "Who else is speaking tonight?"

Our next speaker is a man who is often mistaken for Robert Redford. He tells girls he's the Robert Redford type and they tell him he must be mistaken.

Are there any questions about the material we've covered thus far?

He comes to us from his old job of teaching Cub Scouts to sky dive against their will.

I used to have trouble remembering names until I took that great Sam Carnegie course.

Good evening ladies and gentlemen. It's a pleasure to be here. I have that part of my speech memorized.

Our guest tonight is a man who is young at heart. You can tell he's young at heart by his flashing eyes, his quick step, and his Mickey Mouse cufflinks.

(receiving an award) I'm sure I don't deserve this. But then again, what is my opinion against millions?

He needs no introduction. What he needs is a conclusion.

I have been told that the mind cannot absorb anymore than the seat can endure.

Quiet please. Come to order. It is time for our speaker. You can enjoy yourself some other time.

Before I go any further, I'd like to introduce my spouse. (Lead applause and when no one stands up, shake your head and comment) You know, after that last gas station, I thought it was awfully quiet in the car.

I just received a fan letter addressed to the "Nut in Pennsylvania." What bothered me most was that the post office knew where to deliver it!

That's what I call a Burger King introduction. One whopper after another.

It's always a pleasure to speak to a group so sincerely dedicated to limiting the growth of the money supply, a dedication I first became aware of when I discussed my fee.

I didn't give you much of his background. That's because there isn't any.

His idea of fun is going into Horn and Hardart's and watching an old man wake up his leg.

I'll never forget the first time I met him...but I'm trying.

I've been on the road for three months. I'm a slow driver.

In introducing our treasurer, the good news is--he's as honest as the day is long. The bad news is that for the last five years, he's been working the night shift.

My name is a very old, historic one. It goes back many generations to my great, great grandmother at the Boston Tea Party. In fact, she was the first old bag they threw in the water.

He'll be here soon. He's busy out back practicing firm handshakes.

Here's a guy who moved from Pennsylvania to New Jersey and simultaneously raised the IQ level in both states.

Two bad things happened to me on the way here tonight. Unfortunately for me, I. forgot to bring my watch. Unfortunately for you, I remembered to bring my speech.

I'd like to introduce one of the foremost jugglers of our time--our treasurer!

I want to thank you for those kind and complete remarks. As any speaker will tell you, the emcee they worry about most is the one who says you need no introduction and mispronounces your name.

(after a humorous introduction) Thank you for that wonderful introduction. I won't say how those jokes did, but if you had insurance on them--collect.

(to a fat toastmaster) One more intoduction like that and I'm going to tell Weight Watchers what you really eat!

I want to compliment you on that fantastic display of terminal talent.

Would everybody please take their seats? Would everybody please take their seats? Would everybody please take their seats and put them on chairs?

(response) Mental telepathy must exist. While you were saying all those wonderful things about me, I was thinking the same thing.

(response) He sold me! I'm convinced that you are fortunate to have me speaking here tonight!

We'd like to bring (tall man) up here to the mike to say a few words to you. But, as you know,___is really tall. So tall we'd have to raise this microphone. And you know how management feels about raises.

One thing I like about our next speaker...he was never arrested for embezzlement.

I have been asked to introduce a man who is respected for his integrity, loved for his humanitarianism, and admired for his courage. He is a leader, an individual with vision, a brilliant coordinator, a superb administrator. I have been asked to introduce such a man...but I don't think he's here tonight.

When he asked me how I wanted to be introduced I said, "Why not play down the fact that I'm attractive and brilliant and say something about my humility."

Our speaker tonight will talk to you on leadership. He'll tell you how to be aggressive, forceful, and how to assert yourself. And he will be brief. His wife told him he had to be home early.

For dinner this evening we may have had the margarine as a butter substitute, and Sweet and Low as a sugar substitute, and Cremora as a cream substitute--but our speaker tonight is the real thing!

Isn't he something? He has the kind of smile that could ripen bananas.

Now that we've finished eating our chicken, here comes the baloney.

First, let me thank you for that kind introduction. I won't say what kind.

(opening) I'm sorry I'm late. That wife of mine! She didn't shovel the snow from the driveway this morning. She forgot to put on the snow tires. And halfway here I realized that she hadn't dressed me!

Excuse me if I appear nervous here tonight. You see, I'm with the (poor ball club) and I'm not used to seeing this many people gathered together at one time.

(after being introduced) I'd like to see the piece of paper that Mr. Chairman was reading from. I am sure he left something out. I recall that somewhere in the past I was a newspaper boy.

I'd like to introduce one of the great comedians of our time. This is not my opinion--it is his.

He has not stolen jokes from the top comedians of our era. He has stolen from unknowns, a word which has eventually become synonymous with his career.

The greatest form of flattery is imitation, and he is flattered that for years he has been the imitation of a comedian.

We've heard so much about our speaker--and now we'd like to get his side of the story.

At dinner tonight, I was seated between (name two at head table). Did you ever hear soup in stereo?

The emcee's job is not to bore you, but to introduce the people who will. Tonight, our emcee has done both.

Our speaker needs no introduction. He just needs a conclusion.

Thank you for that marvelous introduction. I haven't felt this good since my wife lost her credit cards.

A guy was travelling in the heart of cannibal country when he happened upon a cannibal cafeteria in the jungle. A sign out front advertised the cost of each entree. He saw fried missionary for $3.50, boiled hunter for $4, and sauteed safari guide for $5, and baked Baptists (or other group to which you are speaking) for $20.
"Why do they cost so much more?" he inquired.
"Ever try to clean one of them?" the chef replied.

I would have given him a long introduction, but I called his office for information, and they said, "The less said about him, the better."

A community-minded person, last week our speaker did a telethon for ingrown toenails...all the spectacular diseases had been taken.

(intro for a fat person) And now, here he is, our extra-padded attraction...

They're truly a refreshing act. Everytime I'm at one of their appearances I always feel so refreshed after I wake up.

We asked him to speak his mind, so at least we know this will be a brief speech.

Now I know why they call him the toastmaster. Have you ever heard anyone buttered up like that before?

Our next speaker is a news writer whose column has appeared in every major parakeet cage in the United States.

Here's a guy that's going places...and the sooner the better.

(following a lengthy intro) First, let me thank you for adding something to this program. About ten minutes.

Thank you for those fine opening comments. I'm sure your thoughts, like tonight's dinner, will stay with us for a long time.

I'll remember this evening for as long as I live. How often is it that you see 300 people sit down in a restaurant and all order the same thing?

(response to a roast intro) The accoustics are really bad up here. I heard every word you said.

Our speaker can point to many amazing accomplishments in his lifetime. Unfortunately, none of them were his.

You probably don't realize this, but we have something in common. You don't know what I'm going to say, and neither do I.

Rule number two in public speaking: After a very flattering introduction, never tell the audience you don't deserve it. They'll find out soon enough.

 **INVENTIONS**

He's just developed a new perfume called "Evening in Newark".

If it wasn't for the invention of the television, we'd all still be eating frozen radio dinners.

I crossed my TV with a microwave oven, and now I can watch "60 Minutes" in eight and a half minutes.

If they can put a man on the moon, why can't they invent a parking meter that gives change for a dollar?

For heart patients who can't afford to pay all at once, he invented the coin-operated pacemaker.

I invented an electric shoehorn. Just one kink in it. It sets your socks on fire.

He invented the car with the sunfloor.

I've just invented a knife that'll cut the meat so thin that the in-laws will never come back!

Those drug companies are really trying. One of them just brought out a product that's guaranteed to put you to sleep. Home movies.

He is the inventor of the first toupee with a sunroof and was also the transportation innovator who developed left turn on red.

Cars talk. Refrigerators talk. Why can't they invent a washing machine that talks and tells you what it did with the other sock?

I invented the microwave fireplace. Now I can lay in front of the fireplace for the evening in eight minutes.

He is the inventor of the waterproof sponge and wisdom dentures. He is also the creator of the inflatable sledgehammer.

His latest invention is Teflon-coated peanut butter.

He developed synthetic hair balls for ceramic cats.

He thinks the greatest invention is the Thermos.
"Why?" I asked.
"Because a Thermos can keep something hot or cold. And how does it know?"

I just developed the cellophane newspaper for wives who like to see their husbands at breakfast.

He's ironing the bugs out of his latest invention that keeps you warm in winter without electricity--the wood burning blanket.

He invented reversible roller skates for backward children.

He invented the refrigerator with a peephole for people who want to know if that little light really does go out.

As the patent lawyer said to Dr. Denton: "Your idea doesn't look like much, but it just might be the sleeper of the year."

IBM and Goodyear Rubber have merged to create a computer that makes snap decisions.

He just invented a new kind of candy that doesn't cause cavities...chocolate-covered flouride.

He invented the silent fog horn for clear days.

Here are some of my inventions that are really going to make me rich... Plastic song sheets for people who like to sing in the shower...Bifocal headlights for Model T's...Windshield wipers that won't hold parking tickets...Curtains for window envelopes...A tuna flavored chewing gum--Chicklet of the Sea...Tax forms printed on Kleenex for those of us who have to pay through our noses...Red talcum powder for chafed Indians...

I invented the solar-powered flashlight. The only problem with it is, it only works in the daytime.

I invented the non-alphabetical phone book for people who have a lot of time.

He invented a smoke detector with a snooze alarm.

He invented a digital grandfather's clock.

I developed the upside-down lighthouse for submarines.

I invented soap with a hole in the middle for people who don't like to have those useless, little pieces left over.

It was Alexander Graham Bell who invented the telephone, but it was the teenager who invented the busy signal.

I just invented a case to carry dead batteries in. It's called a flashlight.

I developed a wood stove that sells for $29.95. And with it, you get a free, hand-carved, wooden frying pan!

ITALIAN/POLISH

The godfather speaking to a man who's half-Italian and half-Polish: "I'm going to make you an offer you can't understand."

At Vito Dumbroski College, one student was heard to say, "Did you hear that there's a case of malaria in the dorm?"
"Good!" said one of the undergraduates. "I was getting tired of Pepsi!"

DO-IT-YOURSELF SPACE.

WRITE YOUR OWN JOKE HERE!

JAPAN

The new Disneyland just opened in Tokyo. It'll be kind of interesting to see the Seven Dwarfs towering over the people.

JOBS

How are things going? Well, my resume is in it's third printing.

You can't win. Last week I arrived at the office a half hour early every morning. Friday, the boss came over to my desk and asked me if I was having trouble at home.

He will not drink coffee on the job because he doesn't want to toss and turn at his desk all day.

I can always go back to my old job of selling medicine cabinets to Christian Scientists.

He got a job working at the pharmacy, but he kept breaking the prescription bottles in the typewriter.

You know that your job is in jeopardy when...your new sales territory is in the Mojave Desert...or if you push the button on your intercom and the operator says your number has been disconnected...or if you are moved to a smaller office that stops at each floor.

He used to work for the Philadelphia Inquirer until they took away his paper route.

I asked my son, "What can you do?"
He said, "Nothing."
I said, "Good, I'll get you a job with the government. They won't have to break you in."

He was once a caddy on a miniature golf course.

His last job was for an ad agency where he created the phrase "Good to the Last Drop..." unfortunately it was for an elevator company.

He once worked as a lifeguard in a secretarial pool...
As an elevator operator, but he was fired because he couldn't remember the route...
At Midas mufflers inspecting automobile tailpipes. But he quit after three days because he was completely exhausted...
At a clock factory--making faces.

He had to quit his last job due to illness and fatigue. The boss was sick and tired of him.

He was a door-to-door doorbell salesman who went broke. He said, "People who needed my service never knew I was at the door."

I didn't always do this for a living. I used to be a plant manager for a large industrial firm till one day I forgot to water them and they all died.

He worked in a place with 400 people under him. He was a caretaker in a cemetery.

He just got a job as a lifeguard in a car wash.

He had a job as a novelty worker. It was a novelty when he worked.

He had a job as a night watchman. Then somebody stole two nights and he was fired.

He had a series of unusual jobs: he was a night watchman at a day camp; a deckhand on a submarine; a traffic director in a phone booth, and a cruise director on a Ferris wheel.

He was a specialist in his former job. He was the man who put the one cashew into a can of mixed nuts.

He just became a brush salesman so he could lead a Fuller life.

I worked at a factory where they made fire hydrants. It was a great job, but I couldn't park near the place!

He's all excited because he just bought the rights to sell maps to the movie stars homes--in Des Moines, Iowa.

I could always go back to my old job of selling knee pads to contact lens wearers.

I asked one applicant what he could do and he said, "Nothing." I didn't hire him. I really hate it when someone is after my job!

Husband: I found a great job, good salary, fine health and accident insurance, paid holidays and coffee breaks.
Wife: That's wonderful, dear!
Husband: I knew you'd be pleased. You start Monday.

One day I came home from work all excited and told my wife I had been named vice-president of the company. She was busy cooking dinner and replied curtly, "Vice-president. That's a big deal. A really big deal. Why, at the supermarket I shop at, they have a vice-president in charge of prunes."
I couldn't believe this, so I called the store and asked to speak to the vice-president in charge of prunes. The voice on the other end said, "Packaged or bulk?"

He's a veterinarian who specializes in elephant skin diseases--a pachydermatologist.

Another way that I've reduced pressure on the job...my In basket is a paper shredder.

He left his last job the same way he arrived--"fired with enthusiasm."

I'm not really a huge success in my job. In fact, when a new employee is hired, they first bring him to me, so he can view the company from the bottom up.

He comes to us from his former job as a retirement planner for Kamikaze pilots.

He retired from his old job at the nuclear power plant and moved to coastal New England. He now has a new job in Bar Harbor, Maine, where he is a lighthouse.

It was bad enough that I lost my job to a computer, but what really made me mad was they gave it my parking place, too!

Before joining this firm he had a thriving business of selling old magazines to doctors.

I've learned to cope with pressure on the job. I refuse to take phone calls from home.

I had a tough day at work. The computer broke down and I had to think.

My insomnia's so bad, I can't even sleep at work.

A job application asked, "Ever arrested? Why?"
The applicant wrote, "No. Never caught."

He daydreams on the job. He's the only guy I know whose secretary gives him "While You Were Out" messages while he's still in.

An astronaut was asked about stress on the job and replied, "How would you feel if you were going up in a rocket that had 140,000 parts all supplied by the lowest bidder?"

He used to be a tree surgeon until he fell out of one of his patients.

I'm a great swimmer. I used to be a street cleaner in Venice.

He has a key job with (large firm). He locks up at night.

Dad always wanted to be a garbage man. He thought they only had to work on Tuesdays.

I got this job by replacing a machine that found it to be too boring.

Help wanted ad: Man wanted to work on nuclear-fission isotope counters and three-phase photo-synthesizers--no experience necessary.

A farmer hired a hand who he assigned to cut a large amount of wood. By noon, the worker had the project completed, much to the farmer's amazement.
The next day, the farmer ordered the worker to stack all the wood, a huge job. This again was completed by noon.

The third day the farmer thought he ought to give the worker a break. He said, "Go into the potato bin and sort out all the potatoes. Put the good ones in one pile, the fair ones in a second pile, and the rotten ones, throw away."

An hour or so later, the farmer checked on the worker, and found him passed out cold. When the farmer revived him, he asked for an explanation.

Said the worker, "It's making them decisions that's killin' me."

I had a very responsible position at the last place I worked. Everytime something went wrong, they said I was responsible.

I'm making a fortune in my new job of selling NEXT WINDOW PLEASE signs to the post office and OUT OF ORDER signs to the telephone company.

Before joining the company, he worked in several other fields. He worked in a wheat field, a potato field, a cotton field...

Before joining us, he worked for the Fruit-of-the-Loom underwear company where he was widely known as Inspector 22.

He knows his job so well that he can do it backwards. Maybe that's his problem.

He used to be a consultant--which as we all know is a guy between jobs.

Cab driver: It's not the work I enjoy. It's the people I run into.

When I left my job at the circus as the human cannonball, the ringmaster said, "We'll never find another man of your caliber."

 # JOGGING

Statistics prove that if all the joggers in our town were laid end-to-end, it would be a whole lot easier to drive to work in the morning.

Jogging is a perfect exercise. Thanks to jogging, for the first time in history, people are falling over dead in perfect health.

You should see him jogging. Yesterday, two worms were chewing on a leaf, and one of them looked up and saw him plodding along in his jogging shorts. He said, "Herman, do you see what I see?"
And the other worm said, "Please--not while I'm eating!"

Did you ever see those bumper stickers--Speed Kills--? People who watch him jog think he's going to live forever.

I was to go out jogging this morning, but I got winded putting on my sneakers.

My doctor informed me that jogging could add years to my life. He's right. I feel fifteen years older already.

A middle-aged runner said, "I don't like to brag, but I've got the body of a 20-year-old."
A younger runner said, "Well, give it back. You're getting it all wrinkled."

Who needs jogging? If I want to increase my pulse rate for twenty minutes all I need do is open my wife's Master Charge bill.

I was out running the other morning and was going so slowly that the police arrested me for loitering.

(mourners at funeral) "He sure looks good."
Wife: "Well, he should. He jogged three miles a day."

JURY DUTY

How to escape jury duty...
- Put a tattoo on your arm that says, "Hang 'em High!"
- When attorneys are asking you questions, flip a coin before each answer.

- Tie your necktie in a hangman's noose.
- Bring the prosecuting attorney a birthday cake that says, "Happy Birthday, George."
- Wear a hood and white sheet and keep repeating, "There ain't nobody I'm prejudiced against..."
- Bring your own bagful of evidence and pass it among the perspective jurors.
- Learn to whistle "The Prisoner's Song" very loudly.

DO-IT-YOURSELF
SPACE.

WRITE YOUR
OWN JOKE
HERE!

KANGAROOS

Mother kangaroo to father kangaroo: "I sure hope it doesn't rain today. I hate when the kids have to play inside."

KARATE

Christmas is when karate experts face their greatest challenge. First they break a board in half. Then they break a brick in half. Then they take on the hardest object of all--a Christmas fruitcake!

KIDNAPPED

I was once kidnapped and my wife didn't want to pay the ransom. She said she didn't want to have to break a ten.

KIDS

He grew up to be the kind of kid his mother didn't want him to play with.

A perfect example of minority rule is having a baby in the house.

Proud mother showing infant to neighbors: "He's eating solids now...keys, newspapers, pencils..."

Sarah concluded her prayers: "Amen. Good night, God. And now stay tuned for Karen."

I have three children and find it hard to believe that farmers can possibly grow a surplus of food.

A place for everything, and everything in its place...and my kids agree. Only problem is they think the PLACE is the floor.

There's nothing wrong with teenagers that reasoning with them won't aggravate.

(boy visiting friend's home for dinner) "Bobby, do you need help cutting your meat?"
"No, thank you, ma'am. We often have it this tough at home."

A mother advising her son said, "James, we are in this world to help others."
James said, "Then what are the others here for?"

A mother of three toddlers sent a thank you note to a friend who sent her a playpen as a gift. She wrote, "It's my most valued possession. I sit in it every afternoon and read--and the children can't get near me."

A child excited about his first piano recital, told his parents, "And we're going to have real people there, too. Not just parents."

A youngster writing a thank you note penned, "Thank you for the nice present. I always wanted argyle socks, although not very much."

Speaking of kids--and show me a grandparent who doesn't!

A surefire way to get your kids to do as you say: say nothing!

A boy was sent by his mother to buy Pampers at the store. The clerk said, "That'll be $1.80 plus tax."
The boy said, "I don't need the tacks. Mom uses those tapes on the sides."

A mother brought her newborn home from the hospital. Her four-year-old son noticed the hospital wristband on the baby's wrist and inquired, "Mommy, when are you going to take off the price tag?"

Mother to son: "When Billy threw those stones at you, why did you throw stones back at him, instead of coming and telling me?"
"That wouldn't have done any good, Mom. You can't hit the broad side of a barn."

A busy father was weary of reading "Little Red Riding Hood" to his daughter night after night. Finally he decided to make a cassette of the story. His plan worked for three nights. On the fourth evening, his daughter came to him with the book and said, "Daddy, please read this to me."
The father said, "But you're a big girl. You know how to work the tape recorder."
"I know," said the daughter, "but it won't let me sit on its lap."

"Mom, I promise to be good if you give me a dollar."
"Son, you should be ashamed of yourself. When your father was your age, he was good for nothing."

A child observed his busy father working with papers from a loaded brief case night after night. He asked his mother why.
The mother said, "Your daddy has so much work to do, that he just can't get it finished at the office."
"Well, then," said the boy, "why don't they just move him to a slower group?"

"Are you sure this stuff is healthy to eat? It tastes pretty good!"

A woman with many children named her last three Eenie, Meanie, Miney.
She said, "There ain't gonna be no mo."

Teenagers are like snowstorms. They may be late, but they never fail to show up.

My son keeps a hamster in his room. At first the smell was terrible--but the hamster got used to it.

I said, "Eat your spinach. Think of the thousands of kids who would love some."
My son said, "Name two!"

A man with no children misses a lot. For instance, a man with no children will never know the thrill of officiating at the funeral of a dead goldfish.

A mother put her child to bed for being cross and ill-tempered. The child argued, "It's temper when it's me and nerves when it's you!"

Before I got married, I had three theories about raising children. Now I have three children and no theories.

Mother to fussy son: "Twenty years from now you'll be telling some girl what a great cook your mother was...so be quiet and eat your dinner."

Forget bedtime stories that begin with, "Once upon a time..."If you really want to put kids to sleep, start off with, "Now when I was your age..."

Kids, share your toys with friends. When sledding, you take your sled downhill, and let your friend take it up.

Parents stayed out late. They rushed home and apologized to the babysitter. "We're sorry we're late."
The babysitter said, "Don't apologize. If I had kids like that, I'd stay out late, too!"

It will be interesting to hear what teenagers today tell their children what they had to do without when they were young.

I just wish that there was a way to keep kids at the cute age of two, but I guess taxidermy is out of the question.

A boy came home from school with all A's on his report card. I said, "I guess he gets his intelligence from me."
My wife replied, "He must. I've still got mine!"

It's impossible to overestimate the appetite of kids. Eat? We have a refrigerator that's constantly at room temperature!

A father read that a middle-aged man should not shovel snow because he could have a heart attack. So he said to his teenager, "Son, I shouldn't shovel wet snow. Would you do it for me?"
The son said, "Yes", he'd do it immediately. And the father had a heart attack.

Two kids walk into an art gallery and were looking at a wildly abstract painting. "Let's get out of here," one said to the other, "before they say we did it!"

I've got a three-year-old son. Now I know why tigers eat their young.

She loves finger painting. She painted one of them blue, one of them red...

Did you go to Billy's party?
No, the invitation said 4-9 and I'm already 10.

I just visited an art museum where they had an exhibit of work that was done entirely by children. All of the works were hung on refrigerators.

A little boy and friends were playing in the sandbox making mud pies under the kitchen window. When all the activity suddenly ceased the boy's mother went to the window to see what happened. Just then her five-year-old supervisor of the gang shouted, "We've run out of dirt. Everyone take off his shoes and empty them."

A little girl fell out of bed. When she was asked why, she replied, "I stayed too close to where I got in."

There had been several earthquake shocks in the district, so a couple sent their little boy to an uncle who lived out of the danger zone. A day or two later they received a telegram: "Am returning boy. Please send earthquake."

271

Our kids got us a perfect anniversary gift. Our very own phone!

How do you get your kids out of a tub of water?
Throw in a bar of soap.

I was really proud of my children--that all by themselves they raised $176 at a garage sale, until I noticed that our station wagon was missing!

My oldest son wanted to go into business for himself selling soda in the park.
"First," he said, "I've got to buy a wrench."
I said, "You mean a bottle opener, don't you?"
He said, "No, I need a wrench to turn off all the water fountains."

Mother: "Eat your spinach. It will put color in your cheeks."
Son: "But, mom, who wants green cheeks?"

A boy was crying loudly, and complaining to a friend, "My mom lost her psychology book and now she's using her own judgement."

A boy came running home with blood all over his face.
"What happened?" his mother questioned.
"Some kid bit me," the boy answered.
"Would you recognize him if you saw him again?" the mother inquired.
"Sure," said the boy. "I've got his left ear here in my pocket."

One little boy to another as they watched the escalator going down:
"What happens when the basement gets full of steps?"

"Why don't you take your little sister fishing?"
"Nothing doing. Last time we went fishing together we didn't catch a thing."
"I'm sure she'll be quiet."
"That's not the problem. Last time she went along, she ate the bait."

"Roy, are you spitting in the fish bowl?"
"No, mom, but I'm coming pretty close."

"Why are you home from school so early?"
"I was the only kid who could answer a question."
"What was the question?"
"It was, 'Who threw the eraser at the principal?' "

Maternity nurse: "Well, what were you hoping for?"
Expectant father: "A boy."
Nurse: "Sorry, sir, your wife gave birth to a girl."
Father: "That's okay. That was my second choice."

I have a great idea for putting the legions of unemployed back to work.
How about assigning each one a two-year-old to clean up after?

Our next door neighbors who have five small kids have moved south to
Florida. I think they're moving into one of those pandemoniums.

"Johnny, wash your hands please."
"Both of them?"
"No, just one of them. I want to see you do it."

We named our first boy after my father. We called him Pop.

I can get my kids' attention any time I want to. All I have to do is stand
in front of the TV set.

I'm on the road so much that when I come home the kids call me Uncle
Father.

Times sure change. Remember when kids used to ask to be tucked in?
Now they have electric blankets and at night they ask to be plugged in.

Someday a cereal company is going to make a fortune by creating a
cereal that will drain the energy from kids.

Boy: "I think I'm old enough to start noticing girls, Dad, if you point
them out to me."

A miracle drug is any medicine that you can get the kids to take
without screaming.

"You know the vase that we've been passing down from generation to
generation? Well, this generation just dropped it!"

The doctor said, "Quick, get some boiling water!"
I said, "Is the baby coming?"
He said, "No, the nurse is making coffee."

The baby arrived and I sent a note to my mother, "Congratulations.
You've just become a professional babysitter."

A lady meant to call a record shop but dialed the wrong number and got a private home instead.

"Do you have 'Eyes of Blue' and 'Love That's Real'?" she asked.

"Well, no," answered the puzzled homeowner, "but I have a husband and eleven children."

"Is that a record?" asked the woman.

"I don't think so," replied the mother, "but it's as close as I want to get."

(boy to friend) My dad doesn't have a den. He just growls all over the house."

Our kids are picky eaters. My son thinks that spinach and sauerkraut are forms of child abuse.

My wife has saved countless hours of sewing nametags in our children's clothing by naming them Machine Wash and Tumble Dry.

Rule number one in disciplining your children: Never spank a child on an empty stomach. Be sure you eat something first.

Our kids have the most frustrated pet in town--a turtle that chases cars.

(boy to friend) "You'll have to excuse the way my room looks. I haven't had a chance to dirty it up since my mother cleaned."

(teacher in nursery school) "We share the spirit in America that we are all free."

(youngster) "I'm not free. I'm four!"

I don't need a clock radio, refrigerator, or washing machine that talks back. I've got a teenager for that.

Beware of the amusement parks that say, "One price covers everything." That sentence, of course, does not apply to families with youngsters who eat, drink, like souvenirs and stuffed animals. After five minutes in one such park, our seven-year-old had already earned her black belt in Getmethat.

Father to son: "Now do exactly as your mother tells you. There's no reason you should be an exception."

I know one parent who disciplined his teenager by putting Super Glue on a Lawrence Welk tape and jamming it into his car stereo.

I live with my wife and kids in a five bedlam house.

An interviewer marveled to a mother, "How can you possibly care for eleven children?"
The mother replied, "When I had only one, he occupied every second. What more can eleven do?"

I love to watch the baby put his toes in his mouth. Babies are the only human beings who can make ends meet these days.

A young child observed her sunburn peeling and cried, "Oh, no! I'm only four years old and I'm starting to wear out already!"

The best time to give advice to your kids is when they're still young enough to think you know what you're talking about.

As a kid of five, he ran away from home. The police came to his house, but his parents couldn't describe him.

My mother read a label on an aspirin bottle that said, 'Keep away from children'. And we never saw her after that.

Kids are chauffered everywhere by their parents. One boy threatened to run away from home, and his mother said, "Wait, I'll drive you."

I'm sure company's downstairs. I just heard mom laugh at one of dad's jokes.

Mother describing to daughter the delights of her childhood on a farm: "I used to ride horses and slide down haystacks."
Daughter: "Wow, mom. I wish I had met you sooner!"

A six-year-old insisted on sewing a button on her dress. She moistened the thread and said to the needle, "Okay. Open your mouth and say, 'Ahhh.' "

Boy to mother: "The teacher asked whether I had any sisters or brothers, and I told her, 'No, I'm an only child.' "
"And what did your teacher say?" the mother asked.
"Thank goodness!" said the boy.

"When I was born it cost $100. Today it costs $2500 to have a baby in a hospital."
"Yeah, but look how long they last."

My wife said to my son, "Finish all your meat and you'll grow up to be just like Daddy."
Now he only eats vegetables.

"I found a quick way of putting the baby to sleep. I toss it up in the air again and again," a friend reported.
"How does that put the baby to sleep?" I asked.
"We have very low ceilings."

My kid's a born doctor. He can't write anything anyone can read.

(kids in audience causing disturbance) Children are like New Year's resolutions. Sometimes they need to be carried out.

Dad came home from work and was met by his five-year-old daughter.
"Is something wrong, honey?"
"Yes, all day long I've been having trouble with your wife!"

My family loves books. In fact, my little daughter just finished War and Peace. That's amazing when you consider that that's over 1,000 pages to tear out.

First child: I helped by washing the dishes.
Second child: I helped by drying the dishes.
Third child: And I helped by sweeping up the pieces.

A grandfather was visiting with his grandson who kept pestering him:
"C'mon, grandpa. Let's go out and play football."
After numerous requests, the grandfather said, "I don't play football. I never have. Why do you keep asking?"
"Because," said the lad, "my dad says when you kick off we can get a new car."

"C'mon now, Billy. Kiss your Aunt Mary."
"Why, mom? I didn't do anything!"

They say my son looks just like me. But what should it matter as long as he's healthy?

What's a home without kids? I'll tell you what it is...quiet!

I was going to help my son with his homework but he insisted on getting it all wrong by himself.

I had to check out our homeowner's policy the other day. Some workers were putting new carpeting in my son's room, so now we have to check to see if our policy covers "Shock".

My wife really knows how to build self-esteem in our children. Why just this morning I heard her tell my son, "You're getting to be just like your father!"

I am teaching my children that they should accept the things they cannot change, and that their socks and underwear are not among them.

Our quiet Saturday afternoon was disrupted when our seven-year-old began trimming his nails--in the food processor.

We're so proud of our kids that not only do we claim them as exemptions on our income tax forms each year, we also send along their school pictures.

I spent a huge amount on my son's teeth and an even larger amount on his education. The only difficulty is, he still uses his teeth.

He really begs for sympathy. He's the only kid I know who limps when he has a head cold.

I put an extra room on the house especially for the kids. But my wife went and spoiled it. She forced me to put in a door.

They had twin girls and called them Kate and Duplicate.

KNOWLEDGE

Never pride yourself on knowledge. Even a head of lettuce knows more than you do. It knows if that little light really does go out when the refrigerator door is shut.

DO-IT-YOURSELF
SPACE.

WRITE YOUR
OWN JOKE
HERE!

LATE

It seems whenever I'm late...the boss isn't...I break a shoelace...I get behind a $13 order in a fast food place...the self-serve pump won't work...the commuter train is early...the light gets stuck on red...I knock over a cup of coffee into the desk drawer...my plane leaves from the furthest gate of the terminal.

LAUGHS

He who laughs last usually has a tooth missing.

What has 100 legs and eats cottage cheese? My wife's aerobic class.

LAUNDRY

I just developed a talking washer and dryer that will tell you what it did with the other sock.

I go to an old-fashioned laundry where they tear the buttons off by hand.

This is an imported shirt. I know, because the washing instructions say, "Beat against flat rock."

LAWNS

I don't know what makes crab grass so crabby. It's always winning!

LAWYERS

A grateful client said to the lawyer, "Oh, I'm just so thankful for your great work. How can I ever repay you?"
The barrister responded, "Ever since the Phoenicians invented money, there's been only one answer to that question."

My lawyer says that giving legal advice gives him a grand and glorious feeling. You give him a grand and he feels glorious.

My lawyer advises me that the ideal contract is made of words too big to understand and print too small to read.

He's such a successful lawyer he owns his own ambulance.

(witnessing the collision of two cars) "I'm a lawyer. I saw the whole thing, and I'll take either side!"

In our town, white mice are being replaced by lawyers in scientific experiments. In the first place, there are more attorneys than white mice in our town, and in the second place, you don't become emotionally attached to them.

He really found out that crime doesn't pay. His lawyer's fee turned out to be more than he embezzled.

If you can't get a lawyer who knows the law, get one who knows the judge.

We should be thankful for lawyers. Lawyers are the people who get us out of the difficulties that we would never have gotten into if it hadn't been for lawyers.

Lawyers never smile for photos. A smart photographer corrected the problem. He said, "Gentlemen, say fees!"

As a young lawyer his first client was hanged. But he didn't give up. He sued the jury for whiplash.

A convict called the family lawyer. "Look, they've shaved my head, cut a slit in my trousers, asked me what I want for my last dinner. What should I do?"
His lawyer answered, "Don't sit down!"

They keep saying that crime doesn't pay. But every lawyer I know drives a Mercedes.

"You cheat," shouted the lawyer's client. "You've kept me hanging for months and got rich on my case alone!"
"That's gratitude," said the lawyer sadly. "And right after I named my new yacht after you."

Did you hear about the lawyer who was injured in an accident? The ambulance accidentally backed up.

"I've just come up with some new evidence," said the lawyer as he begged the judge for a new trial.
"What kind of evidence?" inquired the judge.
"I've just discovered that my client has another $2,000."

"Look at this item on my lawyer's bill!" complained the client. "For waking up in the middle of the night and thinking about your case: $25."

"Before I take your case you'll have to give me a $50 retainer," said the lawyer. "Now that entitles you to two questions."
"$50 for two questions?" the defendant asked. "That's kind of expensive, don't you think?"
"Yes, I suppose it is," replied the lawyer. "Now what is your other question?"

A lawyer is a man who helps you get what's coming to him.

Humpty Dumpty sat on the wall,
Humpty Dumpty had a great fall;
"The bricks on the wall," said his lawyer, "were loose;"
"We've got a good case, so we'll sue Mother Goose."

I had a clumsy lawyer. Once he threw himself on the mercy of the court and missed.

He's such a dedicated lawyer, that he even named his daughter Sue.

I had a great lawyer. I got a ticket, and he had the charges reduced to second degree manslaughter.

If you have the law on your side, hammer on the law.
If you have the facts on your side, hammer on the facts.
If you don't have the facts or the law on your side, hammer on the table.

How can a lawyer write a document of 5,000 words and call it a brief?

His lawyer offered him a great deal..."$100 down and the rest when he gets out of prison..."

My lawyer asked, "How much money do you have in the bank?"
I said, "I don't know. I haven't shaken it recently."

My lawyer swallowed a nickel, two dimes and three pennies. Doctors treated him for weeks, but there was no change.

LAZY

Her brother is so lazy. He watches "The Today Show" and if it's raining any place in the country, he doesn't go to work.

LEFT-HANDED

You have a left and a right side to your brain. The left side controls the right half of your body, and the right side controls the left half. Therefore, lefthanders are the only people in their right minds.

Anybody here lefthanded? (applause) Hey, that's pretty good. Usually we have trouble clapping. Lefthanders have a tough time. Just look at our image.
Leftovers--they're not too good. Lefthanded Compliment. Two Left Feet. Left Out.
Have you ever heard of a criminal named Righty? Righthanders have an advantage.
Right On. The Bill Of Rights. Right of Way. You go to a party and look around. Nobody's there. What do you hear..."They all Left!"

I have a left-handed ear, nose and throat specialist. You can bet he charges an arm and a leg.

LENT

Here's a list of things I'm giving up for Lent: Fig Newtons, trampolines, dog sledding, porcupine plucking, Rolls Royces, and the metric system.

LIGHT

One thing about the speed of light...it gets here too early in the morning.

Teenagers really brighten up a home. They never turn the lights out.

LINCOLN (ABE)

Isn't it crazy? We learn from history that Lincoln once walked nine miles to borrow a book--so now they close the libraries on his birthday!

We are told that Abraham Lincoln had the qualities of the common man. If that's true, how come there are no photographs of Lincoln taking out the garbage?

LITTLE LEAGUE

Last night I umpired my first little league game. Now if you've never gone to one, it's something like World War II with innings.

Little League is where the kid on the mound has five basic pitches--a fast ball, a slow ball, a curve, a sinker, and one that reaches the plate.

LODGE MEETING

We regret to announce that the Grand Invincible Potentate of the Lodge couldn't make it to the meeting tonight. His wife wouldn't let him come.

LUCK

Before the big game, I walked into the locker room and saw one of our players ironing a four-leafed clover. I asked, "What are you doing?" He said, "Just pressing my luck!"

DO-IT-YOURSELF
SPACE.

WRITE YOUR
OWN JOKE
HERE!

MANNERS

His manners have improved. A girl dropped her purse, and he drop-kicked it back to her.

MARRIAGE

Whoever claims that marriage is a 50-50 proposition doesn't understand women or fractions.

A salesman inquired, "Are you the head of the household?"
Husband: "I certainly am. My wife's out grocery shopping now."

Judge: "I've reviewed the case and have decided to give your wife $250 a week."
Defendant: "That's really generous of you, judge. And every now and then I'll try and send her a few bucks myself."

He attributes his many years of happy marriage to the fact that before marriage he and his wife resolved that she'd make all the little decisions, and he'd make all the big ones. And it's worked out perfectly. So far, nothing big has come up.

Husband to wife: "Well, I worked out the budget, but one of us will have to go."

You know that the honeymoon is over when your wife starts complaining that you're making too much noise while you're getting breakfast.

My wife says she'll always remember our wedding day because it was the last time she walked down an aisle without a shopping cart.

When I was first married, I'd come home from work after a hard day, the dog would race around barking and my wife would bring me my slippers. Now everything's changed. My wife barks at me, and the dog brings me my slippers. I guess I shouldn't complain. I'm still getting the same service.

"Young man," boomed the father to the suitor, "are you prepared to support a family?"
The prospective groom replied, "No, sir. I'm prepared to support your daughter, but the rest of you will have to shift for yourselves."

A husband who hadn't given his wife an anniversary present in years was feeling sentimental on the eve of their 25th wedding anniversary. He asked, "Darling, what kind of flower do you like best?"
"After 25 years," snapped his wife, "you ought to know it's Pillsbury!"

"Dear, this is the seventh time you've gone back to the buffet table for food. Aren't you embarrassed?"
"Why should I be?" said the husband. "I keep telling them it's for you."

He's so cheap he got married in his backyard so the chickens could eat the rice.

Husband: "Would you go to the show without buying a new gown?"
Wife: "Absolutely not!"
Husband: "That's what I figured, so I just bought one ticket."

Webster wrote the dictionary because of his wife. Everytime he opened his mouth, she said, "Now what's that supposed to mean?"

Friend: "When are you thinking of getting married?"
Single girl: "Constantly."

My little daughter was looking at the wedding album. She asked, "Are these pictures of the day when mommy came to work for us?"

He boasts that he runs things in his house---and he does. He runs the washing machine, the lawn mower, the vacuum cleaner...

I know my husband will love me when my hair turns gray. He's loved me through three shades already.

An archaeologist is the best husband to have. The older a wife becomes, the more interested in her he becomes.

The Smiths next door are taking an adult education course in the Korean language. They've adopted a Korean baby and want to understand what she says when she begins to talk.

He married her for her looks, but not the ones he's been getting lately.

I'm not saying he married late in life, but Medicare picked up 80 percent of the honeymoon.

For them a big night out is to sit on the front porch and watch TV through the window.

Bride-to-be: "Mother, I don't want to leave out the simplest detail."
Mother: "Don't worry. I'll make sure he's there."

Frustrated wife to husband: "Next Sunday we'll trade jobs. You get the children fed and dressed, and I'll go out in the car and honk the horn for ten minutes."

At license bureau: "How much does it cost to get married?"
Clerk: "It's four dollars for the license and one paycheck a week for the rest of your married life."

He's so henpecked he cackles in his sleep.

Now that I'm married, I know why they call English 'the Mother Tongue'. Father never gets a chance to use it.

On our wedding day we received lots of gifts marked "His" and "Hers". Her brother gave us something marked "US". It was a green Army blanket.

When I said, "I do," her mother said, "You'd better!"

My wife and I have a mutual understanding. I don't try to run her life and I don't try to run mine.

You can tell that a marriage is off to a bad start when a bride is halfway down the aisle and asks if anyone has an aspirin.

He never knew what true happiness was until he got married. And then it was too late.

They say that brunettes have sweeter dispositions than blondes and redheads.
Don't believe it. My wife has been all three, and I can't tell the difference.

A few husbands in the audience are celebrating their 25th wedding anniversaries--and we're going to have three minutes of silence for them--perhaps the first they've ever heard.

His favorite trick is running his wedding movies backwards so he can watch himself walk out of church a free man.

He used to subscribe to the theory of male superiority until his wife cancelled his subscription.

Isn't it ridiculous to say to a mother at a wedding: "You're not losing a daughter. You're gaining a son." At her age, all she needs--more children!

Marriage is like twirling a baton, turning handsprings, or eating with chopsticks...it looks easy until you try it.

Marriage teaches you loyalty, forbearance, self-restraint, and a lot of other qualities you wouldn't need if you stayed single.

A husband is a person who is under the impression that he bosses the house--when in reality he houses the boss.

You know that the couple that is getting married is too young when there are four figures on the wedding cake--the bride, the groom, his dermatologist and her orthodontist.

I know a couple that got a divorce the morning after the wedding. Incredible! I mean, could the breakfast have been that bad? The biggest problem they had was deciding who got custody of the toaster.

My wife bought me a book on etiquette. I think I embarrass her when I use the wrong fingers when I whistle for the waiter.

Love is never having to say you're sorry. Marriage is never having the chance to say anything.

Marriage is when you see a fellow in his slippers and bathrobe taking out the garbage on a cold night, and you recognize him. It's you!

The phone rang in the maternity ward and an excited voice on the other end said, "This is George Brown and my wife's about to have a baby. I'm bringing her in."
"Calm down," said the operator, "is this her first baby?"
"No," shouted the husband. "I told you this is George Brown!"

"I'll never marry again," said the man. "My first wife died of eating poisoned mushrooms, and my second wife died of a fractured skull."
"Did she have a bad fall?"
"No, she wouldn't eat the poisoned mushrooms!"

They celebrated their porcelain anniversary--one year to the day since she threw a teapot at him.

Charles was 93 and Myrtle was 91. They were married in a beautiful ceremony on the first of June--and they spent the first two days of their honeymoon trying to get out of the car.

I read that last year 4,153,237 people got married. I don't want to cause problems, but shouldn't that be an even number?

Marriage is a lot like the United States Constitution. A man starts out by laying down the law to his wife--and ends up by accepting all her amendments.

I told my wife that a husband is like wine--he gets better with age. So she locked me in the cellar.

Nothing encourages a man's belief in flying saucers as much as marriage.

She was married to a banker, an actor, a minister, and an undertaker. One for the money, two for the show, three to get ready, and four to go.

The groom asked the minister, "How much do I owe you?"
The minister replied, "Give me what you think she's worth."
The man gave the minister 50 cents.
The minister lifted the veil, took one look at the bride, and gave the groom a quarter and said, "Here's your change!"

The husband encouraged his wife: "Remember, dear, the hand that rocks the cradle rules the world."
She handed him a diaper and said, "Well, take over the world for three hours while I go get my hair done."

I never argue with my wife. I might win and then I'd be in real trouble.

I just found out why my neighbor's wife left him. He came home from work and she said, "Guess what I made for you on your birthday? Bird's nest soup, oysters on the half shell, pheasant under glass, homemade blueberry pie, and fresh brewed coffee." He shook his head and said, "I had it for lunch!"

He's glad to be living in a free country where a man can do exactly as his wife pleases.

They had a big difference of opinion about getting a dishwasher. His wife says he doesn't need one.

When she suggests going out to eat, he says forcefully, "We're not going to a restaurant and that's semi-final!"

When he was hanging the "Home, Sweet Home" plaque she said, "No, on the other wall, stupid!"

He's really handy around the house. Why just the other day he caulked up all the holes in the waffle iron.

When my wife and I got married, we couldn't afford a honeymoon trip to Niagara Falls. Instead, we took a slow ride through the car wash!

My niece married a guy who's unemployed. At the wedding, everyone threw food stamps.

He's so thoughtful. For her birthday he got his wife a mop in her school colors.

He's been happily married for nine years...and nine out of twelve isn't a bad average.

They really don't go out very much. To give you an idea of how little they go out--their car still has half a tank of Esso.

In our marriage we made a decision never to go to bed mad. We haven't had any sleep in three weeks.

When we married, my wife and I agreed that through the years she would make all the little decisions and I'd make all the big decisions. It's worked perfectly! So far, nothing big's occurred.

A woman goes to a lawyer and says she wants a divorce. The lawyer says, "Do you have a grudge?"
She replies, "No, we have a carport."
He says, "Well, do you have grounds?"
She says, "Yes, sir, about an acre and a half."
He says, "Does he beat you up?"
She replies, "No, I'm up an hour before him."
The lawyer says, "Well, why do you want a divorce?"
She answers, "We just don't seem to communicate."

I told my wife that I read an article that reported that the longer a couple is married, the harder it is to communicate...She said, "I don't want to discuss it."

They say that after many years of marriage, a husband and wife start looking like each other--my wife is very concerned.

The kids next door are just starting out...the wife came over last night to borrow a cup of money.

"Honey, you look the same as you did when I married you fifteen years ago."
"I should. I'm wearing the same dress."

He wears the pants in his house--under the apron.

The last big decision she let me make was whether to wash or dry.

The doctor told the husband that his wife needed sea air so he fans her with a mackerel.

I asked him how he got his tremendous physique. He said, "I owe it all to my wife. When we were married, I vowed that anytime my wife would bug me, rather than argue, I'd take a walk around the block. So, this magnificent body that you see here is the result of twenty years of outdoor living."

My wife looked up from her breakfast cup of coffee the other morning and asked, "Do you know what today is?"
I checked the date at the top of my newspaper and failing to connect it with any momentous occasion in my life I replied, "Other than being Tuesday, I don't know."
"It was just a year ago today," my wife said, "that you forgot that our wedding anniversary was tomorrow."

He has a tendency to place his wife under his pedestal.

We divide the chores in our home. I wash the dishes, and my wife sweeps them up.

A year after we were married there was the pitter-patter of little feet around the house. Her parents were midgets.

The other day she threw him out of the house. Unfortunately they live in a mobile home and were doing seventy at the time.

Someone asked his wife, "How do you rate your husband on a scale of one to ten?"
She thought for a few seconds and said, "Do you take fractions?"

He takes his wife out every night, but she always finds her way back.

He had a fight with his wife the other night, but she came to him crawling on her knees yelling, "Come out from under the bed, you coward."

(newlyweds) "Dear, don't expect the first few meals to be great. It takes time to find the right restaurant."

We were so poor when we started out married life that my wife had to go on the honeymoon alone.

My wife and I have agreed that if I don't like the way she does something, I can do it myself.

He sometimes places his wife on a pedestal--that is, when he vacuums around her.

Marriage is a real grind; you wash the dishes, make the beds, and two weeks later you have to do it all over again.

Wife: "I'm ready now. I thought you said you were ready awhile ago."
Husband: "I was. But now you'll have to wait for me. I've got to shave again."

Did you ever notice how rapidly a woman's voice can change when she stops arguing with her husband to answer the telephone?

I attended a Japanese wedding last week. Instead of rice, they threw transistor radios at the bride and groom.

Bride to husband: "There you are, dear. My first meal cooked just the way you'd better like it."

He's been so busy that he only sees his wife once a week for one hour. But he says that the hour passes quickly.

Their marriage is a 50-50 deal. Half the time she's right, and half the time he's wrong.

Since I've been married, I've never had any trouble meeting expenses. My wife is always introducing me to new ones.

When he got married, he said he'd be the master of the house or know the reason why...now he knows the reason why.

I'm always the first person to admit my mistakes. But with a wife, a mother-in-law, and three children, it's usually a very close race.

In his marriage, the only time he gets to open his mouth is when he yawns.

He is truly an inconsiderate husband. When he won a trip for two to Hawaii, he went twice.

A husband was looking at a birthday card for his wife. He read one which said, "Your love is worth the world and all its treasures." He noticed the price of $1.50, and asked the clerk, "I love this card's message, but don't you have one that's a little cheaper?"

Wife: I've changed my mind.
Husband: Thank goodness. Does it work any better now?

I stopped calling my wife the 'little woman' when she started calling me 'the big mistake'.

MEDICINE

They say that the way to a man's heart is through his stomach. I don't know who said that, but I do know that I wouldn't want him to be my doctor.

MEMORY

I have a photographic memory but sometimes I forget to take off the lens cap.

I had a terrible experience last week. I enrolled for a memory course and forgot why.

I could never remember names until I took that great Sam Carnegie course.

MEN'S CHARACTER

Everything happens to me. Who else do you know who gets threatening calls from information?

He's a naturally evil person. You know the toothpaste test on TV? He roots for the cavities!

Unlucky? You're looking at the only guy who ever found four-leaf poison ivy!

Shallow? If it wasn't for bumper stickers, he wouldn't have any opinions at all!

But he's really a wonderful man. If I asked him for it, he'd give me the shirt off his back. Why not? It's mine.

He's the kind of fella who'd go to a night club with a show featuring Frank Sinatra, Wayne Newton, Bob Hope and Barbra Streisand, and complain about the relief band.

MEN'S CLOTHES

It's all right to be fastidious--but who puts shoe trees in sneakers?

For months now, I've had the feeling that old age has been creeping up on me. But it was only cheap underwear.

MENTALLY UNBALANCED

The Reader's Digest reports that one out of every three people is mentally unbalanced. Now think of the two people next to you. Do they seem OK to you? If they do, then you're the one!

MICROPHONE

(squealing mike) If you had to listen to as much nonsense as this mike, you'd squeal too!

I'm having a little trouble with the microphone. Bob used it to pound the heel back on his saddle oxfords.

MIDDLE AGE

When you get to be my age, you go to the beach and turn a wonderful color. Blue--from holding in your stomach!

You're reaching middle age when it takes longer to rest than it did to get tired.

Middle age:
• is when everything starts to click: your elbows, knees, neck;
• is when you realize that you'll never live long enough to try all those recipes you've clipped from magazines; it's not only later than you think--it's sooner than you suspect;
• is when you're faced with two temptations, and you choose the one that gets you home before nine o'clock.

MIDGET

A midget fortune teller escaped from jail...headlines read "Small Medium At Large".

That's about as much fun as trying to short-sheet a midget.

I performed for a midget's convention. I got a standing ovation and didn't even know it! It's amazing when you think that every joke I told was over their heads!

MIDWEST

I've always been fascinated by Cincinnati. No matter how you spell it, it always looks wrong.

They say it took the pioneers two months to go from the Mississippi River to California. You can still do it. Let your wife read the road map.

MIRRORS

Be kind to your mirror. Even though it never lies, it never laughs.

MISTAKES

To err is human, but to really louse things up requires a computer.

My secretary is not a good typist, but she can erase 75 words per minute.

Learn from the mistakes of others because you can't live long enough to make them all yourself.

 **MONEY**

I admire the way she spends. She's a real credit to her card.

A mugger stuck a gun in a frugal man's ribs and said, "Your money or your life."
After a long pause, the tightwad said, "I'm thinking. I'm thinking!"

"After looking at our budget, dear, how do you feel about storing up nuts for the winter?"

In the old days, men rode chargers. Now they marry them.

A dollar does go farther these days. You can carry it around for a week before you can find anything you can buy with it.

After looking through my bills, I think I can make it through the rest of the month if I don't eat anything or turn anything on.

I can't live on what I'm earning. I can't even live on what I'm spending.

I received a collection letter: "We're surprised we haven't heard from you."
I wrote back, "Don't be surprised. I didn't send anything."

The only thing that'll give you more for your money than it did ten years ago is the penny scale at the drug store.

I've put all those little monthly payments into one large monthly payment that I can't meet.

I have a great idea to save husbands' money--a seat belt that won't unbuckle when the car stops at garage sales.

I figured a way to put off paying the bills. I filled out one of those change of address cards at the post office and then I didn't move.

Let's face it, there's only one thing money can't buy--poverty. You need credit cards to do that!

We always have too much month left over at the end of our money.

Prices are unreal. Would you believe that the Girl Scouts now offer a cookie layaway plan?

Maybe I worry too much about money, but you'd worry too, if your wife was just elected to the MasterCard Hall of Fame.

Actually I now have enough money to last me the rest of my life, provided I walk across freeways.

I have enough money to last me the rest of my life, provided that I die tomorrow.

I'm so broke, I have to save up to be truly needy.

I've got enough money to last me for a lifetime--if I don't buy anything.

It's easy to meet expenses--everywhere I go there they are!

We took all the money we were saving for a new car and blew it all on a movie.

How can we teach our kids the value of money in America? We can't even teach our Congressmen!

I have too many organizations to which to pay dues. I think my tombstone will read: "Here lies_____. Clubbed to death."

Money isn't that important. After all, Henry Ford had millions and never owned a Cadillac.

I read somewhere that poverty is a blessing in disguise. Well, it's the perfect disguise for me.

I was always warned that one day I would squander my money recklessly, but I never thought that it would be on gasoline, coffee and postage stamps.

Yesterday I did some calculating, and discovered that the only way I can come up with enough cash for a backyard swimming pool is to sell the backyard.

My latest investment hasn't been doing too well. I put three thousand dollars into the Howard Cosell Charm School.

Poverty is hereditary. You get it from your children.

My current financial status is all based on liquid assets. In other words, my finances are all going down the drain.

I never have money problems. Lack of money problems, yes...

My money problems are over. My investment broker just got me the Draino contract for the Alaskan pipeline.

MORNINGS

I just couldn't wake up this morning. Fortunately I snapped out of it just after I sprinkled Draino on my toothbrush.

Nothing has gone right today. Here it is, the first day of the rest of my life, and I don't even have clean underwear!

Some mornings I feel like life is the Indy 500 and I'm a '56 Plymouth.

No wonder I couldn't sleep last night. When I awakened this morning, I discovered that my electric blanket was on extra-crispy.

MOTELS

Some resort motels have towels that are so thick and fluffy that you can hardly get your suitcase closed.

They have running water in every room. I just found a spring in my bed last night.

The rooms are so small. I stuck my key in the door and broke a window. So small that the mice are hunchbacked. I closed the door, and the doorknob got in bed with me!

My motel room was so small that I had to use a folding toothbrush.

It was so small that twice a day I had to step outside just to let my mosquito bites swell.

The motel was really expensive. They charged $15 for breakfast. For breakfast! I didn't even know that they made designer pancakes!

MOTHER-IN-LAW

Sorry I have to leave now. My mother-in-law is arriving on the five o'clock broom.

My mother-in-law was so exhausted the other evening that she could hardly get her mouth open.

I never complain about my wife. What can you expect from a woman who was raised by my mother-in-law?

Behind every successful man stands two women: his wife and a flabbergasted mother-in-law.

A bomb shelter in the home makes sense. It's the ideal place to hide if that terrible event occurs--a visit from your mother-in-law.

I just flew in on the "Mother-in-Law" flight. It's non-stop.

My wife asked, "Why did you tell the babysitter that we were going to the movies when we were going to see my mother?"
"I didn't say that," the husband replied. "I just told the sitter that we

were going to see the creature from the black lagoon, and she just assumed that we were going to the movies."

She has such a big mouth that she can play a tuba from the wrong end.

He was married in a civil ceremony. His mother-in-law couldn't come.

She has a mind of her own. Who else would want it?

You know what a mother-in-law is? The bark from the family tree.

My mother-in-law lives with us. That way I get nagged in stereo.

He discouraged her from returning by putting a school of piranha in the hot tub.

He lent his mother-in-law their Scrabble game, but he hid all the vowels.

His mother-in-law ate all the ice cream except for one spoonful, and then put the carton back in the freezer.

His mother-in-law asked, "Did you miss me?"
"No," he replied. "They opened up an aggravation parlor downtown, and they deliver."

Having your mother-in-law visit for a month is like having Howard Cosell for a roommate.

Did you hear about the cannibal who ate his mother-in-law and she still disagreed with him?

I'm trying to get my mother-in-law nominated for vice-president. That way, if she's elected, I won't hear from her for another four years.

The only time his wife doesn't get the last word is when she's talking to her mother.

He put a sign in his mother-in-law's room: "Your American Express Card is Welcome Here."

He sneaked into his mother-in-law's closet and took the wire coat hangers and reversed every other one.

He put a burlap towel in the guest room.

His mother-in-law got back at him, though. She used his entire stamp collection to mail her Christmas cards.

He kept his mother-in-law from visiting by selling every part of the house except one room.

My mother-in-law needed a blood transfusion but we had to give up on the idea. We couldn't find a tiger.

She missed her nap today. She slept right through it.

My mother-in-law has been visiting with us.
Oh, really? When is she leaving?
Sixteen hours, thirteen minutes and twenty-seven seconds.

Stereo is when you listen to two speakers at the same time. I'm an expert on stereo. I have been living with my wife and mother-in-law for years.

My mother-in-law is extremely well-informed. She can complain on any subject.

We decorated the guest room for my mother-in-law. It's surly American.

If he had my mother-in-law, Confucious would not have said. He would have listened.

I just created a new perfume called "Mother-in-Law." It smells like trouble.

We've been married fourteen years and my mother-in-law only visited once. She came the day after the wedding and hasn't left since.

My mother-in-law's dentist is a rare man. He's the only person who has ever seen her with her mouth open when she's not talking.

My mother-in-law doesn't try to hide her feelings. Like when she calls me she makes it a "person-to-it" call.

My mother-in-law reminds me of a saint. Mount St. Helens.

Billy's maternal grandmother had just come for a visit, and he was ecstatic. "Now Daddy can do his trick," squealed Billy.
"What trick is that?" Grandma asked.

"Well," answered Billy, "Daddy said that if you stayed a whole week, he'd climb the walls, and I've never seen him do that before!"

"I keep having recurring dreams of my mother-in-law chasing me with a man-eating alligator. It's terrifying to see those awful, yellow, bloodshot eyes, dry, scaly skin, those ghastly, sharp teeth."
The doctor nodded, "That sounds nasty."
The man said, "That's nothing--wait till I tell you about the alligator!"

An earthquake is caused by two massive forces pushing against a fault. It's like your wife and your mother-in-law.

My mother-in-law is coming to visit us and I'm getting ready for it. I spent a quiet weekend picking the letters out of our welcome mat.

I'm so shrewd. We've been married ten years, and my mother-in-law doesn't even know we have a guest room.

Last night the whole house started shaking. I thought it was an earthquake. Turned out it was my mother-in-law doing her exercises.

My mother-in-law is into a physical fitness kick. She calls it aerobic nagging.

We now have a law that prohibits outside agitators from crossing state lines. I sent a copy of it to my mother-in-law.

My mother-in-law came over last New Year's Day and had a wonderful time. She must have. She never left!

And being subtle doesn't help. Like yesterday we did over her room in a brand-new style--Early Roadmap!

Bigamy is a crime whose extreme penalty is two mothers-in-law.

Double trouble is a mother-in-law with a twin sister.

I just came back from a pleasure trip. I took my mother-in-law to the bus station.

Have you heard of those Indian gurus who have something profound to say about everything? They're like a mother-in-law with a beard.

I don't do mother-in-law jokes because my mother-in-law is really a wonderful woman with a lovely disposition. For those of you who have never met my mother-in-law, just picture Howard Cosell in curlers.

I'm dedicating tonight's program to my mother-in-law--Fidel Castro in toreador pants...No, I really shouldn't compare her to Castro. His speeches only take four hours.

My mother-in-law took up oil painting. I came home the other night and sure enough, there she was making a scene.

My mother-in-law was kidnapped. The kidnappers said that if I didn't send $10,000 they'd send her back!

Japanese women make the best wives. They care for you, pamper you, stay with you, and best of all your mother-in-law lives in Tokyo.

Mixed emotions is watching your mother-in-law drive over a cliff in your new car.

She speaks 140 words per minute, with gusts up to 180.

The wedding got started on a rather sour note when my mother-in-law came down the aisle and lobbed a grenade into my family's pew.

We must watch the Macy's Day Parade. This year my mother-in-law blew up three of the balloons.

My mother-in-law is so near-sighted that she nagged a coathanger for an hour.

MOTHER'S DAY

Last year on Mother's Day the whole family got together for a big dinner and afterward when I started to clean up my son said, "Mom, don't bother with those dishes. Today is Mother's Day. Leave the dishes. You can always wash them tomorrrow."

I can remember when I was a kid. Every year we'd give Mom a great big box of her favorite candy...Mom always got the first piece, and if she was really quick, she got the last.

I finally found a Mother's Day card that expressed my feelings for my mother in real terms. It said, "Now that we have a mature, adult relationship, there's something I'd like to tell you. You're still the first person I think of when I fall down and go boom!"

I called my Mom on Mother's Day. I just loved the excitement in her voice as she accepted the charges.

Mom to son: "You sent me three beautiful roses, and I'm glad, but was there any special reason for sending three?"
He said, "There sure was. Twelve of them cost $25."

I purchased a high-speed camera for Mother's Day so that I could get a picture of my mother-in-law with her mouth closed.

MOTORCYCLES

You can always tell a happy motorcyclist by counting the number of bugs on his teeth.

Here are things <u>not</u> to say when traveling behind a motorcycle gang's road rally:
• My Aunt Betty had a pair of earrings just like that.
• Is that your beard or did you drive through a moss bank?
• Are you guys the road company for the Richard Simmons Show?
• Hey, did you lose one earring, or did you find one?
• Hey, dummy, can you show me the fastest way to get to the hospital?

Motorcyclists always wear leather because chiffon wrinkles so easily.

I wear winter undies when I ride my motorcycle. They're called long Hondawear.

 # MOVIES

The Hollywood tycoon was determined to create the greatest epic ever filmed. "I will use two armies for the battle scene", he cried. "Twenty-five thousand extras on each side."
"Fantastic!" cried the director. "But how will we pay them?"
"That's the best part of my plan," replied the tycoon. "We'll use real bullets."

Why don't they make he-man movies anymore? I just saw a new adventure film, "Tarzan Opens a Boutique".

Movies today are terrifying. I went to one the other day and I never saw such violence, sex, and vulgar language--and that was at the popcorn stand!

The movie had a happy ending. Everyone was glad when it was over.

I don't mind folks eating popcorn and candy at the movies, or even bringing a bucket from the Colonel...but setting up a hibachi in the aisle is going a little too far!

The sign at the movie window said: "Five dollars--popular prices." The moviegoer asked the girl, "You call five dollars popular prices?"
She said sweetly, "We like them."

Haven't you found that most 3-D movies lack depth?

He saw Guess Who's Coming to Dinner? twice and guessed wrong both times.

A couple went to the drive-in movie and nearly froze to death. "Closed for the Season" was showing.

MUSIC

Song titles:
- I Wouldn't Take You to a Dog Fight Even if I Thought You Could Win
- Don't Cry Down My Back, Baby, You'll Rust My Spurs
- The sequel to Mack the Knife--Irving the Fork

A boy practiced the violin for fifteen minutes and the dog howled continuously. In desperation, the father yelled, "Tommy, will you please play something that the dog doesn't know?"

He sings through his nose by ear.

Song title: "If Today Was a Fish, I'd Throw It Back In".

On a card in front of a neighbor's house, a sign read, "Drum set for sale."
In the window next door, another card appeared which said, "Hooray!"

A novice concert-goer rushed up to the conductor after the band performance and said, "I think it only fair that you know that the fellow who plays that instrument that slides in and out only played during those intervals that you were looking right at him."

The accompanist said to the singer, "I can play all the white keys and all the black keys, but you're the first singer I have ever played for who could sing between them."

Next on the program we have a musician who is not without a lack of talent, and she manages to play the simplest pieces with the greatest difficulty.

The band has really improved. Now you can tell when they're tuning up.

"I didn't send for a piano tuner!"
"I know. Your neighbors did."

Father: "Stop practicing the clarinet or I'll go crazy!"
Son: "Too late, Dad. I stopped an hour ago."

The orchestra was so bad it sounded like someone had tied a knot in the string section.

They eat, breathe, and sleep music. Too bad they can't play it!

What lung power! He used to blow up the Goodyear Blimp.

And now for their next number, the band is going to take the instruments out of their cases.

She's never sung better. Kinda sad when you think of it.

He used to be a drummer until he lost one of his sticks. Then they had to make him the conductor.

He sings like a prisoner. Behind eight bars and looking for the right key.

In all the years I've been singing, not once have I had throat trouble. And that's because I sing through my nose.

I can't sing well tonight. This morning I yelled at my kids through a screen door and strained my voice.

I was recently on that TV show, "Maim That Tune."

He's one of the greatest singers of our day. Unfortunately he doesn't sing that well at night.

Presenting the first musical score of the evening: Brahms 6, Beethoven 2, at the top of the fifth.

They have a style that kind of grows on you...sort of a musical fungus.

My music has improved. You can tell when I'm tuning up now.

How about a great big hand for the boys in the band? Let's face it--they've tried...I mean if you don't have it, you can't fight those things.

Four carpenters formed a tuba group and called themselves the "Tuba Four"

I was in a drum and bugle corp that was so bad, the drums carried the tune.

Each of these fine musicians is an artist in his own right. It's just that when they play together that they have a problem.

He has a great ear for music. It looks just like a tuba.

When I was younger I wanted to play in the high school orchestra. I even had private tootering on the trumpet...Until the teacher wouldn't take anymore of my lip, so I took up the guitar instead...but the orchestra picked on me until I became completely unstrung. And then I saw that there was a spot open at the accordion. But someone squeezed me out. And when I couldn't make it on the maracas I was really shaken. But I finally found out that I had a natural talent for playing the trombone. I excelled by just letting things slide.

At the end of the concert, I asked the pianist why he had chosen to play Beethoven's Fourth Concerto. "Because that's what the orchestra was playing," he replied.

As a musician, he only knows two numbers. One is "Chopsticks" and the other one isn't.

She's been playing the piano for fifteen years now and her fingers are really tired.

Wow, what a voice! When he gets finished carrying a tune you can see fingerprints on it!

She has an unusual voice, sort of like asthma set to music.

Next, this fine medley of songs, "If You Knew Susie Like I Knew Susie, You'd Go Out With Sally," and, "I Tried To Look Into Her Eyes, But They Were Too Far Apart," and "Get Out Of The Wheat Field, Grandma, You're Going Against the Grain."

Last night the high school orchestra played Beethoven and Beethoven lost.

He plays the violin just like Heifetz--under his chin.

It was one of those restaurants with quiet background music. Well, not too quiet. The first number put ripples in my soup.

It helps to think of rock music as youth's way of getting even for spinach.

His voice fills the hall with music. And while he was singing, I noticed some of you leaving to make room for it.

Tonight, I'd like to play like I've never played before--in tune!

Next I'd like to sing for you, "My Girlfriend Looks Like a Total Stranger Since Her Face Got Caught in the Record Changer".

They call it a five-piece band because that is all they know.

His voice has been compared to Pavarotti's--unfavorably, of course.

I sing all my songs fast. I want to get through them before I make mistakes.

What a musician! Once destined to be the world's greatest organist. But then his monkey died.

Our high school band was terrible. The way we played, it was a good thing we kept moving.

Our college band consisted of 110 members, each of whom hoped the other could play.

Our band was so bad that the cymbals always carried the melody.

I'm really into music. In fact, there isn't an instrument I can't play. I can't play the guitar, I can't play the banjo, I can't play the piano...

If you want a career as a musician or songwriter, persevere. Just remember, it took Brahms five years to compose his memorable lullaby. He kept falling asleep at the piano.

The way he sings, he should play a pirate in an opera. He's murder on the high C's.

What a powerful voice. When the doctor slapped him on the day he was born, he cried and shattered the window in the delivery room.

DO-IT-YOURSELF
SPACE.

WRITE YOUR
OWN JOKE
HERE!

NECKTIES

The nice thing about narrow neckties is that they give gravy a much smaller target.

NEW JERSEY

The government has just invented a rapid transit train that can go through New Jersey at 150 m.p.h.. Which, when you think about it, is the only way to travel through New Jersey.

NEWSCAST

The National Rifle Association claims that taking guns away from people violates the rights of hunters. After all, how else could they clear out the caribou herds in Toledo?

Mad dog terrorizes city. Foam at eleven.

Respirator illness sweeps community. Phlegm at eleven.

A freighter carrying a load of yo-yos hit a reef and sank 132 times.

An 80-year-old lady is marrying a 26-year-old man. Guests are asked to throw rice underhand.

Man hit by bus critical...well, you can't blame him!

The United Nations has just started a campaign to wipe out hunger and illiteracy at the same time, by giving out 800 zillion tons of alphabet soup.

The Nuclear Regulatory Commission reports that the atomic accident has caused no changes at 2 1/2 Mile Island.

Another massive recall in Detroit, General Motors had to recall 67% of all the cars sold in the third quarter...but they hope to have both of them repaired shortly.

Bulletin! Water has just been discovered under Lake Erie.

The Coast Guard reports that two ships have collided off the coast of Florida. One ship was carrying red paint; the other was carrying purple paint. First reports indicate the passengers and crews of both ships were marooned.

A man has barricaded himself into a house downtown. However he is unarmed and alone, and no one is paying attention.

The Doomsday Society has determined that the world will come to an end this Friday at 7:30 p.m.. All are invited to attend. Refreshments will be served and there will be a discussion afterwards.

Franco-American has announced that it will merge with Timex and begin producing self-winding spaghetti.

Also in today's news, another senseless killing. Irving Senseless was found dead in his driveway.

In sports, boxer Arnold Sussman is hanging up his gloves so that he can return to his first love ---beating up ordinary people.

And now, the stock report. Empire Hemlines are up . . . 7 Up is down..International Harvester is stable and Pampers remain unchanged.

Crossword puzzle addict Bessie Snidley has inserted a new clause in her will stating that when she dies she wants to be buried six down and three across.

This month's meeting of the Clairvoyants Club has been cancelled due to unforeseen circumstances.

Two-thousand pounds of human hair fell off a truck in New Jersey today and blocked the highway. Police are still combing the area.

In sports, the East German pole vaulting champion has just become the West German pole vaulting champion.

A minor earthquake hit Iran today causing $2 billion worth of improvements.

The fortune tellers and the Clairvoyant's Association will be holding their annual picnic next Sunday. In case of rain, the event will be held Saturday.

A dog exploded today at a busy downtown street corner. No one was killed but 12 people were overcome by fur. Police estimate that 50 to 60 fleas lost their lives in the blast.

A 65-year-old man, Ralph Thompson, was asleep in his downtown hotel room last Thursday, when he was awakened by the sound of a barking dog. When he woke, he found his room was full of smoke; he could not see, and the dog led him out of the room, down the hall, and into an elevator shaft where he plunged eight stories.

Next year, NASA plans to put 20 head of cattle into orbit. It'll be the first herd shot 'round the world.

An eight-year-old escaped serious injury downtown today when a case of Coke flew off a delivery truck and hit him in the head. Fortunately, it was just soft drink...

Today's meeting of the earthquake readiness committee was adjourned with a motion from the floor.

A gas stove explosion rocked the Cranston house last evening, blowing Mr. and Mrs. Cranston through the front door and out onto the street. Neighbors report that it is the first time the Cranstons have gone out together in 15 years.

A Lancaster resident was hauled into court for failing to pay his check at the doughnut shop. He was charged with impersonating an officer.

War has broken out in Africa between Zulus and the Pygmies. Battle casualties are seven wounded, 20 captured, and 39 stepped on.

In center city today, a wine truck collided with a cheese truck, resulting in a $3,000 fund raiser.

A tragic accident occurred in a sawmill today when a man lost his entire left side. He was immediately rushed to the hospital and doctors report that he's all right now.

A new attempt is being made to wipe out malaria. I wonder what those poor Malarians have done this time?

The State Department has some good news and bad news. The good news is that last week an American on a pleasure cruise fell overboard and was rescued by a Russian sub. The bad news is that he went overboard off the coast of Florida.

In the field of medicine, Dr. Seymour Savem has announced that he will spend the rest of his medical career seeking a cure for wheat germ.

NEWSPAPER

The sportswriter for our local paper doesn't suffer from insanity. He enjoys it.

A reporter for a Chinese newspaper got his first scoop, rushed into the office and called to the editor, "Hold the back page! Hold the back page!"

A person whose character was defamed in a newspaper article, went to an associate for advice. The friend advised, "Do nothing. Half the people who got the paper never read the article. Half who read it did not understand it. Half who did understand it didn't believe it. Half of those who believed it are of no importance anyway."

NEW YEAR'S EVE

We're so broke, my wife and I stayed home and toasted the New Year--she had whole wheat, and I had rye.

If you really want to save a lot of hassle this New Year's Eve, try this. Stay home, eat a bad meal, spill a beverage on your trousers, put a dent in your fender, rip up $140 and get the same effect.

On New Year's Eve I call friends all around the country, but the different time zones are confusing. Like last year I was tallking to the operator in New York and I said, "How far behind New York is Los Angeles?"
She said, "Literally or culturally?"

I had a terrific fight with my wife on New Year's Eve. She called me a procrastinator. So I stopped addressing Christmas cards and left.

Happy New Year? What's happy about it? Your car has depreciated $1,000 and your wife's clothes are out of style.

The New Year is celebrated too early. The Procrastinators' Club of America waits until August to see if it's worth celebrating.

NEW YORK

A guy asks me, "Do you know where Central Park is?"
I replied, "No."
He said, "Okay, I'll mug you here."

NOSTALGIA

I'll never forget the first girl I ever danced with. I said, "You'll have to forgive me but I only know two steps--the fox trot and the tango." She said, "No kidding? Which is this?"

NURSERY SCHOOL

I send my four-year-old to a day school and she just loves finger painting. Yesterday she painted one of them red, one of them blue, and another one...

And today was the crowning achievement of them all--she learned to tie her shoelaces. To each other. She's probably the only four-year-old in the world who minces.

OFFICE

We just bought a new conference table. It's nine feet wide and thirty feet long and sleeps twenty.

I don't want to complain about the size of my office, but it is a little embarrassing when you have to wheel your desk chair all the way out to the lobby just to swivel.

People are so inconsiderate. My last boss thought nothing of calling me and waking me up--right in the middle of a sound work day.

OIL

One oil company's public relations man said, "Of course we spilled 800,000 gallons of oil in the ocean, but after all, who wants a squeaky ocean?"

OPENING

I am grateful to be invited to speak here tonight. You see, I'm married, and what I'm usually invited to do is listen.

Good evening, ladies and gentlemen. You'll be happy to know that when I gave my speech to the secretary to be typed, I asked her to eliminate all that was on the dull side. So, in conclusion...

Folks, my jokes are so fresh tonight that I brought them to the show in Tupperware.

I am going to begin my speech tonight by reciting some wisdom I once learned from a Publishers Clearinghouse envelope.

 # OPTIMISTS

The optimist fell out a window on the top floor of a skyscraper. As he passed the tenth floor he was heard to say, "Well, so far, so good."

He's the kind of guy who comes home from a laundromat to fold his clothes and says, "Look, I found an extra sock!"

An optimist is a guy who goes out fishing for Moby Dick in a rowboat, carrying a jar of tartar sauce.

He's so optimistic that he puts his shoes on when he hears a speaker say, "Now in conclusion..."

When he goes fishing he takes along a camera and a frying pan.

He saves the illustrations from the seed catalogs to compare with what he grows in his flower and vegetable gardens.

A real optimist is a guy who pulls up in front of a shopping mall to meet his wife and leaves the motor running.

An optimist is a person who looks forward to enjoying the scenery on a detour.

He's such an optimist that he walked into a restaurant and ordered oysters, feeling that he'd find a pearl to pay his dinner check.

A nurse at a blood bank inquired of the donor: "Do you know your type?"
"Oh, yes," replied the donor, "I'm an optimist."

I was optimistic when I installed my own telephone. Now I get a dial tone on the electric can opener.

DO-IT-YOURSELF
SPACE.

WRITE YOUR
OWN JOKE
HERE!

PANHANDLER

"Could I have a dollar for a cup of coffee?"
"A dollar. That's ridiculous!"
"Just tell me yes or no. Don't tell me how to run my business."

"Can I have twenty dollars for a cup of coffee?"
"Twenty dollars!"
"Can I help it if I'm a big tipper?"

A passerby asked a bum who was stretched out on a park bench, "Why don't you go to work?"
The vagabond answered, "What--to support a shiftless, lazy no-good like me?"

"May I have $3 for a cheeseburger?"
"But a cheeseburger is only $1.50."
"Yes, but I have a date."

A panhandler asked me for five dollars. I said, "That's a little steep, isn't it?"
He said, "Yeah, but I want to knock off a little early so I can play tennis."

A panhandler said to me, "Mister, I haven't tasted food for a week." I said, "Dont worry. It stills tastes the same."

A guy says to me, "I haven't had a bite in two days."
So, I bit him.

"Do you think it's proper going door-to-door begging for food?"
"No, but they refuse to bring it to me."

"I haven't eaten in four days."
"Boy, I wish I had your will-power."

A panhandler approached me and asked for a dollar for a cup of coffee. I said, "But coffee is only fifty cents."
"I know that," he replied, "but won't you join me?"

I asked a panhandler, "Have you ever been offered work?"
He said, "Only once. Apart from that I've been treated with nothing but kindness."

He's the outdoor type. That's because no one would dare to let him in their home.

 ## PARACHUTE

Did you hear about the Ethnic parachute that opens on impact?

Rule number one in parachuting is never have an agrument with your wife while she's packing your parachute.

I always wanted to be a skydiver but nothing ever opened up for me.

Skydiving. Now there's a sport that's down to earth. Good to the last drop.

If your primary chute doesn't open, and the reserve chute doesn't open either, well, that's what you call jumping to a conclusion.

Now let's all sing the skydiver's theme: "It Don't Mean a Thing if You Don't Pull That String."

In basic training, skydivers were learning to jump. Just before one soldier was about to leap, a sergeant said, "Just a minute, private. You're not wearing a chute."
The private returned, "I didn't think I needed one. Didn't you say this was just practice?"

PARENTHOOD

Parenthood is hereditary. Chances are if your parents didn't have children, you won't either.

PARKING

It's not as easy as you think to get parking tickets. First you have to find a parking place.

And let's have a big round of applause for the parking lot attendants. They're certainly doing a bang up job out there. I understand that there are a lot more compacts leaving this place than ever came in.

PAYCHECK

It's called "take-home" pay because you are too embarrassed to take it anywhere else.

I give my wife my pay envelope each Friday. If she saves very carefully, by the end of the year she'll have 52 envelopes.

I found a note in my paycheck which read: "Your raise will become effective as soon as you do."

My wife said she wanted to see my paycheck go further...so she mailed it to Australia.

It's getting so that take-home pay can hardly survive the trip.

He designed curtains for window envelopes.

The businessman explained, "We pay every two weeks, because you can't buy anything with one week's pay."

I just got my paycheck, and I see that the government just gave itself another raise.

I'm not very high on the employee salary list. In fact, the post office delivers my paycheck by junk mail.

I opened my paycheck last Wednesday and saw a blank check. That didn't surprise me. I knew that sooner or later my deductions would catch up with my salary.

PAYDAY

Many women today are getting men's wages, but haven't they always?

PERFORMANCES

I performed at the Weight-Watchers Convention in Gainesville,

Florida; the Contortionists' Convention in South Bend, Indiana, and the Plumbers' Convention in Flushing, New York.

I also performed for the President. At least, I think I did. After the show, some guy came backstage and said to me, "If you're a singer, than I'm President Reagan."

Am I available for your program? Only on days of the week ending with the letter "y".

Last week I appeared at the Academy of Music and drew a line two blocks long. Then some wise guy came along and took away my chalk.

My career is taking off. Bigger things than ever are starting to fall through for me. I've had some things fall through for me lately that I thought I'd never get close to.

(if you close the show) I'm glad they finally put me on. I've been standing out there for 45 minutes with my suit and material slowly going out of style.

I performed at an arts and crafts festival last week. It's the first time I ever saw a macrame Volkswagon.

I sang at a music festival and asked a girl, "Are you enjoying the concert?" She said (VERY LOUDLY), "Yeah and I was lucky enough to get a place right by the speakers!"

His performances are always refreshing. The audience always feels good when they wake up.

During one of his performances a man got up and walked out. His wife said, "Please excuse my husband. He's always walking in his sleep."

A critic reviewed an entertainer's opening performance. The entertainer told him, "That's a fine way to dress for my opening! Your suit looks like you slept in it."
"Now that you mentioned it," the critic replied, "I just woke up."

My last performance was so bad that it was reviewed on the obituary page.

I gave a one-man show and a critic wrote, "There were too many in the cast."

Last week I entertained a lodge in New Jersey. Seated next to me was an officer. I asked, "What's your title?"

He said, "Supreme Dictator of the Universe."

I said, "Oh, you head this organization?"

"Not exactly," he answered. "Actually, I'm the lowest office in the lodge."

A reviewer wrote of my most recent performance, "For the first time in my life, I envied my feet. They were asleep."

Last night he had the audience glued to their seats. Wasn't it clever of him to think of that?

A self-centered entertainer sent two tickets to his opening performance to the mayor, along with a note saying, "Bring a friend if you have one."

The mayor sent the tickets back with a note which read, "Due to previous engagement I cannot attend. I'll purchase tickets for the second show--if there is one."

My publicity agent did have one other well-known client--the Unknown Soldier.

I was in Swan Lake. It was the kind of role I could throw myself into.

PERSONALITIES

I have an unusual uncle. He won the three-legged race at the picnic. What made it so unusual was that he didn't have a partner.

Ugly? Did you ever see a mosquito that would bite somebody with its eyes shut?

Believe me, a model who weighs 90 pounds doesn't have an easy time of it. She has to worry about long hours, bright lights, and strong vacuum cleaners.

Talk about hairdos. Picture shredded wheat with bobby pins.

PETS

We had a terrible tragedy in our house yesterday involving our daughter's pet. Up until today, I never realized until I sat in my favorite armchair that it was gerbil colored.

The used pet store ran a sale on a near-sighted owl and an elephant that had amnesia.

PHILADELPHIA

Philadelphia had a 21-inch snow fall, and it brought the entire city to a halt. My question is: "How could they tell?"

A mugger walked up to me on Broad Street the other day and was so friendly. He said, "Can you help a poor, hungry man who's down to his last dime, and has nothing left in the whole world, except for this loaded revolver?"

A friendly tip for those of you who live in Philly. If a holdup man threatens to blow out your brains if you don't give him your money, don't give in to him...you can live in Philadelphia without any brains, but not without money!

Philadelphia isn't really dull. It just seems that way because it's across the river from exciting Camden, New Jersey.

I like Philadelphia. I spent two weeks there one Sunday.

PHILOSOPHY

If you can keep your head while all the others around you are losing theirs--get somebody to explain the situation to you.

Did you every get the feeling that life is one big basketball game and you're Mickey Rooney?

PIANO

Now there's a person who was born to play the piano! Did you notice? Every other finger is black.

He started out playing the trumpet, but he likes the piano better. With a piano, you don't have to stop and shake out the spit between verses.

PIG

A little girl was visiting a farm and she saw her first sow. It was a huge animal, squatting in the pigpen.
The farmer commented, "Big isn't she?"
"She ought to be," exclaimed the little girl. "I saw her a few minutes

ago, and she had eight little ones underneath her blowing her up."

PLANTS

I have one plant I never talk to. He thinks he knows everything!

PLUMBER

My plumber is such a slow reader when it comes to following directions. In fact, he had to go to the eye doctor twice just to read the eye chart once!

"I'm sorry it took so long to get here."
"That's okay. While we were waiting, I taught the kids how to swim."

The plumber said, "Your basement's not too bad. Just pretend you live in Venice."

A person who can laugh when things go wrong is probably a plumber.

Meat prices are so high these days the plumbers are even beginning to notice.

After receiving a bill from the plumber for unclogging our bathtub, the expression "Paying the piper" has taken on a whole new meaning.

My wife answered the door, and the plumber asked, "Where's the drip?" She said, "He's upstairs in the bathroom trying to fix the leak."

POLICE

He was stopped by the police, and the officer asked to see his license. He said, "Okay, if I can shoot your gun."

A rookie patrolman was asked in an examination what he would do to break up a crowd. His answer indicated a deep understanding of human nature. He wrote, "I'd take up a collection."

POLITICS

In today's politics you can be on the cover of Time one week and be doing time the next.

The opinions expressed by the speaker were his own and not those of this station--or for that matter, of anybody else in his right mind.

We have a crisis in leadership in this country. Where are all the Washingtons, the Jeffersons, the Jacksons? I'll tell you where they are! They're all wide-receivers on pro football teams!

I love to visit Washington--if only to be near my money.

All the candidates are out raising money. The Republicans are having $1000 a plate dinners and the Democrats are throwing Tupperware parties.

He is spending $20 million to get his party's nomination. That may sound like a lot to you, but it just works out to $2 a promise.

I know what's wrong with this country. We're trying to run it with just one vice-president.

He introduced a bill that would create 20 million jobs. He proposed to build a bridge across the Mississippi--lengthwise.

He's one of the finest representatives money can buy.

After hearing his speech, 30 percent of the audience was undecided, and the other 70 percent will be polled when they wake up.

"Ol Man River, he don't know nuthin', he don't do nuthin'..."
Sounds just like our Congressman.

When a bureaucrat makes a mistake and continues to make it, it usually becomes a new policy.

As a safety tip: Do not attempt to drive a car or to operate heavy equipment after hearing one of (candidate's) speeches.

Campaigner's wife plops into chair: "What a day! I'm exhausted."
"You're exhausted? What about me? I had to give seven speeches in seven towns!"
"I know, dear, but I had to listen to them and smile the whole time."

After a long speech, the candidate asked, "Now, are there any questions?"
Someone in the audience yelled, "Yeah, who else is running?"

Did you ever wonder what the people of city hall do to celebrate Labor Day?

A clever hitchhiker held a sign: "I'm an undecided voter. Pick me up and try to convince me."

Being a politician is a lot like flying a kite. To get anywhere, you need to keep moving and have a lot of wind.

When a group of Nobel Prize winners gathered at the White House for dinner, the President declared, "This is the most extraordinary collection of talent and intelligence gathered at the White House since Thomas Jefferson dined alone."

One candidate promised to balance the budget by tilting the country.

I don't know why everyone is picking on that congressman. After all, he hasn't done anything.

He promised to help all poor people, which is a good thing. If he's elected, we'll all be poor next year.

He's just the man to get this country moving again. If he came to my neighborhood, I know I would!

When the President enters a room, we play, "Hail to the Chief". When Congress convenes, should we play, "Send in the Clowns"?

I don't have to do this for a living. I have the hemlock concession at Democratic headquarters.

Election returns were forming a pattern. Mrs. _____ went up to her husband and said, "_____, I've got some good news and some bad news for you. First the good news. You won't have to buy a new suit for the inaugural."

I just picked up a marvelous bargain in a second-hand car. It was only used by (losing candidate) in inaugural parades.

Yesterday I took my wife to a $100 a plate dinner. I had to. Who can afford restaurants? It's an eerie feeling to go to a $100 a plate dinner. When you drop a french fry you think, "There goes two dollars."

In the United States, everyone's vote counts--and in Cook County, that's true many times over.

How can you tell when a politician is lying? You can see him moving his lips.

Don't be too hard on our politicians. Many of them are doing the work of two men--Laurel and Hardy.

You have to admire the Democrats for astuteness. Yesterday, a Democrat began a speech to his supporters by saying, "As I look over this dense crowd--" Then I realized he knew his audience!

There's no furniture more costly than a government bureau.

Have you noticed how the administration keeps renaming things? The MX missile is called a peacemaker. Taxes are now called revenue enhancers. Next thing you know, unemployment will be known as a vacation extender.

Millions of Americans don't vote. They figure you can't earn your keep under the Republicans and can't keep what you earn under the Democrats.

When a political candidate promises you pie-in-the-sky, you can bet he plans on using your dough.

A candidate got a letter saying, "Dear Senator: I believe in the principles that you stand for. For those principles, I'd climb the highest mountain, swim the deepest ocean, fight the biggest army. I'd cross the widest desert. Long before the polls open on election day, I will be there---that is if it doesn't rain."

The cheapest way to have your family tree traced is to run for public office.

Timing is very important. One year Haldemann and Ehrlichman were arguing over who would get license plates number two and three. And a year later they were making them.

As Mayor Daly used to say on election day, "Vote early and vote often."

I was at city hall, and the mayor was making one of his decisions. I didn't actually see the mayor, but I did see the coin flip.

Our little daughter asked my wife the other day, "Mommy, do all fairy tales begin with 'Once upon a time...'
My wife said, "No, dear, some of them begin with, "If I'm elected..."

In politics, some men are self-made, but most politicians are machine-made.

He's not a member of an organized political party. He's a Democrat.

Grave marker: "Here lies a politician and an honest man."
Passerby: "Can you imagine? Two people in the same grave!"

We're overlooking one of the biggest sources of natural gas in our country--politicians.

I have to admire the straightforward way the candidates are dodging the issues.

I picked up a matchbook with job opportunity ads on the back. It said, "You, too, can become a Democratic presidential candidate."

This political campaign is really getting dirty. Someone sneaked into one of the candidate's headquarters and let the air out of his speeches.

I ate much better during Eisenhower's administration. I had my own teeth then.

He's an election-day taxidermist. He stuffs ballot boxes.

History always repeats itself because no one was listening the first time.

When electing a President, it pays to exercise extreme caution. Four years can be an eternity. Just ask anyone who tries to get plumbing or TV repair work done.

I like political jokes unless they get elected.

I got an invitation to a political fund raising dinner that read, "$100 a plate--blue cheese dressing 25¢ extra."

Now there's a candidate who doesn't take any chances. A reporter asked him what his favorite color was and he replied, "Plaid."

I was on the Metro in Washington, and inquired, "How do I get to the White House?"
The native replied, "Well, first you've got to enter the primaries..."

I always love the bobsled even in the winter Olympics. The bobsled is said to be the fastest way of going downhill without being a part of (politician's) campaign.

I attended one of those $1,000 a plate fund-raising dinners. Then I went home and discovered that every carrot on my plate had cost me $14.75.

A politician from Los Angeles was campaigning in New Hampshire for three days, and was terrified. "Why are you so afraid?" a reporter asked.

"I've been breathing air for three days that I couldn't even see," the politician answered.

They've a special plaque for him in the Capitol rotunda. It reads: "(politician) slept here--through two administrations."

His slogan is, "Honesty is the best policy." He should know, he's tried both.

In the last election he was a victim of accurate counting.

I got a letter from the President in reply to one I had sent. He told me that when the time comes, he wants me to serve in an advisory capacity. Well, those weren't his exact words. It was more like: "When I want your advice, I'll ask for it."

The party asked me to run for President, but I turned them down. After all, if I were elected, there would be no chance for advancement.

Our chief of police has done a super job of getting crime out of the alleys and back onto the streets where we can all see it.

Why does (candidate) want to eliminate poverty? That's all most of us have left!

There are only three ways to become a millionaire in this city: inherit money, get lucky, or get elected.

Most politicians shake hands well--
They've mastered that maneuver.
The trick's to find a shaker, pal,
Who also is a mover.

Today, an honest politician is one who when bought, will stay bought.

He claims to be "the man of the hour." Well, he better check his watch--he's running a little slow.

(about losing candidate) I can empathize with (loser). With a wife, mother-in-law, and a boss, I know just how it feels to be outvoted.

I went to a $1,000 a plate political fund raiser last week where the guest list was limited to 525 persons. Beyond that they would have to open another can of Bartlett pears.

He's running for President because "it's inside work, and there isn't any heavy lifting".

He's got the cleanest mind in politics, and that's because he changes it every hour.

POOR NEIGHBORHOOD

There's one advantage to being poor. It's very inexpensive.

We were really poor. I had so little to eat one year, I forgot how to swallow.

I wasn't born in a log cabin but my folks moved into one as soon as they could afford it.

The ground we lived on was so poor that we had to put fertilizer around the house just to raise the windows.

We had a lot of things money can't buy...unpaid bills, for instance.

We were so poor as kids we though that Irregular, Marked Down and Clearance were brand names.

POST OFFICE

Columbus went in the wrong direction from Spain looking for India...landed in the Bahamas and decided that he had discovered America. If he were alive today, he'd be working for the post office.

A guy walks into the post office and says to the clerk, "I'd like $20 worth of stamps."
The clerks asks, "What denomination?"
The guy replies, "Baptist!"

Postal rates are going up again. Customers are taking more of a licking than stamps!

The post office has been in business for over 200 years and is still unhindered by progress.

Old postal clerks never die, or if they do, it's very hard to tell.

I got a package in the mail the other day that had written on the front: "Photographs: Do Not Bend." And underneath the postman had written, "Oh, yes they do!"

I've learned one thing from dealing with the post office: if you're getting your neighbor's mail, and he's getting yours, there's only one thing to do to straighten it out--swap houses.

Post office employee to boss: "Sir, may I present Joe Johnson. He's retiring from the post office after thirty years."
Boss: "Well, Johnson, what have you learned after thirty years with us?"
Johnson: "Don't mail my check."

People usually get what's coming to them...unless, of course, it's mailed.

I still say that our coast-to-coast mail service could be improved. Maybe fresh horses would help.

This week they're holding the finals in the post office's annual pass, punt and kick competition.

This year they had a softball league for postal workers. The first game lasted all summer.

I know how to put off a postal increase for another two years. Have them request it by mail.

I handed the guy in our post office a compliment and he dropped it.

I don't want to be uncharitable to the post office, but the mailman just delivered my TV Guide. It has Ed Sullivan on the cover.

The post office has speeded up. I mailed a letter yesterday and got it back today.

I saw a package in the post office that said, "Fragile: Throw Underhand".

The post office is raising their rates again and it makes sense. Do you know what it costs these days to lose a letter?

Have you heard of the new wine called Post Office Red? You mail five pounds of grapes in a container marked "Fragile".

I was frightened while standing in line at the post office this morning. I heard one mailman yell, "Hey, Roy! Do you see that package marked FRAGILE over there? Kick it over here, will ya?"

Neither rain nor snow nor sleet nor gloom of night shall stay these couriers from the swift completion of their appointed rounds. We're referring to joggers, not postmen.

If you are what you eat, the post office must eat escargot.

This year I'm getting back at the postman for slow service. I'm mailing his Christmas gift.

There's always a lot of criticism of parcel post at this time of year but it's certainly unjustified. They're smashing as fast as they can.

On the average, one out of every three pens works in the post office...that's about the same ratio as the clerks.

Should have known better than to let my mailman show me his home movies...everything was in slow motion.

I see the arrival of spring is a little late this year. The post office must be delivering it.

A lady at the post office purchased stamps and said to the clerk, "Shall I stick them on myself?"
"Positively not," said the clerk. "They'll accomplish much more if you put them on envelopes."

They say, "Bad news travels fast..." Not if you mail it!

The post office is our only hope to whip inflation. If they can't slow it up or lose it, no one can.

I can always spot the picketers at a postal workers strike. They're the ones carrying signs and moving at a snail's pace.

"Tomorrow never comes"--particularly if the post office is delivering it.

This is the time of year for dumb mail. Yesterday, I got four envelopes with $15 million that I "may have already won".

I don't like to complain, but this morning the post office delivered my new credit card, and it expired last month!

I just got a C.O.D. package from the post office...Crushed On Delivery.

The other day I drove by one of those signs that say: Slow Children-- and underneath it someone scrawled: Grow Up To Work For The Post Office.

The new post office commemorative has a picture of a long line of people waiting to buy stamps.

My young son was asking me to explain how slow motion works. I was searching for a simple explanation, and fortunately, the postman walked by.

He saves money on postage by dropping his letters in the mailbox without stamps when no one is looking.

PREACHER

"I've always said that the poor are welcome in our church, and judging by today's collection, I see that they have come."

He was such a great preacher that at the close of each sermon there was a great awakening.

"Mom, did you say the preacher's name was 'Reverend' or 'Neverend'?"

A rural preacher said, "I don't know what the word 'procrastination' means, but I think it's something that Presbyterians believe in."

 **PRISON**

A governor giving a speech to prisoners said, "Fellow citizens--" Realizing his error, he started over. "Fellow convicts..." Laughter erupted. The governor continued, "I'm glad to see so many of you here."

"My son is coming home from prison next week."
"Why I thought he had another year to serve?" stated a neighbor.
"He did. But he got paroled for good behavior."
"Well," the neighbor continued, "You can certainly be proud to know that you have such a good son."

The ladies' auxilary was writing letters to cheer prisoners. One woman was perplexed as to how to open her letter, for she only knew the prisoner's number. Finally, she began, "Dear 3962974, or may I call you 396?"

A group of prisoners was headed to chapel on a Sunday morning. One group filed toward the Catholic chapel, another toward the Protestant chapel, while one lone prisoner headed for the main gate. A guard stopped the wanderer and asked, "Just where do you think you're going, Sam?"
Sam responded, "Well, I was told I could go to the church of my choice and it's in Dallas."

PRIZES

And don't forget, the winners of our Pat Williams and Ken Hussar Look-Alike Contest will get gift certificates to the plastic surgeon of their choice.

For those of you who have been following our Orson Welles Look-Alike Contest--First prize went to Cincinnati.

First prize tonight: A dart board with an automatic return.

First prize: A 20 day cruise to the Bermuda Triangle.

Second prize: A two-week vacation to one of the islands--Three Mile.

Third prize: Twenty-seven minutes of uninterrupted root canal work.

Tonight's prize is a free ride on the Goodyear Blimp through Libyan air space.

The good news is that you have just won seven glorious days and six romantic nights in beautiful Hawaii. The bad news is, they're in separate weeks.

Tonight's prize: A weather rope. It works beautifully. You take it outside, hang it on a tree branch. If the rope's wet, it's raining; if it's swinging, it's windy; if it's white, it's snowing.

Tonight's prize: A trip to Rangoon for the annual malaria season.

Second prize: A trip to Outer Mongolia in time for the annual famine.

Tonight's grand prize: A brand, new Mercedes--windshield wiper.

Another great prize; A 112-piece dinner set--a box of toothpicks and a can opener.

PROCRASTINATORS

Congratulations to_____. The Procrastinators Club of America has just named you past president.

The Procrastinators' Club of America claims to have 600,000 members, but only 3,300 of them have gotten around to joining.

The Procrastinators' Club led a successful protest against the War of 1812--in 1967!

PROFOUND QUESTIONS

If Americans throw rice at weddings, do the Chinese throw hot dogs?

If you didn't have a nose, would your eyes bump into each other?

If dolphins are so smart, how come they don't have off-shore drilling rights?

I hate when my foot falls asleep during the day, because that means it's going to be up all night.

Never invest your money in anything that eats or needs repainting.

If you take off your right glove in very cold weather, the key will be in your left pocket.

What do they call the coffee break at the Lipton Tea Company?

A philosopher is one who keeps learning more and more about less and less, until he finally knows everything about nothing.

New evidence that women are more coordinated than men, in general: otherwise how come they don't make soap-on-a-rope for women?

Will designer jeans ever replace the tourniquet?

Why is it that the people who forget to turn off their car headlights always remember to lock their cars?

If olive oil comes from olives, where does baby oil come from?

Just remember this: This is the first day of the rest of your life. Unless, of course, you live on the other side of the International Dateline, in which case, yesterday was the first day of the rest of your life.

If I mail a boomerang, must I put a return address on it?

If the formula for water is H_2O, is the formula for an ice cube H_2O squared?

If a dentist can save $20 a month by cutting his son's hair, how much per month can a barber save fixing his son's teeth?

Have you ever wondered what chairs would look like if your knees bent the other way?

Why is living in California like eating a bowl of Granola? After you get done with the fruits and nuts, there are still a lot of flakes left.

Did you ever worry that the guy who invented Musak may be working on something else?

How can you tell when you're running out of invisible ink?

How come we park in a driveway and drive on a parkway?

Does it make you nervous when you're eating alphabet soup, and someone is reading over your shoulder?

Have you ever passed a 7-11 store that doesn't have a sign in the window that says: "Night Manager Wanted?"

Did you realize that 200 years from now most antiques will be made out of plastic?

How come when you cook bacon, the fat splatters in every direction--but when you eat it, it all accumulates in one or two places?

Ever notice that when you send a package by car it's a shipment, and when you send it by ship it's cargo?

If a woman's work is never done, how come she doesn't start earlier?

Think of how smart we all would be if we retained as much of what we read as of what we eat!

If you don't think there's strength in numbers, consider the snowflake. If enough of those fragile things stick together, they can paralyze an entire city.

I don't understand food stamps. Do poor people have that much food to mail?

Japanese people look so much alike. Can you imagine an armed robbery in Japan with an eye-witness?

I believe in being positive...I think.

How come 'fat chance' and 'slim chance' mean the same thing?

"No two snowflakes are alike" is an observation about nature.
"No two flakes are alike" is an observation about California.

Believe me, illiteracy is nothing to write home about.

What do you give a sick florist?

Was Robin Hood's mother known as Mother Hood?

Why is it that while everyone else is getting a piece of the pie, I'm still holding a Twinkie?

How do you explain counter-clockwise to someone with a digital watch?

Have you ever seen a security guard who looks like he's in good shape?

Don't you think hurricanes should be given tougher names, like "Hurricane Butch" or "Hurricane Chuck"?

Why is it always the third car back that is the first to see the light turn green?

Why does sour cream have an expiration date?

If a man can swallow an aspirin at a drinking fountain, don't you think he deserves to get well?

Why is it that it's day that breaks, when it's night that falls?

If it's such a small world, how come it costs so much to run it?

If people can really communicate with plants, why doesn't someone ask poison ivy, "Hey, what's your beef with us, anyhow?"

Why is it that when I go to the supermarket the woman ahead of me always has a loaded cart, no driver's license, and a check drawn on the Bank of El Salvador?

If the world is getting smaller every day, as some say, why is the price of airline tickets continually rising?

Don't you think more people would be interested in politics if the electoral college had a football team?

Why is it that the kid who can't hear his mother calling him from the kitchen can always hear the ice cream truck when it's nine blocks away?

Did you ever notice that people are always saying, "Have a good day..." but that they never tell you how?

If modern medicine has done such wonders in increasing our life spans, how is it that you never meet a woman who's older than 39?

If the bank repossesses the car while you're living in it, can you live in the bank?

If the city really wants to solve its parking problems, why don't they hire the guy who squeezes 25,000 units of Vitamin C into those tiny little capsules?

If the United States manufactures five billion ball-point pens a year, how come I can never find one by my telephone?

What did pioneer mothers do about static cling and ring around the collar?

Isn't it amazing that Lincoln and Washington were both born on holidays?

Did you ever feel so weak in the morning that you had to use both hands to brush your teeth?

The colder the x-ray table, the more of your body you will be asked to put on it.

Do you think that it's a coincidence that the first airline meal and the first air sickness bag were introduced on the same day?

Have you ever gone to a discount store that has shopping carts that work?

Have you ever driven down a country road that has a No Shooting sign that isn't all full of bullet holes?

If the owl is so smart, why doesn't he get on the day shift?

Some profound thoughts from bumper stickers:
    *Look-out for the guy driving in the car behind me.
    *Oink if you're a road hog.
    *Real men don't stop for yellow lights.
    *I don't care what you love, what your other car is, or what you'd rather be doing.
    *I Hate Bigots.
    *Warning! I do not brake for liberals.
    *Honk softly, I've had a lousy day.
    *Support the crisis of your choice.

"Do you believe in coincidences?" "Funny, I was just going to ask you the same thing!"

Did you ever see a healthy-looking person come out of a health food store?

Do parking lot attendants have drivers' licenses?

PROGRAM HIGHLIGHTS

I saw the sword swallower that we had lined up for our halftime show swallowing pins and needles. He told me, "I'm on a diet."

A man walked into the office of our halftime coordinator carrying a large and a small suitcase. He explained, "The climax of my act comes when my assistant takes a rock and places it on my head. He then takes a hammer out of the little suitcase and smashes the rock to little bits."
"Interesting," said the coordinator. "Tell me. What is in that large suitcase?"
"Aspirin," the entertainer replied.

And next on our program, ——————— will do his famous impersonation of Guatemala.

And for you kids, we'll demonstrate how you can make a fantastic four-passenger skateboard out of mom's ironing board.

Later on in the show, those fine Filipino contortionists, The Manila Folders!

From Dover, Delaware, the remarkable Dover twins, Ben Dover and Eileen Dover, who will demonstrate their unusual hobby of twisting animals into the shapes of balloons.

Tonight we have a galaxy of international stars performing for us: from Indonesia, Mr. Frank Sumatra; from South America, the gorgeous Bolivia Newton-John; from Chile, Mr. Andes Williams; from Bermuda, the acrobatic midgets, the popular Bermuda Shorts, and the Olympic Czechoslovakian Trampoline team, the sensational Bouncing Czechs.

Tonight we will feature a sword swallower who will swallow a five-and-one-half foot sword. What makes it really amazing is that he's only five feet tall.

Next on the program we have something that is guaranteed to bring delight to everyone in the audience: a sky diving contest for political candidates.

Later on we'll have Humpty Dumpty out here to perform some more of his off-the-wall humor.

We were expecting to have a man entertain us at halftime (intermission) who first jumps off a 50-foot tower into a tank of water, and then a 100-foot tower into a barrel of water, and finally a 150-foot tower into a damp rag. He'd be doing it tonight, but unfortunately, during rehearsal, somebody wrung out the rag.

This act is just back from working the mountains--the Himalayas.

Next on the show, the State Police Barbershop Quartet--the fabulous Coppertones.

PSYCHIATRISTS

Psychiatrist to patient: "What do you do for a living?"
Guy says, "I'm an auto mechanic."
Psychiatrist says, "Okay, get under the couch."

He told the doctor, "I'm schizophrenic."
Doctor says, "Well, come on in. That makes four of us."

I've got some good news and some bad news. The bad news is that my psychiatrist says that I'm afraid of success. The good news is that he says I have nothing to worry about.

Psychiatrist to patient: "If you think you're walking out of here cured after only three sessions, you're crazy!"

There are only two things to do if you have a nervous breakdown. Go away for a long rest in the country--or get a job in the National Basketball Association where it won't be noticed.

He told the psychiatrist, "No one takes me seriously."
The psychiatrist said, "No kidding?"

But it's great the way psychiatrists throw those big words at you. I went to one and he said, "Yes, I see you're suffering from Cashew-Maraschino Syndrome."
I said, "What's that?"
He said, "You're nutty as a fruitcake."

I have a friend who's a deaf psychiatrist. It's a great arrangement. He can give all the answers, and he doesn't have to listen to any of the questions.

The psychiatrist said, "I've got some good news and some bad news for you. The good news is that you don't have an inferiority complex. And the bad news is, you _are_ inferior!"

We can thank modern psychology for being the #2 preventer of insanity in our country...#1 is the opening of school.

Schizophrenia beats living alone.

Neurotic: Builds castles in the air.
Psychotic: Lives in the castles.
Psychiatrist: Collects the rent from both.

He was so ugly that when he went to the psychiatrist the shrink told him to lie on the couch---face down.

I went to the psychiatrist and told him everything I know. Now he's out doing my jokes.

Wife: "Could you please stop my husband? He thinks he's a baseball manager, and he keeps throwing baseballs at me."
Psychiatrist: "Tell him to stop!"
Wife: "I'm afraid to. He keeps threatening to trade me to Cleveland."

Psychiatrist: "So what if you like eating grapes so much? There's nothing wrong with that!"
Patient: "Off the wallpaper?"

"Doc, you gotta help me. I'm obsessed with pancakes. I love 'em. They're all I think about."

The shrink says, "Well, there's nothing wrong with enjoying pancakes. As a matter of fact, I love them too."

"Wow, that's great, doc. Why don't you come over to my house tonight? I've got a whole basement full of 'em."

"Look, the whole world's not against you. Maybe people in the United States can't take you, but not the whole world!"

A man walks into a shrink's office with a duck on his head. The duck quacks, "Hey, doc, will you get this guy off my tail?"

My psychiatrist has two baskets on his desk, one marked Outgoing and the other marked Inhibited.

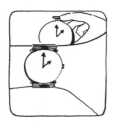

PUNCTUALITY

The trouble with being punctual is that, nine times out of ten, there's nobody there to appreciate it.

I've cut down on my mistakes at work. I arrive late and leave early.

He's the most punctual player on our team. He always showers before practice because he says there's less competition for a shower stall then.

RAILROADS

Trains are great. They let you off in the old sections downtown. Why if it wasn't for trains, muggers would have to commute to work.

The railroads publish a monthly joke sheet. It's called a timetable.

Timetables are so precise. They tell you that you'll arrive in St. Louis at 10:23 a.m.--give or take a few days.

I asked the ticket agent, "Is there any way I could get to Boston sooner?"
He said, "Sure, take the first car on the train."

An experienced train rider never orders soup that doesn't match his pants.

Railroads are carrying fewer and fewer passengers. I called the station and asked, "What time does your train for Richmond leave?"
The agent said, "When would you like it to leave?"

REPLIES

(reply to a tricky question) That's what I call a loaded question. It's like your wife asking, "How do you feel today?" which indicates either an interest in how you feel today--or that she wants the maple tree transplanted.

RESTAURANT

"Waiter, there's a fly in my soup!"
"Well, there's a fly that knows good soup!"

Sign: "We not only honor credit cards, we love and respect them."

A waiter carrying a flaming shish kebab was asked by a customer, "What is that?"
"A customer who didn't leave a generous tip," the waiter answered.

The waiter said, "Your dinner will be along shortly, sir. In the meantime, would you care for another candle?"

I dined in a posh restaurant, and two men approached my table. One said, "Good evening. I am Pierre, your waiter. And this is Mr. Samuels. He'll arrange the financing."

Two fellows go into a restaurant. One says, "I'll have the iced tea and make it very weak."
The second says, "I'll have the iced tea also, but I'd like it very strong. And make sure it's in a clean glass."
The waiter returned and said, "Now I forget. Who gets the clean glass?"

A restaurant offered a special: Dreaded veal cutlet.

I went to a new restaurant that specializes in Mexican/Jewish food. It's called the Casa Haddassah.

I went to a restaurant on my vacation. I told the waiter, "It's been ten years since I came in here."
He said, "Don't blame me. I'm working as fast as I can."

The roof leaked so badly, I finished my soup three times at lunch today.

Two-fifty for a cup of coffee! But you get a choice of three different types of cups--small, medium and clean.

It's one of those restaurants that always serves pumpernickel because it is nutritious, tasty, and doesn't show the dirt.

I'd like to send my compliments to the kitchen crew. It's the first time I've ever been served roast beef, coffee, and ice cream all at the same temperature.

The restaurant advertised, "Homestyle Breakfast". And sure enough, the waitress wore a bathrobe, had her hair in curlers, and served burnt toast, weak coffee, and lumpy oatmeal.

You know you're in a bad restaurant if the waiter asks, "Would you like another handful of mashed potatoes?"

When you go into a restaurant, do you ever wonder what the ham had before it was cured?

Patron to waiter: "May we have a bag for our leftover meat? We want to take it home for the dog."
Kid: "Oh, great, Dad. Are we getting a dog?"

They had three waiters for each table. One to give you the check, and the other two to assist you to your feet after you fainted.

The waiters were independent. They took orders from no one.

There was a sign in the restaurant: "Watch Your Coat and Hat." While I was watching them, somebody stole my soup.

You say you're my waiter? Somehow I was expecting a much older man.

"Are you the waiter who took my order?"
"Yes, I am."
"Well, you're looking well. By the way, how are the grandchildren?"

Menu notation: "Our eggs are so fresh that the hens haven't even missed them yet."

Isn't one of the worst feelings in the world being in a restaurant and hearing a sneeze from the kitchen?

Waiter, there's a fly in my soup.
That's funny. When I left the kitchen, there were two of them.

Waiter, there's a fly in my soup.
Just wait 'til you see the main course!

"I'd like a pork chop, and make it lean."
"Which way, sir, to the left or to the right?"

There's still something you can get for a nickel these days...the waitress' opinion of you.

Never go to a restaurant whose traditional placesetting is a fork, a spoon, and a flyswatter.

The restaurant advertised "blended coffee".
I asked the waitress, "What coffees go into the blend?"
She said, "Yesterday's and today's."

They serve soup that is three days old, but they're very clever. On the menu they call it "Soup Deja Vu".

They don't have much variety or originality at that restaurant. Take one item they have on the menu, for instance: "Soup of the Year".'

I won't comment on the size of their portions. Suffice it to say that the steak I had was good to the last bite--which, incidentally, was also the first.

A panhandler went to the famous George and the Dragon Restaurant and knocked, asking for a handout. A woman answered the door and yelled, "We have no food for slimy beggars! Get out, you scum!" Undaunted, the beggar asked, "May I speak to George, please?"

I ordered the entire meal in French, and the waiter was truly impressed. It was a Chinese restaurant.

We got a little suspicious when everytime there was a wedding in town, the restaurant would run a special on rice pudding.

They're closed on Mondays. That's when they do the dishes.

Their soup du jour comes from the finest du jours grown today.

And wasn't the service at this dinner something? I didn't know that the post office catered.

I saw a cockroach in a restaurant that was really tough...he was bench pressing a bread stick.

I asked the waitress to warm up my coffee, and she stuck her cigarette in it.

I told the waiter that the soup was awful and asked who made it. He said, "I had a hand in it."

They didn't have food to go. I asked, "How come?"
The guy at the counter said, "We used to, but people kept bringing it back."

You can tell something about the food in a restaurant when you see speed bumps between the tables and the rest rooms.

I saw a touching thing at the restaurant. Two of the waitresses were singing "Happy Birthday" to several of the doughnuts that had been under the plastic dome for a year.

I asked the waitress, "What's the time?"
She said, "I'm sorry, this isn't my table."

Never go to a restaurant that has a sign that says Prisoners Welcome and don't go to any restaurant that owns its own ambulance.

I went to a seafood restaurant and asked, "What's the catch of the day?" and the waiter replied, "Hepatitis."

I went to one of those restaurants that advertise "Breakfast Anytime" so I ordered pancakes from the Renaissance Period.

I went to a very tough restaurant. They had a special--"All you can eat for $10." After two forkfuls, Vinnie came over and said, "That's all you can eat."

Will the hot cakes be long?
No, sir, they'll be round as usual.

It has been said: We pass this way but once. I don't know who said it. It might have been our waiter.

Tough? Their specialty is pheasant under bullet-proof glass.

When you go to restaurant, be sure to get a table near a waiter.

It's the kind of restaurant where nobody bothers you. Not even the waiters.

They have a Detroit salad bar. You know--where they change the oil every six months.

When my wife and I were dating I took her to a nice restaurant. She looked over the menu and said, "I guess I'll have the steak and lobster." I said, "Guess again!"

Sign on a restaurant cash register: Sure we'll cash your personal check if you're over 80 and accompanied by your parents.

Restaurant sign: "Shoes are required to eat in restaurant. Socks may eat wherever they wish."

One restaurant owner stated: There will be no increase for New Year's Eve. The restaurant's normal exorbitant prices will prevail.

Just once I'd like to meet the waiter with enough courage to leave the check face up on the table.

I really impress people when I take my wife to dinner and order everything in French. The employees at McDonald's are amazed!

We go to one of those very swanky health food restaurants. Their specialty is rack of soybean.

Sign on a restaurant window: Come on in. Everything else has gone wrong today.

The food in the restaurant was so bad that the humane society wouldn't let them give out doggie bags.

I went to a Sushi restaurant whose specialty was Chicken Kamikaze. A live chicken walks into the kitchen and does a jackknife onto the grill.

I asked the waiter, "May I have a glass of water?"
He said, "To drink?"
I said, "No, I want to do my high diving act."

He claims to have gone 44 days without food. He should have given his order to another waiter.

I asked the waiter if he had any suggestions and he said, "Yeah, don't wear that tie with that suit again and get a decent haircut."

McDonald's has recently opened in Mexico. Their new advertising pitch is, "You deserve a break, Jose..."

Sign in a restaurant window with a filling station out front...Eat Here And Get Gas.

I asked the waiter if he had pig's feet and he said, "No, but the cook is pigeon-toed."

I knew I was in trouble when I discovered that they had Pepto-Bismol on tap.

The restaurant was so cheap that there were only two beans in the three bean salad.

I said to the waiter, "What is our offense? We've been on bread and water for over an hour now!"

A fellow at a restaurant ordered a breakfast of warm orange juice with pits and pulp, two eggs sunny-side up but very lightly done and gooey, burnt toast, and cold coffee in a dirty cup with lipstick smudges on the rim. The astonished waiter said, "But, sir, we can't make such a breakfast!"
To which the man replied, "Why not? You did it yesterday!"

Our food is untouched by human hands. We have a baboon for a cook.

What a restaurant. Terrible service! I think the 'vegetable of the day' was our waiter!

I asked the waiter what looked good in the kitchen and he said, "The new Pest-Strip!"

Waiter: "We practically have everything on the menu."
Customer: "Yes, I can see that. Would you mind bringing me a clean one."

Customer: "Why is the blue-plate special less expensive than the

white-plate special?"
Waiter: "The white-plate special is the one on clean dishes."

A salesman walked into a restaurant and ordered two eggs fried very hard, two pieces of toast burned to a crisp, and a cup of coffee, cold, weak, and almost undrinkable. Then he asked the waitress, "Now, will you sit across the table and nag me? I've been on the road for two weeks and I'm homesick."

Here's a tip: Avoid restaurants that have signs in the window that read: <u>Same Day Service.</u>

How did you find your steak?
Easy. I moved the potato over, and there it was.

He went to a restaurant to get dinner, but then turned around when he saw a sign in the window that said "Home Cooking".

When you walked into that restaurant you were going down two steps--literally and socially.

It even had monogrammed napkins. What class! At least I thought so until I saw my monogram crawl away.

I said to the waiter, "I understand that fish is brain food."
He said, "Yes, I eat it all the time."
I said, "Well, there goes another scientific theory."

I went to a Chinese restaurant in Tennessee. The Chattanooga Foo-Chu.

On their menu they had "Western Sandwich". I ordered one, and now I know how it got its name. Two slices of bread and wide-open spaces.

I ate in a restaurant in San Antonio, and on their menu the dessert suggestion read, "Remember the alamode".

"Waiter, what's this button doing in my salad?"
"Well, I suppose it came from the salad dressing."

"Waiter, there's a fly in my soup."
"I suppose the heat must have killed him."

The restaurant I went to last evening was making money hand-over-

362

fist selling Indian appetizers. You know, those are the things you munch on while you're waiting for your reservation.

I won't say what the size of their servings are like, but I asked the waiter to put my steak on my credit card--and it fit!

Their house specialty was Pollo con Pontiac. That's a chicken that has been run over by a car.

My steak was smothered with mushrooms. Judging from its size, I think it was a mercy killing.

What class! They even hired a midget waiter to serve shrimp cocktails.

My roast beef was so thin that I could see right through to the plate.

RETIREMENT

He worked for a cheap company. Spent forty years with the firm and they gave him a testimonial coffee break.

He still has some difficulty adjusting to retirement. Every morning he struggles downstairs to the kitchen and punches his time card in the toaster.

A retirement party is when the boss says all those nice things about you that he never said when you asked him for a raise.

In his years with this firm, he's kept his ear to the ground. I'm told he can sleep anywhere.

Look at the crowd that has assembled to honor you on your upcoming retirement. Who was it who said, "Give the people what they want, and they come out in droves"?

The years have been kind to you, Bob. But those weeks in between have really knocked you for a loop, haven't they?

Retirement won't change you that much. You'll find that all those things that you never had time to do become all those things that you don't have the money to do.

He told me, "When I retire, I'll finally be able to finish the book I started thirty years ago."
I asked, "What book are you reading?"

He's at that difficult stage in life where he's too old to work and too poor to retire.

We wanted to get something for you, Bob, but no one would start the bidding.

When we heard you were leaving, we all decided to get together and give you a little momentum--I mean memento.

We all wanted to get you a gift to prepare you for your retirement, Bill, and the staff made a unanimous choice. It's a book on etiquette. Don't worry, Bill, it has lots of pictures.

Retirement is that stage of life where the only thing you have to take a stand on is the bathroom scales.

Since his retirement, he's started a career in the take-out business. His wife tells him every day, "Take out the garbage...take out the dog...take out the weeds."

The first big shock of retirement is when you realize that there are no days off.

As a symbol of our gratitude, we have created this special gold watch to serve as a reminder of your many years with the company. It needs a lot of winding up--is always a little late--and every day at quarter to five, it stops working.

In preparation for this dinner the office staff produced a thumbnail sketch of all his accomplishments during his 35 years with the company. It's called a thumbnail sketch because that's what it fits on.

I hear that the biggest challenge of adjusting to retirement is sitting around and doing nothing. With Bill this won't be a problem. With our company alone he's had over 25 years of practice.

He never spent his time in daydreams--mostly because they'd interfere with his naps.

We have two wishes for your future--that your bowling score will be as high as your hopes, and your golfing score will be as low as your pension.

It was a little embarrassing planning this event. When Bill announced that he was going to retire, it came as a complete surprise to most of us--because most of us thought he already had.

You know that you're ready for retirement when you take off your shoes, put on your slippers, and even they hurt.

You can always tell the guest of honor at a retirement dinner. He's the one who yawns when the boss is telling his favorite jokes.

A retirement dinner is where the foreman says, "John Jones will be leaving us after fifty-three years of faithful service, but he'll always be in our memories."
And the boss says to the personnel manager, "Who?"

I retired three years ago. The biggest problem is to keep the boss from finding out.

The problem with being retired is that you never know what day it is, where you're supposed to be, or what you're supposed to be doing. It's much like working for the federal government.

One big shock that comes when you retire after a lifetime of office work is that some people actually buy pencils, pens and paper.

The secret to retirement as I see it is planning ahead. (Pick up a roll from the basket, inspect it and put it in your pocket.)

He took an aptitude test to find out for what he was best suited, and he found out he was best suited for retirement.

Though he's leaving us, we'll all feel a little richer--that's because he won't be borrowing money from us the day after payday.

I won't comment on his work record with the company, but word has it that before he could find his way back to his desk, he always had to start at the vending machines.

He was late for his own retirement dinner tonight. The boss said, "Instead of a gold watch, we're going to give you an alarm clock."

Retirement dinners are when the administration gives the retiree a sterling silver watch case, and the retirement plan gives him the works.

Here's a person who's put in 25 great years with this company--13 if you don't count coffee breaks.

We won't tell you how many mistakes he has made in his years with the company, but as a token of our esteem, we've had this eraser bronzed.

We don't look upon his leaving the firm as losing an employee. Rather, we are gaining a spot at the water cooler.

After you retire, your wife suddenly realizes that she never gave your secretary enough sympathy.

I know all about the mandatory retirement age. I'm just trying to convince the guys in the office that there's a mandatory work age!

 **RICH**

Kid: "When I grow up, I want to be a philanthropist. They always seem to have lots of money."

He's so rich that when he flies his wallet is considered carry-on luggage.

He is insightful. The other day he saw a well-dressed man step into a chauffeur-driven limo, and he said to hiimself, "There, but for me, go I."

Money isn't everything. As he puts it, "I can have as much fun with 900 thousand as I can with a million."

Money hasn't changed him that much. It's made him proud where he used to be arrogant, outspoken where people used to say rude, and eccentric where we used to say crazy.

The wealthy parents gave their youngsters blocks as a wedding gift--49th Street and 51st Street.

The neighborhood is so rich, they have a restaurant--Pheasant Delight.

He's so rich that the IRS just named him poster boy for next year.

He strained his voice by counting his money out loud.

There is only one thing that's keeping me from being rich--money.

He's so rich that his bank gave him bookends for his bankbooks.

His neighborhood is so exclusive that the fire department has an unlisted number.

His neighborhood is so rich that the preacher has stained-glass windows in his Mercedes.

They're so rich that they get TV Guide in the hardcover edition.

Their neighborhood was so rich that the girls go door-to-door selling Girl Scout caviar.

Some people think that because he was born rich, he was spoiled. His parents were very strict, however. Whenever he was bad, they'd take away his slave.

Our town is so rich that every Christmas we distribute food baskets to homes with only one pool.

Don't knock the rich. When was the last time you were ever hired by somebody poor?

Rich is having a bird bath in your back yard--with a salad bar!

A lot of people can't handle prosperity. But then again, most of us don't have to.

He comes from a rich family. At age three months his favorite food was Gerber's Rack of Strained Lamb.

His dad gave him two golf clubs. One has a swimming pool, and the other has a hotel.

You can have a pile of money, but the size of your funeral is going to depend on the weather.

He's so rich he flies his own plane--inside his house!

He's so rich he doesn't count his money. He weighs it.

He's so rich he has bills with pictures of Presidents you've never even heard of.

He's so rich that when he buys a suit, the only thing the tailor has to do is let out the pockets.

Rich? I could live a whole year on the loose change that has fallen from his pockets into the couch and the recliner.

It's a rich community. Where else can you find a restaurant called Pheasant Delight?

Just remember: A rich man is just a poor man with lots of money.

What a sight in front of my house Friday evening! There were three Mercedes and a Rolls Royce parked out front. Who would ever have guessed that the butcher, orthodontist, plumber, and TV repairman would all show up on the same evening?

 **RIDDLES**

What's the difference between a Xerox machine and the stomach flu? One makes facsimiles, and the other makes sick families.

Why did Humpty Dumpty have a great fall? To make up for a rotten summer.

What do you get when you throw a hand grenade into the kitchen? Linoleum blown apart.

What is green, has six legs, and if it fell out of tree could kill you? A pool table.

ROAST

He has a one-track mind, and the traffic on it is very light.

He's tighter than the top olive in the bottle.

"There seems to be a conspiracy of silence against me. What should I do?"
"Join it!"

He's so short he can keep his feet warm just by breathing hard.

He looks like he went to a blood bank and forgot to say when.

That's a nice outfit. Didn't they have it in your size?

If it wasn't for his stupidity, he wouldn't have any personality at all.

I won't say he has a big mouth, but the first time I met him was at a party where I saw him bobbing for basketballs.

He has the knack of making strangers immediately.

He confided in me, "As I was polishing my trophies the other day, I just happened to see my reflection, and now I understand why women are simply crazy about me."

An empty taxi stopped in front of the restaurant tonight, and Harry got out.

He's such a goody-goody that he goes out behind the barn to chew gum.

He's so dumb that if you put his brain in a bird the bird would fly backwards.

He's so short that he can swim ten lengths in his bathtub.

Now there sits a man with an open mind. I can feel the draft from here.

He's all excited because his name is on the cover of Time Magazine this week. I looked on the cover, and sure enough, there it was, right on the address label.

(short) Poor guy. Imagine going through life without ever being able to see a parade!

Some people are consumed by ambition. In his case, ambition lost its appetite.

He's so dull, he's even boring when he listens.

He's in pain. He strained his back holding in his stomach at the beach.

While on the beach, he picked up a seashell, held it up to his ear, and heard, "Why aren't you home working, you bum?" It was his mother-in-law.

He's so cheap that when he goes on an ego trip he travels tourist.

He's paranoid and feels that the whole world is against him. That's not true. Some of the smaller countries are neutral.

He's the kind of guy who would slap a bumper sticker on the rear bumper of your car that would read, "All Cops Are Ridiculously Overpaid".

Cheap? He gets mad if he gets well before his pills give out.

He has a big nose. When he lies on the beach, you can tell time by his shadow. He had it broken once, though, so actually he's about five minutes fast.

What can you say about him that hasn't already been said about warts?

He's a lot of fun to be with if you like to yawn.

He doesn't have a bad personality. He has no personality at all.

He's never bored, but he is a carrier.

He likes to relax in the tub for hours. Sometimes he even puts water in it.

He's no dummy. He knows plenty. He just can't think of it.

We were going to put a statue of him in the park, but then we figured, "Why should we scare the poor pigeons?"

He wanted to be his own best friend, but his mother would never let him hang around with that kind of person.

(short) He's the kind of man you put on a pedestal--to show honor, to show respect, and most important, you place him on a pedestal so you can see him.

Cheap? I don't mind a guy taking a doggie bag home from a banquet, but he's got plastic wrap in the pocket for the soup!

If we profit from our mistakes, this year is going to prove to be a bonanza for Bill.

His family album indicates that his ancestors went West in a covered wagon. And when I saw pictures of them, I realized why the wagon was covered.

Some men are born to greatness, others have greatness thrust upon them. And a few like Ralph duck.

What can we say about a man who has come from humble beginnings, and rose to the top based solely on his intelligence, grit and perserverance, when others might have fallen back? A man who has distinguished himself among his peers in such a way that no one can say a word against him. Well, enough about me--we're here to talk about Bob Smith.

He's been called cold, cruel, arrogant, and egotistical. But that's just his family's opinion.

He's late for everything. It's a family tradition. His ancestors came over on the Juneflower.

He tells me that ever since he joined the "Save the Dolphins" campaign, his life has taken on a whole, new porpoise.

He came down the driveway last night, banged into the garage doors and knocked one of them completely off the hinges. Thank goodness he didn't have the car!

Some people belong to the I.Q. club, Mensa; he belongs to one called Densa.

Sam remembers two things about Will Rogers. He remembers Will saying, "I never met a man I didn't like." And he remembers Will punching him out. It wasn't a fair fight though. Sam said Dale Carnegie was holding his arms.

People say he's outspoken, but I don't know by whom.

Ralph is known for being a continual complainer. After the meal, the waiter came over to him and asked, "Sir, was <u>anything</u> all right?"

As a youth, Ralph had lots of charisma. But lately, it's cleared up.

He paid $1000 to have his family tree traced, and $2000 to have it hushed up.

In all the years I've known him, no one has ever questioned his intelligence. In fact, no one has even mentioned it.

A real intellect. He once told me that he read Shakespeare in the original French.

His day hasn't gone well. This morning he went to the barber for a haircut, and right in middle of it he slipped off the booster stool (or pony).

His life has been full of trials, but so far not a single conviction.

If what you don't know won't hurt you, he must be almost invulnerable.

He is on the dull side. He even has to move his lips when he listens!

We really shouldn't pick on him. He's had a tough time. Earlier today, his pet rat died in his arms.

Why are we honoring this man? Have we run out of human beings?

He's so short he had to wear hand-me-ups.

I don't know what's wrong with you, but if you were a building, you'd be condemned.

He looks like an advance man for a famine.

He finally got it all together, but now he can't figure out what it is.

He's not lazy. He just has a phobia about getting tired.

He's not cheap. He just has low pockets and short arms.

You seem like a nice person. I just can't understand why no one likes you.

He looks like he finished last in the human race.

I thought my razor was dull until I heard him speak.

He went crazy trying to throw away his old boomerang.

When there's a piano to be moved, he's the kind of guy who would grab the piano stool first.

I wish I had known you when you were alive.

He could give Excedrin a headache.

He always hits the nail squarely on the thumb.

He recently returned from a half-year cruise. He was sent up the river for six months.

He has more crust than a pie factory.

I like your haircut. Did you do it yourself or have it sent out?

He's so dull he has a butter knife named after him.

He's so cheap he's keeping all his toys for his second childhood.

I offered him a penny for his thoughts, and he said, "No thanks. I don't want to turn pro."

I've known him for ten years, and he's still the same guy he's always been. In fact, he's still wearing the same suit.

He's such a loser. He showed me pictures of his wedding day, and he isn't included in any of them.

He was born in Minneapolis, which was good news for St. Paul.

What a memory! He never forgets an idea that crosses his mind. After all, it's such a short trip.

He's always easy to spot in a restaurant. He's the one with his back to the check.

A true conservationist, when the Sierra Club asked him for suggestions on how to save trees, Bob told them, "Shoot the woodpeckers."

I really admire the way that this man can take a firm, neutral stand on any important issue.

We wanted to put a bronze statue of him in the lobby, but the sculptor said it wouldn't stand up with one foot on the ground and the other in the mouth.

He's quite a reader. He has 400 books, but he just doesn't know where to put them. Nobody will lend him a bookcase.

When I think of him, two things come to mind--talent and humility, neither of which he has ever possessed.

(refer to another person on the dais) Look at Bob Jones here. Take away his dignity and grace and charm, and what do you have? That's right--Bill (roastee).

I was responsible for bringing together all the people who love and respect him. They're all waiting outside in the phone booth.

I've been asked to say something nice about him. He doesn't shed.

But success hasn't changed him. He's still the same arrogant clod he always was.

Say what you want, but there is only one Sam Dawkins. I found that out by looking in the telephone directory.

Is this guy a talker! He had worn out two sets of lips before he was twenty.

Friends? Why, he has friends he hasn't even used yet!

He started out years ago searching for that pot of gold at the end of the rainbow. Well, at least he's found the pot.

Warm? He donated his blood to the Red Cross, and it kept freezing up.

Cheap? If you do him a favor, he says, "Thanks a hundred."

He has an open mind which probably should be closed for repairs.

Sam says, "There are two ways that you know that you're getting old. The first is you lose your memory, and the second one I can't remember."

Some men thirst for riches, others thirst for power, Bob only thirsts after salted peanuts.

He is listed in the Guiness Book of World Records...under the <u>lowest</u> recorded tippers.

He's about as memorable as Whistler's father.

He's a very humble man, and after you hear him you'll know why.

First of all, my compliments to the organizers of this event. How they ever felt they could bring this off without funny speakers or material will never cease to amaze me.

Now that he is done, we all know the meaning of the expression comic relief.

You mean those were your best shots? Are you through? That's kind of like being stoned to death with popcorn.

He's good to his family, folks; he hardly ever goes home.

He stayed in his hometown until he was twenty-six. He wanted to finish high school.

He bragged to me, "When I give advice, it lasts a lifetime."
I said, "How do you know?"
He answered, "They never come back for more."

Look at this guy. He has all the warmth and charm of a Southern sheriff.

He wasn't always this way. Someone once gave him some bad advice that he followed. They said, "Be yourself."

He knows the secret of winning friends and influencing people, and he also knows how to keep that secret.

I introduced him to a doctor friend of mine at a party. Right away Bill began describing his symptoms to him.
My friend said, "Look, I'm not an M.D. I'm a doctor of philosophy."
Bill thought about that for fifteen seconds and then said, "Okay, what's the meaning of life?"

Aggressive? His secretary said, "Have a nice day," and Bill shot back, "Don't tell me what to do!"

He went through school on a tether ball scholarship.

He's very indecisive. Sort of like a centipede who's told to put his best foot forward.

He hasn't been well--suffers from a rare ailment--sclerosis of the charisma.

His destiny was set when his mother didn't make it to the hospital, and he was born in the family car--an Edsel.

Stylish? Who else do you know who orders a Perrier Slurpee?

He's the only guy I know who failed fire drill in school.

His idea of an exciting evening is to go down to the supermarket and fool with the electric doors.

What can you say about a man who not only wears a clip-on bow tie but also wears a clip-on suit?

Sir, I have listened to your humble opinion--and it certainly has every right to be a humble opinion.

I had dinner with him. I won't say he's cheap, but before he reached to pick up the check, the restaurant had changed ownership three times.

I don't want to imply that he's short, but yesterday I saw him playing handball against the curb.

He's learned to cope with the pressures of this world. He sleeps for 22 hours each day and in the afternoon takes a two-hour nap.

I tried to contact him through a mutual friend, but I found he didn't have any.

Here's a man who has proven that no matter how humble your origin, you can always sink lower.

He had a terrible experience. Earlier this week, a mugger broke into his brain and walked away empty-handed.

He says, "The things that baffle me most are the things I just don't understand."

He's so vain, he refuses to wear glasses. At a party, the only way he can tell the difference between the coasters and the cookies is that the coasters are chewier.

He is the most uncoordinated person I've ever seen. When he sneezes, it takes him three tries before he can get his hand to cover his mouth.

He's the prototype of the born loser. The other day on the beach, he picked up a seashell, held it up to his ear, and it said, "Get off the beach!"

He's so lazy that he uses an electric cart when he plays miniature golf.

Did you ever notice that his typical expression is that of a guy who has locked his keys in his car and the motor is still running?

He's so unpopular that his phone doesn't even ring when he's in the bathtub.

He remembers when he got to sit in the barber's chair without having to use the booster seat. That was the biggest thrill of his life. Still is!

This has certainly been an evening to remember. I say that because I want to remember everything correctly for when I talk to my lawyer in the morning.

He had his head examined but they couldn't find anything.

If there's an idea in his head, it's in solitary confinement.

He said the moth balls he bought were no good. He threw a whole box at them and didn't kill a single one!

He's one person who would make a perfect stranger!

His idea of a big evening is if he gets his bunny slippers on the right feet the first try!

He likes to drive friends crazy by sending wires that read, "Ignore first telegram."

With Bob there's never a dull moment. The whole day's dull!

He's the kind of man who comes through when the chips are up.

And now, here he is, Harold Stassen's charisma coach.

He has only one fault. He's unbearable.

They make him take all the family pictures. That way he's never in them.

He said, "I ran all the way home behind the bus today and saved fifty cents. Tomorrow I'm going to run home behind a taxi and save five dollars."

He has a millimeter mind in a megaton world.

When he went boating, he took along a shotgun because he wanted to shoot the rapids.

He's so far behind the rest of the pack he thinks he's in first place.

I like to congratulate him, but I can't think of anything to congratulate him on.

That's a beautiful dress you're wearing. It looks like a Goodwill bag with feet.

When they made him, they threw away the mold. It must have been done as a safety precaution.

He's the kind of guy who plants and fertilizes poison ivy.

Don't feel badly if there's a cold in your head...at least that's something!

Get this information in your brain and you'll have it in a nutshell.

He hates to go camping because he can't see the forest through the trees.

He sold his house for $85,000...and it really upset his landlord!

He owns beach-front property--a sandbox in Buffalo.

He even wrinkles his brow when he reads the comics!

They named a Chinese restaurant after him--Low I. Queue.

He's really something. He has the strength of a rabbit and the speed of an ox.

You ought to go to work for Maytag...as an agitator.

I've always suspected that he could be brainwashed with an eye-dropper.

Don't insult his intelligence. That would be like a mercy-killing.

Tonight brought back many memories. In particular, it brought back the memory of the time I spent in the Kansas City hotel immediately beside the stockyards. And this evening I can truthfully say I've never heard so much bull in all my life.

He never makes the same mistake twice, but he does have a great way of finding new ones.

After a speech like that may I say--may you be a light sleeper, and may the guy upstairs take a correspondence course in polka and breakdancing.

That was really a wonderful speech when you consider the handicap he's working under--terminal talent.

Isn't he sweet? In his spare time he's a heckler at telethons.

Some men make their mark in the world while others learn to write their names.

He was so excited when he was promoted to sixth grade that he could hardly shave without cutting himself.

He can always be counted on to hit the nail squarely on the thumb.

Is that your face or did you block a kick?

His life is so dull, that he actually looks forward to dental appointments.

The best part of his family tree is underground.

He's so generous that he'd give you the sleeve out of his vest.

In the game of life he came with batteries not included.

Strange things happen to him. Last week he was gored by a live moose in the lobby of the Denver Hilton.

He's not himself today...and I've noticed the improvement!

They say that "what you don't know won't hurt you", and he's a man that must feel no pain.

I won't say he's windy, but he can blow up a kiddy pool in thirty seconds.

He's the kind of guy who would put hamburger in your trunk while you're driving through Lion Country Safari.

I think the world of you. And you know the condition the world is in.

Talk about being clumsy. He's the only guy I know who can walk down the beach and kick sand in his own face!

You've heard of Who's Who. He's listed in Who Cares?.

He keeps a bowl of wax fruit on the table hoping that some night a group of mannequins will come over.

We didn't expect anything from him, and he came through.

As a kid he was so ugly that they put him in a corner and fed him with a slingshot.

Good looking women ask if he dyes his hair. Absolutely not. It was that color when he bought it!

(responses) You could say that what caffeine is to 7-UP...charisma is to our last speaker. Never had it, never will.

In all fairness to him, he's recovering from a delicate operation. He just had a talent by-pass.

Aren't you proud to be an American? Where else could a person like our previous speaker find acceptance and work?

When his ship came in he was sitting at the bus station.

The Freedom of Information Act hasn't affected him. He still doesn't know anything.

Opportunity knocked at his door once but just to ask directions.

To him, foreign currency is anything over $20.

He tried living within his income once but he got claustrophobia.

Okay, he didn't complete his degree, but certainly thirteen years of college is good for something!

He doesn't know the meaning of the word fear because he's afraid to ask.

He was learning to fly a helicopter. It's up 800 feet, and suddenly it falls to the ground.
I said, "What happened?"
He said, "It got chilly up there so I turned off the fan."

I asked him to spell farm and he said, "E-I-E-I-O."

He's a tough guy to get a gift for. What do you get for a guy who has nothing?

He reminds me of St. Paul. One of the dullest towns in America.

Are your suits made to order? If so, where were you at the time?

He doesn't get ulcers, he gives them. I'm going to name my first ulcer after him.

I make it a practice in a battle of wits never to attack anyone who's unarmed.

He wanted to know whether to go to a mind reader or palmist. His friend advised, "Go to a palmist. It's obvious you have a palm."

Our next entertainer needs no introduction. What he needs is an act.

He has such a big mouth that he can eat a banana sideways.

He starts mystery novels in the middle, so he won't have to only wonder how it will end, but also how it began.

He walked off a bus backwards because he overheard a man say, "Let's grab his seat when he leaves."

He and his wife called it quits after their fourth child was born because they read in National Geographic that every fifth child born in the world is Chinese.

Just the other day he was heard to say, "They're not making antiques like they used to."

He always takes his paycheck to the bank because it's too little to go by itself.

He's so fat he can take a shower without getting his feet wet.

He saved for years to buy a waterproof, unbreakable, shockproof watch, and he lost it.

He didn't get any respect-as a kid, he got batteries, toys not included.

His dad refused to take him to the zoo. He'd say, "If they want you, they'll come and get you."

He just finished his first book. Next week he's going to read another one.

At McDonald's they wouldn't serve him. The girl behind the counter said, "You don't deserve a break today."

He went into a hardware store and ordered some rat poison. The clerk said, "Shall I wrap it, or do you want to eat it here?"

He wasn't very popular in high school. He had to share his locker with a mop.

Looking back there are so many memories. Who can forget that day 30 years ago when out of the hundreds of employees in our company, the chairman of the board took him aside and left him there?

He got a hernia on an elephant hunt...carrying the decoy.

What a personality. He had a charisma by-pass operation.

He has proven beyond a shadow of a doubt that you don't need a pretty face to be successful.

He takes his wife everywhere because she is too ugly to kiss goodbye.

Here's a man who's been just like a brother to me. In fact, just yesterday he beat me up and took my bicycle.

He's such a procrastinator. He got a birthmark when he was eight.

He loves to play with Slinkies on escalators.

He's Mr. Intrigue. He even knows the serial number of the unknown soldier.

When she was 16 she was chosen Miss America. But remember, there were very few Americans then.

Here is a man with his feet firmly planted in mid-air.

Someone called him a perfect idiot--but nobody's perfect.

He's so dumb. His wife asked him to change the baby, so he brought home a different kid.

We honor tonight a man who started at the bottom and stayed there.

Here is a man who turned the family business into a million dollar business. Of course, it had been a multi-million dollar business.

His favorite song is Tea for One.

He's very charitable. Each year he offers $50,000 to the wife of the unknown soldier.

He used to be miserable and depressed. But now he's turned that all around. He's depressed and miserable.

I love this place. I've come back here for six consecutive years and I look back on them as the best years of my life. Which gives you some kind of idea of the miserable life I've been leading.

He has two legs and two arms just like everybody else, except in his case, they all touch the floor.

Mean? Do you know anyone else who would rearrange the chocolates in a Whitman's Sampler?

He's really mad tonight. He spent 40 minutes combing his hair and forgot to bring it with him.

I've seen him get hate mail from Quakers.

I've been at parties where the Surgeon General has offered him a cigarette.

In honor of you, a tree has been uprooted in Israel.

An illegal alien has been named after you.

As you get older you know more and more about less and less, and now you know everything about nothing.

He found that it cost ten dollars a year to feed a child in China, so he sent his whole family there.

His folks weren't exactly proud of him. Early home movies show his parents sneaking out of the hospital with bags over their heads.

For years his father used to carry around the picture of the kid who came with the wallet.

He ran through a screen door and strained himself.

He's so organized. It took him three and a half hours to finish dinner tonight. Who eats alphabet soup alphabetically?

Here's a guy who reads so slowly that he moves his lips to read a STOP sign.

I don't like to talk about hygiene habits, but let me put it this way. He never has to worry about missing a phone call when he's in the shower.

Here's a man who is educated beyond his intelligence.

Trying to lose him as a friend is like trying to get out of the Book-of-the-Month Club.

To his credit, he's never let failure go to his head.

He won the three-legged race at our picnic. What made it so unusual was that he didn't have a partner.

In etiquette class he was voted as the one most likely to return.

His manners have improved. A girl dropped her purse, and he drop-kicked it back to her.

He's put his foot in his mouth so many times that he had to switch to sugar-free Desenex.

He's so dull that when he pulls into a gas station the bell doesn't even ring.

If it's true that we learn from our mistakes, he'll be the best ever in his profession.

At an early age he showed signs of belonging in the theatre. He put gum under his high chair.

I am sorry to announce that we have two disappointments. Robert Redford couldn't be here and _____ could.

He has the Midas touch. Everything he touches turns into a muffler.

If you had your life to live over again, do it overseas.

I think the world of him, and you know the condition the world is in today.

He won a Gold medal in tennis and had it bronzed.

He bet his IQ in the state lottery and won. It was the first time a two-digit number ever won.

He robbed a bank in Israel and escaped with $2 million worth of pledges.

He was a real loner as a boy. He went to Boys' Town, and Father Flanagan took one look at him and said, "Get lost."

He has meant to his profession what water skiing has meant to the economy of Arizona.

A lifeguard found him at the beach and took him to his mother and said, "Is this your little boy?"
His mother said, "Finders keepers."

Alert? This man is a former lookout on the Titanic.

He's willed his body to science, and science is contesting his will.

He's a modest man. But then again, he has so much to be modest about.

Self confident? He's the first guy I ever met who does crossword puzzles on a typewriter.

Relaxed? He wears a medic alert bracelet that says, "Trust me. I'm alive".

For those of you who want to know the secret of his success, there is no secret because there is no success.

He's the type who likes to walk up to people who are overweight in the supermarket and say, "Haven't you had enough already?"

He was a four-letter man in high school. He never did learn the rest of the alphabet.

He has a great outfit on tonight. It's not often that you see a suit and toupee made out of the same material.

Here he is...a legend in his spare time.

What an outfit. Don't let anyone tell you that burlap doesn't hold a crease!

He's so dumb, he thinks that Taco Belle is a Mexican phone company.

This man is a household word. And that word is wax-buildup.

He's not the greatest looking guy. In the high school play, he was the only guy who could play a hit-and-run victim without using any makeup.

He's more than a friend to me. He's a total stranger.

As a kid, he always had his nose in a book. He never had a handkerchief.

He's just like the guy next door--if you live in a very weird neighborhood.

He belongs to a club for introverts. At their meetings, no one ever shows up.

He's half Mexican and half Jewish. His father was a migrant stock broker.

He's really fat. When he was in the Navy he served as an anchor.

He's the idol of his family. He's been idle for years.

He doesn't drink coffee in the morning because it keeps him awake all day.

He likes to reminisce with people he doesn't even know.

He's the strong, silent type because he can't talk and hold his stomach in at the same time.

I asked her what she thought of Red China. She answered, "It's all right, as long as it doesn't clash with the table cloth."

He gives the kind of performance that gives failure a bad name.

He used to be spic and span. Now he's more span than spic.

He's so fat, that if he gets on an elevator, it better be going down!

He's a man who cares. When I was in the hospital, and I was given three months to live, he sent me a calendar. You don't forget things like that. He also had the courtesy to tear off nine of the months.

This man is responsible for selling more radios than anyone I know. For when he went on the air, I sold mine, my sister sold hers, and all the neighbors sold theirs.

He's a little weird. He came to the dinner wearing one black shoe, one brown shoe, and three white socks.

He never forgets a friend...big deal. He only has two!

He tried to join Paranoids Anonymous, but they wouldn't tell him where they held their meetings.

As a kid he was an only child, and he wasn't his father's favorite.

Earlier today his doctor examined him for an insurance policy and couldn't find one.

He hasn't many faults, but he makes the most of the ones he has.

His ship finally came in, and sure enough there was a dock strike.

His wife married him, because she couldn't resist anything fifty percent off.

It's a miracle that he can speak to us tonight. He's recovering from an unusual accident. He was struck by a thought.

He has what every man wants--respect, admiration, a Snoopy lunchbox.

He walked into a clothing store and asked, "What do you have for a man in my size?"
The clothing salesman said, "Pity."

He arrived here from New Jersey. Broke. Illiterate and uncouth...and nobody has ever been able to take that away from him.

He has the perfect face for radio.

He was lonely as a child, so he thought he'd become involved in extra-curricular activities in high school. He decided to go out for the debating team, but other students talked him out of it.

Here is a man with his shoulder to the wheel, his nose to the grindstone, and his ear to the ground. Worst posture you ever saw.

He's dejected today. He bought a whirlpool for his bathtub and lost three of his best ships.

I will say only one thing for him. He's always given this company an honest day's work...sometimes it's taken him a week to do it.

He really has it. I hope it's not contagious.

Cheap? He works all his crossword puzzles up and down so he doesn't have to come across.

He's aquadexterous. He can turn the hot and cold bathtub faucets off and on with his toes.

He's a lactomangulator. He always destroys the pour spout on a milk carton trying to get it open.

He took a dollar out of his wallet, and Washington was blinded by the light.

You have a beautiful future behind you.

He's very meticulous. Who else do you know that eats potato chips with a knife and fork?

He's just a guy who's trying to get ahead...and he certainly needs one!

He's really morbid. He's the only person I know who knows all the words to "Taps".

He's so morbid, that he goes through the newspaper's obituary page every day and crosses out the names in the phone book.

He's got a great head on his shoulders, which shows what plastic surgery can do.

Who wears your good clothes?

He's in the stationery and hardware business. He sells pencils in a tin cup.

He's so anemic. Two vultures flew over him the other day, and one looked at the other and said, "We're too late. Somebody already beat us to him."

I knew he was thrifty when I borrowed a vice from him and there was toothpaste on it.

He's a real gem. After they finished with him, they threw away the shovel.

He used to go to school every day with his dog. But then one day they separated. His dog graduated.

There's a guy who goes through life being a horrible example.

Here's a man who has definitely proven that anyone can grow up to be an also ran.

He's a dynamic guy. His emotions run the gamut from A to B.

He's superstitious. He won't work on any day that ends in the letter "Y".

He's a real nature lover--in spite of what it did to him.

One good thing about him. He's such an egotist that he never goes around talking about anyone else.

He's such a loser that even his junk mail arrives postage due.

He reminds me of a blister. He never shows up until the work is finished.

He told me, "I may never have graduated from Colgate, but I do use their toothpaste."

Once again our guest of honor served his fellow man. Today he let a guy with just two items go ahead of him in the supermarket. Those two items were a note and a gun.

He's suffering tonight from food poisoning. He bit his tongue.

He can count his friends on the fingers of a catcher's mitt.

He never lets his mind wander. It's too small to go out by itself.

He read that just as many accidents happen in bathtubs as do in airplanes, so he hasn't been in either one since.

He was an ugly kid. He went to parties and played spin the bottle. If you didn't want to kiss him, you had to pay him 25¢. Would you believe that by the time he was twelve he owned his own home!

I'm proud to say that I'm a friend of _____, and it isn't easy being a man's only friend.

Being short really isn't such a handicap. Did you realize that he's gone through his entire life without ever having been told to duck?

He took a course in speed reading, and it really helped. Now he moves his lips a lot faster!

He's somewhat awkward. For example, yesterday he cut his knee while shaving.

He's just been named "Man of the Year". And that gives you an idea of what kind of year it's been.

You have about as much promise as a tuba player with asthma.

I think that it's great that you've willed your brain to science, but don't you think you should have waited until you were dead?

I need you like a trombone player needs arthritis.

He's so unlucky. Why if today he bought a carnation green house, tomorrow they'd cancel Mother's Day.

If you gave it a decent home, maybe your mind wouldn't wander.

He dislikes Daylight Saving Time. That's because he looks so much better in the dark.

Here is a man who has always taken the time to listen to our problems-- and add to them!

Our honoree has the hands of a surgeon. They're always gripping a golf club.

He was so lonely as a kid that his mother hung a pork chop around his neck so that the dog would play with him.

In all the years I've known him, no one has ever said a bad word about him. It usually takes several paragraphs.

Always a gentleman, as a youth he helped little old ladies across the street. Which wasn't easy. He lived in Venice.

It has been said that the human body is the apex of fine art. His is more like a cave painting.

He has a lot of polish, but it's all on his toenails.

His talent has never been questioned or even mentioned.

Here is a man of rare gifts. I know, because I never got one from him--nor has anybody else.

If I ever wanted to get a heart transplant I'd want his--it's never been used.

Here is a man with no equals--only superiors.

Here he is, a legend in his own mind.

You could say that our guest tonight is talented, witty, urbane, intellectually gifted. You could say that--but not if you're under oath.

He hurt his face at a party last night--bobbing for french fries.

He recently had a head transplant performed and it was considered minor surgery.

He does the work of three men--Harpo, Chico, and Groucho.

He is a man who has a firm grasp of the obvious.

He has more talent in his little finger than he does in his big finger.

I won't say anything about his efficiency. However, his previous job was with the post office--but he couldn't keep up with the work pace.

You might say he lacks savoir faire. Who else do you know that goes to the ballet and asks, "May I cut in?"

He's not a born loser. He had to work at it.

He's a confident individual. You can tell by observing the forceful stride he takes while being walked to work by his mommy.

What's the difference between Harry and a canoe? A canoe tips.

There's nothing I wouldn't do for Bill, and there's nothing that he wouldn't do for me. And that's the way we are, going through life doing nothing for each other.

Just a word about Harry's character. If he had been George Washington, he would have double-crossed the Delaware.

He's so dumb, he once tried to knock on a revolving door.

He once took an IQ test and couldn't spell IQ!

He drooled so much during the Miss America pageant that they had to put downspouting on his La-Z-Boy.

I won't say he's an animal, but the only one who'll go near him is Marlin Perkins.

He's so absent-minded. On his way to work this morning he slammed his wife and kissed the door.

Some people climb the ladder of success. He walked under it.

Yesterday, someone told him he had a great memory--but he can't remember who it was.

He regularly practices TM--that's Total Mediocrity.

He's so polite that the doormat in front of his home says, "You're More Than Welcome..."

Tonight we honor a man whose limitations are limitless.

He's a real pessimist. He wears a medic alert bracelet that says, "In case of accident, I'm not surprised."

After him, they didn't break the mold...they fixed it!

When it comes to diplomacy, the art of communication and how to make friends and influence people--our guest of honor is a man without peer--although_____ (name a dull person) comes pretty close.

(response) Obviously a thought just entered his head in search of privacy.

If you had lived, sir, you'd have been a very sick man.

Unlucky? You're looking at the only person who had his luggage lost on a flight to Fantasy Island.

He's the only guy I know who wears a medic alert bracelet that says his next-of-kin don't want to be notified.

He's the fastest comedian around. He has to be with his act.

He's the king of the one-liners, alright. That's because he can't remember two lines.

Talk about unlucky. Today his artificial flower died.

He has no class. For him, soap on a rope is jewelry.

When he started out, he didn't have a nickel in his pocket.
Now after thirty years of hard work, he has a nickel in his pocket!

He's so lazy that he stands in a revolving door and waits.

Money goes through his fingers like glue.

We've all heard the expression, "The worst is yet to come."
Well, he just arrived.

He has a very even disposition...always rotten.

He's a vicious guy. He gives half of his money to piranha research.

His mind seems to wander but fortunately it's too weak to go very far.

He said, "What's the idea of telling everyone I'm stupid?"
I said, "I'm sorry. I didn't know it was a secret!"

He said, "What kind of idiot do you think I am?"
He replied, "I don't know. What other kinds are there?"

He's a fugitive from the law of averages.

In a world of tuxedoes, he's a pair of brown shoes.

He's not himself today, and it looks as if he got the best of the deal.

He has the makings of a perfect stranger.

He has no luck. Last week his swimming pool burned down.

He hates to get up in the morning. It keeps him awake the rest of the day.

He's a little strange at a party. Who else orders Perrier with club soda?

He sleeps just like a baby. Every two hours he wakes up crying.

He's such a meathead that he shampoos with Beef and Shoulders.

(to a short person) He recently did a benefit for "Save the Shrimp".

(dull) He's on the dull side. As a kid, every Halloween he used to dress up as a librarian.

Everytime he gets in an elevator, the operator says the same thing: "Basement?"

The apartment supervisor tells me to wipe my feet in my apartment before I go out in the hall.

He's so short it looks as if somebody pressed the down button on his elevator shoes.

He's a real practical joker. He drives people crazy by putting "Page Two" at the tops of telegrams.

He's the kind of guy who would fill a neighbor's bathtub with hot water and pour in fifteen boxes of Jell-o.

He's listed in Who's Through.

You have a very striking face. How many times were you struck there?

Why don't you send your wits out to be sharpened?

He's got about as much chance to succeed as a guy with a wooden leg in a forest fire.

Your photo does you an injustice. It looks like you.

He's so unlucky that his wax fruit went rotten.

He won't use Listerine because he heard their ad, "It kills germs on contact," and he doesn't like the idea of anything dying inside his mouth.

Here's a very productive man...a man who has made up in apathy what he lacks in ambition.

The psychiatrist said to him, "Here are some sleeping pills."
He asked, "When should I take them?"
The psychiatrist said, "Whenever you wake up."

Cautious? He was told that most accidents occur 20 miles from home, so he moved to a town 50 miles away.

His father gave him a bat for his birthday. The first day he played with it, it flew away.

His wife said, "Take out the garbage." He said, "I already did." She said, "Go out and keep an eye on it."

For three years his son's been going to a private school, and his son still won't tell him where it is.

Last week he told his wife, "A man is like wine. He gets better with age." So she locked him in the cellar.

He was fired from his job as an elevator operator because he couldn't remember the route.

He bought new snow tires, and the next day they melted.

He invented a parachute that opens on impact.

He bet $10 on a football game and lost. Then he bet another $10 on the instant replay and lost again.

Through the years he's constantly risen to new heights. I know. I've seen his expense accounts.

He's been compared to the Vice-President of the United States. No one can figure out what either one does.

For 80 years he's put his nose to the grindstone which means it must have been a beaut when he started.

You've been listening to the famous Chinese toastmaster, On Too Long.

I don't know how to put this, but you've given dullness a bad name.

People say that he stands out in a crowd. Of course he hangs around with the Seven Dwarfs.

Here is a person of limited skills who did not master the art of waving bye-bye until he was eleven-years old.

His face looks like his hobby is stepping on rakes.

He's so ugly that mosquitos close their eyes when they bite him.

When I told him that Michaelangelo painted the Sistine Chapel on his back, he said, "Wow, didn't it come off when he took a shower?"

Men like him don't grow on trees, they usually swing from them.

He could make enemies at a Dale Carnegie course.

When he came into the room someone told him to go to the end of the line. He said, "I can't. Someone is already there."

Tonight we salute him for having done so much for the city...he did so, by moving to the suburbs.

He had another great weekend. He went over to the court house and ran through the sprinklers.

He should go on a diet. He discovered this morning that he could touch his toes...but only with his stomach.

In gym they made him quit climbing the rope because he kept getting lost.

He's dull. He spent another great weekend rearranging his sock drawer.

He took a Bufferin, but it lost interest on its way to the brain.

Eat? Halfway through Thanksgiving dinner he called out for pizza.

Ladies and gentlemen, here he is, the world's only living brain donor.

He's a marvelous public speaker who got his start in the business announcing the blue-light specials at K-Mart.

Something came into his mind and then went away. Maybe it was lonely.

He got his good looks from his father. His father was a plastic surgeon.

"I read your book last week and enjoyed it. Who wrote it for you?"
"I'm glad you liked it. Who read it to you?"

Someone gave him a pair of cufflinks, so he had his wrists pierced.

When he was born, his parents were disappointed. They were hoping for children.

Here's a guy who's living proof that you don't have to be nice to finish last.

Tonight we salute _____ ,last year's poster boy for Dull.

When he walks through the electric eye at the supermarket, the doors don't even open.

It's one thing to be neat, but who has a crease in his socks?

Tonight we honor a man who doesn't know the meaning of the word fear, he doesn't know the meaning of the word quit. And so we all chipped in to get him this dictionary.

(if you go on late) I know the hour is late, and it's been a long evening, but I don't intend to leave this mike until I've told you every good thing I know about our guest of honor. (Pause). Thank you and good night.

That's a beautiful rainbow tie you're wearing. Look, it has a pot at the end.

One of his outstanding features is his glorious head of hair. I feel it's nature's way of compensating for what's underneath.

He and his wife nearly froze to death at the drive-in movies. They went to see Closed For The Season.

Since he's become more decisive he does the wrong things more quickly.

He named his pet zebra Spot.

He's mean. A rattlesnake wouldn't bite him out of professional courtesy.

He's so dumb, he bought a motorcycle with an air-conditioner.

He's so dumb, he follows the Miss America pageant on radio.

He just got a set of matching luggage--two A&P shopping bags.

He's so short, he wasn't born and raised. He was born and lowered.

They asked me to say a couple of words about him--how about short and cheap?

As Marc Antony once said, "We come to praise him, not to bury him." But the vote was pretty close.

This man is to his profession what a gum ball is to a gourmet dinner.

He was eliminated from the eighth grade spelling bee on the word M&M's.

I believe he has delusions of adequacy.

He's not an only child, but his mom says if he had been born first he would have been.

He had trouble with the new bathtub he just bought so he called the plumber. "The water keeps running out..."
The plumber said, "Did you remember to put the plug in?"
He said, "I didn't even know it was electric."

We were puzzled as to why he only scored 42 on his IQ test, and then we learned that he had used the wrong end of the pencil.

I'm here to squash all those nasty rumors that he wears a toupee. He just has naturally cheap looking hair.

For the last few years he has worn an executive beeper so he can be consulted on all important decisions like sugar or plain, regular or black, doughnuts or Danish.

I sacrificed a lot to be here for _____. Mostly my self-respect.

Usually we roast the ones we love, but today we break that tradition.

I'd like to thank our previous speaker, a man of many talents. As we all observed, humor isn't one of them.

The thing I like most about him is that I never get the feeling that he knows something that I don't.

I didn't even know that they made designer jeans in chubby.

He's so lonely that he has a doormat that says, "Amway salesmen welcome."

Fat? For his birthday I bought him something that was form-fitting. A tent.

He's an amazing man. He can write the Gettysburg Address on the head of a pin. What makes it truly amazing is that he does it with a crayon.

If we learn from all our mistakes, someday he's going to be a very smart man.

When he gives a speech there's never a dull moment. Hours, yes!

In a raucous world here is a quiet man. He speaks quietly, never lifts a hand in anger, and is always ready to settle a dispute through compromise. If there was just one word to describe him, that one word would be "Chicken".

His parents were in the iron and steel business. His mother used to iron and his father used to...

He wanted to take One-a-Day vitamins but he couldn't figure out the dosage.

His mom was embarrassed because he was so ugly. She knitted him a turtleneck sweater with no hole.

He was born at home, and when his mother took a look at him they had to send her to the hospital.

I went over to his house the other night and found his wife and him dancing to the Nixon tapes.

I'll remember this evening for as long as it takes me to get to my car.

He was so ugly when he was born that the doctor slapped his mother.

He's so bland he walks into an empty room and fits right in.

That's a nice suit you're wearing. Do you think it will ever come back in style?

They call him Sanka because he has no active ingredients in the bean.

I wouldn't have recognized him, for I hadn't seen him in four years. But I never forget a suit.

They named a town after him--Marblehead, Massachusetts.

He lost his mind when a butterfly kicked him in the head.

He has all the charm of a wrong number.

He is always lost in thought--that's because it's unfamiliar territory.

He had his name legally changed to Hilton, so that it would match the name on his towels.

He is a man of letters. He works for the post office.

He is a model husband--but not a working model.

He's so dull he couldn't even entertain a doubt.

He's so polite that he wouldn't even open an oyster without knocking on the outside of the shell first.

He could write the story of his life on a piece of confetti.

He's so dull, he even looks forward to dental appointments.

His mind is in terrific shape. He rarely uses it.

I just hope you live as long as your jokes have.

He enjoys Scotch taping worms to the sidewalk so he can watch robins go crazy.

(muscular athlete) There he is...body by Nautilus, brain by Mattel.

He's not exactly ready for the computer age yet. He just figured out how to work his View Master.

He's so slow, it takes him an hour and a half just to watch 60 Minutes.

What an ego! Who else do you know who sends himself a Valentine's card?

I wish you were somebody so you could make a comeback.

He's laid so many eggs, chickens now picket his act.

He was adjusting his tie in front of the mirror tonight before this awards dinner and asked his wife, "Honey, how many great men do you think are in the world today?"
"One less than you think," his wife replied.

He's so short that when it rains he's the last one to know.

I like the way you wear your teeth--parted in the middle.

I like the way you dress. Who cares whether or not it's in style?

He's a self-made man, and it's sure nice of him to take the blame.

I've enjoyed talking to you. My mind needed a rest.

I think you're great. But what do I know?

In honor of him, they recently tore down the house in which he was born to make room for a vacant lot.

Nobody is perfect, but you really take advantage of it.

Childhood impressions can last a lifetime. When he was a kid, his father said, "Now don't go getting any bright ideas..." and sure enough, he hasn't!

Optimistic? If he had been on the Titanic, he would have said, "Oh, it's nothing. We're just stopping for ice."

Just last year, our guest of honor won an award for originality and creative imagination. The bad news is that it was from the IRS.

Are you always this stupid, or is this a special occasion?

Aren't you glad now that you didn't throw away that suit ten years ago?

He is always lost in thought--and that's because it's unfamiliar territory.

He's a man of few words but he keeps on repeating them.

He has a strapping physique. Unfortunately the strap is broken...

Don't say he's full of hot air. But if summer rolls around, and you want the kids' pool blown up, he's definitely the man to call.

He was an imaginative kid. Instead of painting swastikas on synagogues, he went around painting Rx's on Christian Science reading rooms.

He's an aggressive man. You know those paper towel dispensers that say Take One? Well, he takes two!

He's so strong, he can pitch horseshoes while they're still on the horse.

We learned he just redecorated his home. He put new padding on the walls.

ROTTEN DAY

For kids. How to be rotten inside when the weather is rotten outside.

- Cut out all the pictures in the encyclopedia and send them to Grandma.

- Pour red food coloring in your bath water and become an Indian from the waist down.

- Dig out Mom and Dad's wedding pictures and laugh uncontrollably for an hour.

- Play trampoline on the couch.

- See if you can make bubble gum from scratch. Heat one cup of white syrup until it boils and then add two balloons.

- Color your parent's marriage license.

- Get a ruler and find out how much toothpaste is left in the tube.

- Call the phone company and find out how much it cost to put an extension phone in the shower.

- Try to teach your dog to roller skate.

I feel like the guy who has lockjaw and seasickness at the same time.

The way things have been going for me lately, if I bought a pumpkin farm they'd cancel Halloween.

Dates? Hey, my phone doesn't even ring when I'm in the bathtub.

It was a nightmare. When I finally got to sleep, I dreamed that I was awake.

 **RUSSIA**

The youths have a great game in Russia. Like hide and stay hidden.

We just worked out a reciprocal trade agreement with Russia. We're sending them 4,000 cars from Detroit--and they're sending us 20,000 parking spaces from Siberia.

Names of Russian TV soap operas:
- One Day to Live
- The Last Day of Our Lives
- Bowling for Food
- Marx and Mindy
- Love Barge
- Leave it to Brezhnev

But the best one was about a man who had the opportunity to leave Russia and go to the United States but didn't. It's called, "That's Incredible."

The slogan for the Russian Express Card is "Don't Leave Home."

People in Russia can complain about the government all they want-- once! That is if they give their names, addresses and telephone numbers.

A Russian marathon runner was asked the secret to his success. "The team uses the Russian border as the finish line," he replied.

The American coach inquired of the Russian coach as to how his Olympians had broken three world track records in the dashes.
"That's easy," answered the coach. "We use real bullets in the starting guns."

The Russians now have a submarine that can surface and resubmerge in 22 seconds. You really have to take your hats off to them--especially the ones that are left on deck.

The party is upset because someone just broke into the Kremlin and stole the results of next year's election.

DO-IT-YOURSELF
SPACE.

WRITE YOUR
OWN JOKE
HERE!

SALARY

An employee found a note in his paycheck which read: "Salary is your personal business, a confidential matter, and should not be discussed." Signing his receipt, one of the workers added: "I won't mention it. I'm as ashamed of it as you are."

SALES

We will close this sales meeting with one last bit of advice. Hang in there, and remember that no sale is complete until the customer's invoice is loused up by the computer.

Somebody once did a painting of our sales department. It was a still life.

I'm good at making excuses for our sales department. It could be that we have such a great product that we hate to part with it.

"We appreciate your business, but your account has been overdue for ten months now. Already we've carried you longer than your mother did."

I see the sales charts have hit a new high. I looked at them upside down.

Have you ever had the feeling your sales department couldn't sell batteries on Christmas morning?

Talk about super salesmen! He could sell carbon paper to Xerox.

Did you ever get the feeling that your sales force couldn't peddle pickles in a maternity ward?

An example of redundancy is a still-life painting of our sales department.

 **SALESMEN**

My hero at the sales meeting is the one who moves that the minutes of the last meeting be accepted without even hearing them read.

Lady to a salesman: "I am not in the market for a vacuum cleaner. But the Smiths next door are. We borrow theirs all the time, and it's in terrible condition."

A judge said to a salesman: "Do you mean to tell me you need to get off jury duty because your company can't do without you?"
Salesman: "No, sir, I know they can do without me. I just don't want them to find out."

A salesman began his pitch to a housewife: "I want to show you an article that several of your neighbors told me you couldn't afford."

My real estate agent is such a super salesman. He sold me a lot last week that is two feet under water. When I went back to complain, he sold me a houseboat.

Boss to salesman: "I'm not saying you're in imminent danger of being fired, but you might have noticed, Henderson, that I did loosen your pin on our sales map."

A super salesman remarked, "When times get tough, I only work half days. And you know, it never seems to matter which twelve hours I work."

We used to have a man who said, "I take orders from no one." And that cost him a job in our sales department.

This weekend I read some light fiction. Last week's expense accounts.

Our salesmen have great imaginations. The trouble is that they put it all in their expense accounts!

We have one salesman who couldn't sell Blue Cross to Humpty Dumpty.

Salesman: "If you buy this freezer, you could save enough on food bills to pay for it."
Housewife: "But we're buying a car on the busfare we save, paying for a washer on the laundry bills we save, and paying for a house on the rent we save. We just can't afford to save anymore right now."

I was a brush salesman, and a woman opened the door in her negligee, which is kind of an odd place to have a door.

I know a fella who is making a fortune selling Think Big signs to pygmies.

A fella wrote to a company and said, "I'm interested in your product but don't send any salesmen." Three days later, a salesman appears. The fella says, "I thought I said, 'No salesmen.'"
The salesman replied, "I'm the closest thing to 'no salesman' that we have."

Boss said, "You've been like a son to me. Insolent, surly, unappreciative..."

I try to stick up for our salesmen. Maybe we have such a great product that they hate to part with it.

He's received offers from four publishers for the fiction rights to his expense accounts.

He's so persuasive that he could get Leonard Bernstein to conduct a jug band...he could sell an Indian blanket to Mrs. Custer...sell a carton of cigarettes to the Surgeon General...sell a marrriage manual to the Pope.

The salesman claimed, "This encyclopedia will tell you just about everything you need to know."
"See, I told you I don't need one," replied the man of the house. "I'm married!"

Sales have really skyrocketed since the boss came up with the idea of taking the pins out of the map and sticking them into our salesmen.

SCHOOL

Student: "The Declaration of Independence was really important. It was all written in italics."

The teacher was giving away Snowball, the class' pet rabbit. Billy begged his mother to send in a note saying he could be eligible for the drawing. Not wanting another pet, but figuring the chances were 28 to one that Billy would win, she consented.
That afternoon, Billy raced through the front door with Snowball saying, "I won! I won!"
The mother questioned, "You mean out of the whole class, you won the bunny?"
"Not exactly," said Billy. "I was the only one with a note."

Parent to teacher: "We realize our son is hyperactive. We just don't know what to make of him."
Teacher: "How about a nice rug?"

The three best things about teaching? Motivating young people, shaping the next generation, and opening up young minds. Or perhaps it's June, July and August.

Student: "Well, I was close to the right answers on the test. They were only two seats away."

He has a rather weak educational background. He attended a school for emotionally disturbed teachers.

Teacher: "Who was the smallest man in history?"
Student: "I suppose it was the Roman centurion who fell asleep on his watch."

It's a wise father who burns all his old report cards.

A student offered this answer on an astronomy test. "The moon is more important than the sun. The moon gives us light in the evening when we need it, but the sun only shines during the day when we don't need it."

He started a protest against a tuition hike at his correspondence school by beating up the mailman.

He dropped out of correspondence school complaining that there was no one to play with at recess.

The teacher announced to the class: "Today is Groundhog Day."
A boy whispered, "Boy, am I glad I packed my lunch today!"

A student wrote in an essay, "Life in Colonial times wasn't easy. Kids had to play video games by candlelight."

The teacher asked, "What cultural contribution did the Phoenecians make?
A bright lad called out, "Blinds!"

A student wrote on his exam paper, "Views expressed on this paper are my own and not necessarily those expressed by the textbook."

An elementary student wrote in an essay, "We get our parents when they are so old that it is very hard to change their habits."

The boy's report card read, "Alan is a fine student, but he talks too much."
The father's written reply read: "You ought to meet his mother!"

I know that a lot of you envy teachers, but any teacher will tell you that ten weeks in the summer is not nearly enough time to allow their eardrums to heal.

A school librarian said to a noisy student: "Please be quiet. The people in here can't read."
The boy said, "Why, they should be ashamed of themselves! I learned to read in first grade!"

Principal to second grader: "It's very generous of you, Tommy. But I don't think that your resignation would help relieve our over-crowded situation."

Billy, what is an indentured servant?
A slave with false teeth?

Teacher: "If we breathe oxygen during the day, what do we breathe at night?"
Student: "Why nitrogen, of course."

Teacher: "What happens to the human body when it is immersed in water?"
Student: "The phone rings."

Teacher: "If your father made $300 a week and gave half to your mother, what would she have?"
Student: "Heart failure!"

A third grader going through the cafeteria line on a day when peanut butter and jelly sandwiches were being served: "Finally, a home-cooked meal."

A parent asked his child what a zero was doing at the top of his paper. The lad said, "Mrs. Fisher ran out of stars so she gave me a moon."

How would you punctuate this sentence: 'I saw a $5 bill on the sidewalk.'
Student: "I'd make a dash after it."

He was the teacher's pet in school. She couldn't afford a dog.

I asked a student, "If the President of the United States died, who do you think would get the job?"
He replied, "Probably a Republican undertaker."

Child: "Today we're invited to a small P.T.A. meeting. Just you, me, and the principal."

He used to write answers on his fingernails. He once became so nervous during a test that he ate the entire Preamble of the United States Constitution.

I got an "F" on my report card, and my father was really proud. I told him it meant phenomenal.

My high school teachers really respected me. They had to. I was older than they were.

I got two "A's" on my report card...one in Pat and the other in Williams.

I was kept after school so often I got two diplomas...one from day school and the other from night school.

I asked my father, "Dad, where are the Himalayas?"
He answered, "Look, you lost 'em, you find 'em!"

A kindergarten teacher is one who knows how to make little things count.

My mother visited my teachers so often, the kids elected her class president.

At our high school, the guy voted most likely to succeed didn't graduate.

Have you noticed that teachers never put kids down anymore? My son had a comment on his report card that he was very skillfull at using visual aids for learning. I called the teacher and asked the meaning and she said, "He copies from the kid in the next seat."

My daughter brought home a health quiz with an essay question, "What are rabies, and what can you do about them?"
Her answer was, "Rabies are Jewish priests, and there's nothing that can be done about them."

Teacher: What are the three great American parties?
Student: Democratic, Republican and Tupperware.

Thinking back on my school days, words fail me. In fact, so did half of my teachers!

I didn't exactly play football in high school, but I was towel boy for the glee club.

Educators say that at least 50% of students graduating today can't do simple percentages; well, it could be worse...it could be four times that!

Has your boy's education been of any value?
Yeah, it's cured his mother of bragging about him!

Not all Texans are fabulously wealthy...someone has to teach school.

The teacher took her class to a museum of natural history. When the first grader got home from school that day, the father asked, "What did you do in school today?"
The boy replied, "Well, first we went to a dead circus."

My son refuses to study history. He claims they can make it faster that he can learn it.

First grade teacher to husband, after returning to first day of classes after summer vacation: "It's like trying to hold 27 corks under water at the same time."

September is the time of the year when parents realize why teachers need three months off every year.

Aren't you concerned about the Seven Dwarf Syndrome that afflicts our schools today? One out of every seven students is Dopey.

His latest report card reveals that he's courteous, attentive, prompt, and dumb.

A little learning is a dangerous thing--but it still beats total ignorance.

We had a tough gym teacher. He made us play bombardment with golf balls. I mean when you were out, you were really out!

My nephew prefers young teachers. He thinks it's fun to watch them age.

Some people think that we should get rid of all the guns, knives and brass knuckles in our school, but I don't agree. The teachers need something to protect themselves with!

"I know I don't get the best grades in school, father," a boy said. "But do you get the highest salary at your office?"

A boy walked into the living room and announced, "Dad, I've got good news for you. Remember when you promised me $5 if I passed school this year? Well, I'm sparing you that expense."

A successful businessman was invited to give a commencement speech. He offered, "Remember, class, there's nothing as important as education. Through education we learn two twos are four, four fours are eight, eight eights are--and then there's geography."

A teacher asked her pupil, "Is the world round or flat?"
The child thought a minute and replied, "I guess it's neither because my dad's always saying it's crooked."

I'm a little worried about the students' lack of basic geographical information these days. Like the senior who told me he planned to go to Hawaii this summer on his Harley Davidson.

A kindergarten girl came home all excited. "Mom, I won a prize today in school for guessing how many legs a hippopotamus has. I said, 'Three'."
"Three? How did you ever win with an answer like that?"
"I was the closest," the little girl replied.

A teacher asked her students to list the nine greatest Americans of all time. Albert was taking a long time. His teacher asked, "Are you almost through, Albert?"
"Yes," Albert replied, "but I'm having a really tough time picking the shortstop."

Our school superintendant reassured us that the quality of education in our district is tops in all 48 states.

Summer's almost here, so remember, kids, you only have several more weeks to give your teachers nervous breakdowns.

When your children come home from school and you ask them what they've learned that day, do you ever get the idea that they're majoring in shrugging?

Teachers really need more money to do their jobs. Do you realize what a gun, whip and chair cost these days?

High school seniors will soon be getting their pictures taken for the yearbook. What a challenge! The kid has got to act natural without looking stupid.

I was thinking about my old rival from school the other day, who told me before he graduated, "Someday I'm going to be a household word." I wonder what Joe Draino is doing?

The teacher said, "Order, order."
Some kid from the back row says, "I'll have a Big Mac, fries and a Coke."

I once played hooky from school, and my mom got a thank you note from the teacher.

Principal says, "What would you do if you were in my shoes?"
A kid answered, "I'd polish them."

He was in school for two terms...Nixon's and Johnson's.

The president of our class was someone who could read his diploma without moving his lips.

Not all kids are smart. They need role models, too. That's why schools have gym teachers.

Just remember, old principals never die, they just lose their faculties.

September is when millions of bright, shining, happy faces turn toward school. They belong to mothers as they wave good-bye to their children.

When I was in kindergarten, I flunked nap. To make it up, I had to sleep all summer.

In school, he was a four-letter man. And those letters were D-U-M-B.

My teacher told me that I'd never grow up to be President, but with my absentee record I might make it to the Senate.

Wife to husband: "Sam, you'd better help Johnny with his homework while you can. Next year he goes into the fourth grade."

"Nobody likes school," he complained. "The teachers don't like me, the kids don't like me, the superintendant wants to transfer me, the school board wants me to drop out and the custodians have it in for me. I don't want to go to school."
"But you have to go to school," replied his mother. "You are healthy. You have lots to learn, you have something to offer others. You are a leader. And besides, you are 45 years old and you are the principal."

A report card convinces parents that they don't have to be weight lifters to raise a dumbbell.

I can't say that I was in the top half of my class, but I was in the group that made the upper half possible.

You've got to wonder about some of the students taking tests today. One fella got his name wrong. What makes it so unbelievable is that it was a multiple choice test.

My seven-year-old came home from school and said, "Guess what? Today we learned how to make babies."
I said, "What? Tell me, how do you make babies?"
She said, "Easy. Drop the Y and add IES."

The only fella whose problems are all behind him is a school bus driver.

Can you tell me anything about the great philosophers of the 9th century?
Yeah, they're all dead.

The good news is there's less graffiti in the schools these days. The bad news is that there's less graffiti because the kids can't write.

Where are the tenth graders? I spent the three happiest years of my life in tenth grade.

"Here's my report card, and it's bad again. What do you suppose my problem is--heredity or environment?"

Teacher: "Bobby, where's the English Channel?"
Bobby: "I don't know. We don't have cable."

Teacher: "Who said, 'I have come to bury Caesar, not to praise him.'?"
Bill: "I think it was the undertaker."

Adult education will continue as long as kids have homework.

He was such a bad kid in school that his parents used to attend P.T.A. meetings under an assumed name.

In school we always used to wonder why all the shop teachers were missing one finger.

Did you hear about the school teacher who was injured? She was grading papers on a curve.

I visited the elementary school the other day and saw a familiar figure with snowy, white hair. It was my son, and he had just clapped the blackboard erasers.

Teachers I know say they aren't opposed to school prayer, provided that after morning prayer they can pass the collection plate.

If a little learning is a dangerous thing, most kids in school today have nothing to fear.

He kind of felt left out in school. In the high school orchestra he was given the ukelele part for Beethoven's Fifth Symphony.

My history teacher was so old, she didn't teach history. She remembered it!

The class went to the zoo, and the teacher asked, "What's the plural of lion, Johnny?"
"Lions," Johnny answered.
"What's the plural of sheep, Beth?"
"Sheep," Beth replied.
"What's the plural of hippopotamus, Harry?"
"Who would ever want two of them?" Harry asked.

A first grade teacher was filling out her district's annual medical questionnaire. She came to the question, "Have you ever had a nervous breakdown?" She wrote in, "No, but watch this space for developments."

A school troublemaker was in the principal's office for the fifth straight day. The principal said, "This is the fifth day in a row you've been in my office to be paddled. What do you have to say for yourself?"
"I'm sure glad it's Friday," the kid replied.

An elementary class was on a field trip to a museum. "D-Don't look," advised one of the pupils. "If we look, we'll have to write about it tomorrow."

"Did you make the debating team?"
"N-n-n-o. Th-th-they s-s-aid I w-w-wasn't t-t-tall enough."

When he was in school, the teacher told him to stand in the corner and his head fit perfectly.

A teacher was lecturing her class on the importance of truthfulness and honesty. She illustrated her point: "Now children, if I put my hand into a man's coat pocket and took all his money--what would I be?"
"You'd be his wife!" shouted a youngster.

"The teacher really must like me," a boy reported to his father. "I heard him tell the principal, 'I wish he were my kid for just ten minutes.'"

How about it--computers are now in elementary schools. They even have one in my daughter's kindergarten class programmed to match up the kindergartners with their mittens and boots.

One student wrote on her history test that the first woman doctor was Dolly Medicine.

A little boy said to his teacher, "I ain't got no pencil."
She corrected him, "I don't have a pencil. You don't have a pencil. They don't have any pencils. Is that clear?"
"No." said the student. "What happened to all them pencils?"

The school I went to had 37 students--36 Indians and me. One time we had a school dance, and it rained for 36 straight days.

Discussing a recent fire at school, one first grader said, "I knew it was going to happen. We've been practicing for it all year."

The school I attended was really advanced. One day I dropped my notebook on the floor, and by the time I bent down to pick it up I had missed a year of calculus.

"Don't blame me for flunking history!" cried the boy. "They keep asking me about things that happened before I was born."

The government has a student loan program. Now who do you know that wants to borrow a student?

I'm sure I would have gotten off to a better start in school if they had put "See Spot jump" in simpler language.

It's a little discouraging to send your kid through high school and college and find a parrot has a greater vocabulary.

You can always tell a teacher, but you can't tell him much.

Only one thing kept him from going to college--high school.

SECRETARY

My secretary gets acute depression because she realizes that she spends half her week being put on hold.

She can type fifteen words per minute if the wind is with her.

He asked a secretarial applicant, "How many words can you type per minute?"
"Big or little?" she questioned.

It's hard to describe my secretary. Let's put it this way, she has a manual typewriter and an electric eraser.

(to boss) "I'm not late. I took all my coffee breaks before coming in."

A new secretary complained: "My boss is really bigoted. He thinks that words can be spelled only one way."

I don't think our new secretary is too bright. Two hours ago, I asked her to look up the phone number for Zaleski's Flower Shop. When I passed her desk she looked up at me as she was thumbing through the phone book and said, "I'm already up to the 'G's'."

I asked his secretary how she could be so organized and happy after working all these years with him. She said, "Simple. I just don't listen to him."

He's always trying to impress visitors to the office. He said to his secretary, "After this meeting, I want you to call my broker."
The secretary replied, "Stock or pawn?"

Boss: "You should have been here at nine o'clock."
Secretary: "Why, what happened?"

She's near-sighted. This morning she tried to dial the pencil sharpener.

Boss: "Do you realize the importance of punctuation?"
Secretary: "Yes, sir, I always get to work on time."

She went to secretarial school and took courses in Lunch Hour, Coffee Break, Water Cooler Etiquette, and Office Collections.

She has a four-drawer filing cabinet--just perfect for losing things alphabetically.

Your typing is improving. Only three mistakes. Now type the second word.

"While I was away did you take any messages?"
"Why, are you missing some?"

What a unique secretary I have. The other day she made four copies without an original.

Carbon paper is the wonderful invention that permits your secretary to make eight mistakes at the same time.

I have a very honest secretary. She didn't come to work yesterday. She called in lazy.

My new secretary is really sharp. Just the other day, she discovered that the dictionary is in alphabetical order...One time she took three weeks to look up the word zoology.

I had to tell my secretary that when the bell rings on her typewriter that that doesn't mean that it's time for another coffee break.

Everyday the secretary was 20 minutes late. Then one day she slid snuggly into place only five minutes tardy. "Well," said her boss, "this is the earliest you've ever been late."

Don't forget, this is National Secretaries Week. Why not go all out and have your secretary make an extra-big pot of coffee in her honor?

My secretary stopped answering the phone. She said, "It's always for you."

Good secretaries are hard to find these days. We knew right away that we couldn't hire one applicant when she misspelled P.S. on the application blank.

I have a secretary who files seven hours a day. She has the most beautiful nails...

She can only do 30 words a minute...not typing...reading!

She's very thorough. I mean, who proofreads Xeroxes against the orginals?

I have a complete office staff--a tall secretary for long hand, a short secretary for shorthand, and a midget secretary for footnotes.

My secretary had an awful accident last week. She broke her typing finger.

She has a perfect attendance record. She hasn't missed a coffee break in five years.

She never makes the same mistake twice, but she has a great knack of making new ones.

She asked, "Do you like your letters double-spaced?"
I said, "Yes."
She replied, "Carbons, too?"

SELF-MADE MAN

He claims to be a self-made man...another example of shoddy American workmanship.

He's a self-made man. He must have taken estimates and accepted the lowest bid.

He's a self-made man which makes you wonder why he ever wanted to make himself that way.

He's a self-made man who should have never quit the job before it was finished.

He's a self-made man who should have never hired such cheap labor.

He's a self-made man who should have consulted an expert.

He's a self-made man who's the worst example of unskilled labor I've ever seen.

He's a self-made man who apparently knocked off work too soon.

He's a self-made man. Too bad he left out the working parts!

He's a self-made man. But if he had to do it all over again, he'd probably call in someone else.

 ## SENIOR CITIZENS

The government has a new plan to use midget postmen to make your social security checks look bigger.

You know that you are getting old when you stop laughing at all those health remedies advertised on TV and you start buying them.

I'm at the age that when I bend down to tie my shoes, I'm not sure that it will be a round trip.

You know that you're getting up in years when the newspaper phones and tells you that they'd like to update their obituary files.

You're starting to get old when your kids come home from school and tell you what they're studying in history, and you remember studying that as current events.

You're getting along in years when your insurance company sends you its calendar, six months at a time.

They don't make mirrors like they used to. The ones I buy now are all full of wrinkles.

Little Cindy's grandmother had just had a pacemaker installed. She bragged to her teacher and first grade classmates, "I bet I have the only grandmother in town who operates on batteries."

He knows he's getting older. His bank sent him half a calendar.

Old age is nice. That's the perfect period in life when people come to your birthday party just to stand around the cake and get warm.

He's so old, he recalls having a pet dinosaur. When he went to school they didn't have history.

You know you're getting old when you stoop to tie your shoelaces and ask yourself, "What else can I do while I'm down here?"

A little gray-haired old lady helps you across the street. She's your wife. Do you mind being old? Well, it's not bad when you consider the alternative.

A highlight of the senior citizens' Halloween party was the game "Bobbing for Dentures".

He says that one of the really nice things about old age is that you can whistle while you're brushing your teeth.

One of our senior friends describes arthritis as 'twinges in the hinges'.

Old people shouldn't eat health foods. They need all the preservatives they can get.

I know he must be old. Somebody told me that when he was teaching English, he used to teach Shakespeare.

A new after-shave lotion for husbands over 65: "Old Spouse."

You know you're getting old when you get winded gumming a mint.

When he was a boy, the Dead Sea was only sick.

Two kids were reading the obituary column in the newspaper. One said, "What's an octogenarian?" It says, 'Mr. Herzog was an octogenarian.'
"I've no idea," said the other, "but they really must be sickly. Every time you hear of one, he's dying."

I went to his last birthday party, and all his friends seemed so old. Everytime I put down my glass, someone was putting his teeth into it.

A few years ago we almost lost him. He nearly overdosed on Geritol.

If you think she looks great tonight, you should see her in the morning when all the wrinkles are rested.

His wife stops him from eating between meals. She hides his teeth.

Social Security is backwards. Why don't they let me loaf and enjoy myself now, and have me work when I'm 65 and have nothing to do?

Did you ever notice that the older generation talks about the younger generation as if they had nothing to do with it?

"I just bought the finest hearing aid money can buy."
"How much was it?"
"Oh, about ten after two."

I'm not saying he's old, but his Social Security number is printed in Roman numerals.

Old? He not only remembers when they introduced Daylight Saving Time; he can recall when they switched the calendar from B.C. to A.D.

You're getting old if your feet hurt <u>before</u> you get out of bed.

He forgets things. Like he can't remember if he came over on the Pinta, the Nina, or the Santa Maria.

On his last birthday, he went to blow out the candles, and the heat drove him back.

He's 93-years-old, and he still has that gleam in his eye. And that's because he keeps missing his mouth with his toothbrush.

You know you're getting older when you have to put tenderizer on your puffed rice.

He's at the cereal age. That's when you feel your corns more than your oats.

Bingo was invented for people who are too old to play shuffleboard.

The best way to brush your teeth is to hold the brush in your right hand and hold your teeth in your left hand.

You know you're getting old when...
your little black book contains names which only end in M.D.
you get winded playing chess
your children begin to look middle-aged
you sit in your rocking chair and can't get it going.
your knees buckle, but your belt won't.
dialing long distance wears you out.
your back goes out more than you do.
you sink your teeth into a good steak and they stay there.
everything hurts and what doesn't hurt, doesn't work.

They say that old age is in your head--as anyone with bifocals, dentures, a hearing aid and a toupee already knows.

You know you're getting old when you open the refrigerator, and you can't remember whether you are taking something out or putting something in.

You know you're getting old when you try to straighten the wrinkles in your socks, and you aren't wearing any.

You know you're getting old when you need a transplant, and the surgeon tells you that they no longer make parts for your body.

She's been pressing forty so long it's pleated.

He has a prospectus for an old-age home marked "Urgent".

You know that you're getting old when they light the candles on your birthday cake, and the air-conditioner automatically switches on.

You know you're getting old when the birthday candles cost more than the cake.

His doctor told him to slow down so he got a job with the post office.

You know you're getting old when your favorite exercise is a good, brisk sit.

One thing nice about being seventy. At least you're not constantly being bothered by insurance salesmen.

She's shy about her age--about 18 years shy.

She doesn't look a day over fifty--ten years, maybe.

You know she's really old. Who else do you know who has a recipe for curds and whey?

You know you're getting old when the only thing you can sink your teeth into is a glass of water.

My aunt just turned 36. Before she turned it, she was 63.

He's got young blood, but he keeps it in an old container.

We were able to put all the candles on the cake, but it did take eight matches to light them all.

He's so far up in years, that for his last birthday, his friends gave him an orthopedic cake to support all the candles.

You know you're getting old when the high point of your day is watching your cereal go snap, crackle and pop!

There was an old lady who lived in a shoe, she was on Social Security...what else could she do?

You know you're getting old when you can remember...when Dr. Pepper was an intern...you remember when they gave you a 12-month warranty on your car, and you didn't need it.

"How do you live to be a hundred?"
"Well, first you get to 99 and then you live very carefully for a year."

A newspaper reporter ended his interview of the 99-year-old man with, "Well, I hope I can come back next year and interview you on your 100th birthday." The senior citizen said, "I don't see why not. You seem in pretty good health."

Her last birthday cake looked like a prairie fire.

When we lit all the candles on the cake, we barbecued the ceiling.

She's so old her Social Security number is Two.

She was named after Betsy Ross, and not very long after, either.

It's time to worry when you start receiving get-well cards from your friends, and you haven't even been sick.

A police officer stopped a senior citizen who breezed past in a car while he was directing traffic. "Madam," he asked, "didn't you see my hand raised? Don't you know what that means?"
"Yes," she retorted, "of course I do. I taught school for forty years."

She gets her hair done at a place that picks up and delivers.

He's 75 but looks like a million.

He's so old that the picture on his driver's license was done by Van Gogh.

Old? I had a slice of her birthday cake, and on my slice alone there were twelve candles.

Old? She has a driver's license for covered wagons.

She had the lemon concession at the Boston Tea Party.

She is loyal. Years ago she reached an age she liked and stuck with it.

The toughest part of getting it all together after you're fifty, is that you can't remember where you left the parts.

We had grandma's pacemaker installed with a dimmer switch. To quiet her, we turn it down. But when we need the house painted, we turn it up full blast.

She said, "John, when we were first married, remember how you used to tickle me under the chin? Do it again."
John said, "Okay, but which one?"

You know you're getting hard of hearing when the oil tank explodes in your basement and you say, "Gesundheit!"

He's so old that if you flattened out all his wrinkles he'd be six-feet-ten.

He's at the age where he has to locate his hearing aid before he can ask where his bifocals and slippers are.

I don't mind growing old. It just takes so long.

You know you're getting old when given a choice of two hobbies you choose the one that you can do sitting down.

You know you're getting old when you need that first cup of coffee in the morning in order to stay up during the Today show.

He's at the age where he bends over twice to pick up something once.

You know you're getting old when there is too much room in the home and too little room in the medicine cabinet.

SIGNS

I saw a strange sign in a jewelry shop window: "Ears pierced while you wait."

SKINNY

Skinny? When he answers the door at a party, people hang their coats on him.

He's so skinny that he has only one stripe in his pajamas.

He's so skinny that he has to run around in the shower just to get wet.

He's so skinny that he has to wear skis to keep from going down the bathtub drain.

He's so skinny that he can't keep his seat down at the movies.

SLEEP

I'm not an early riser. If I get on a flight at noon, I call it the "red-eye."

SMALL TOWNS

We had to cancel our parade in Salunga this year due to a severe confetti shortage.

In our town, a highway patrolman will stop you, and holler, "Pull over, boy." Then tell you, "Okay, boy, take this ticket and write down what I tell you."

The death rate in Salunga is one of the lowest in the nation. No one wants to be caught dead there.

The town was so small that the "Welcome to" and "You Are Now Leaving" signs were on the same pole.

For excitement on weekends we go over to the hospital and watch them rip off all the old bandages, and then go over to Woolworth's and watch them throw out all the dead goldfish.

Our town is so small that our power plant is a Die-Hard battery.

Our barber shop quartet only has two members.

They wanted to install a traffic light in Salunga, but they couldn't decide on the colors.

Salunga's annual Ben Franklin Kite Flying competition will be held underlined-outdoors this year.

We finally got a new fire truck in Salunga. They used the old one to answer false alarms.

Our town is so small that the Masons and the Knights of Columbus know each other's secrets, so they formed a coalition, and they call themselves the Masonites.

Our McDonald's has a sign that reads, "Over four sold."

In our town if you own a painted turtle, they call you an art lover.

Our newspaper is "The Daily Denture." It comes out every night.

The only thing we need in Salunga is a good detour.

In Salunga, the "Late, Late Show" starts at 7:30.

Salunga is a typical small town with a post office, gas station, general store, and speed trap.

The nice thing about living in Salunga is that there's no such thing as dialing a wrong number.

The Salunga Park couldn't afford to buy a duck for the pond, so they got a pigeon with swim fins.

The auctioneer at the Salunga Auction interrupted his spiel and announced, "A gentleman in the room has lost his wallet containing $2,500 in cash, and is offering a reward of $500 for its return." A voice from the back of the room said, "525".

Residents of Salunga have long life-spans. In fact, folks in our town are so healthy, we had to shoot a couple just to get the cemetery going.

For excitement on Saturday nights, my buddies and I would go to the gas station and stomp on the hose, just to hear the bell ring.

Salunga is sort of like Cleveland, but without the sparkle.

Happiness is seeing Salunga--in your rear-view mirror.

Have any big men ever been born in Salunga? No, only babies.

The difference between Salunga and yogurt is that yogurt has an active, living culture.

The biggest sport in our home town is sitting on the front porch on a hot day, and watching the tar bubble in the street.

Well, what do you think of Salunga? Let me put it this way. It's the first time I've ever seen a cemetery with a street light and a stop sign.

Our town's number one industry is taking returnable bottles back to the super market.

Our town is so dead that the largest department store is the Decay Mart.

Our town is so small that the town bully is a midget.

They just named the local farmer the fire chief. They had to--they're using his garden hose.

Salunga is so small that the telephone directory only lists first names.

On slow weekends we like to go to the gas station and watch the Coke machine sweat.

Salunga was discovered by a famous explorer looking for a place to die.

Salunga is so dull that our traffic light is black and white.

Salunga finally built a college. They think that it's going to make up for not having a high school.

They've just started integrating with mandatory busing, which is kind of stupid since we only have one school.

If it wasn't for the Salunga Fire Company our home would have burned to the ground in an hour. Those guys kept the fire going all night.

I heard some bad news. The Salunga Symphony Orchestra had to cancel its performance of Beethoven's Fifth. The fellow who played first ukulele quit.

A highlight of our year is the annual linoleum festival.

Our town is so dull that they print the newspaper three weeks in advance.

We live in Salunga near the airport. Once the tower called when their radar wasn't working and asked me to leave the bedroom light on.

The big show on educational TV in our town is Hee Haw.

When they wanted to paint a white line down the center of our highway, they had to widen the highway.

Our library burned to the ground last week and we lost both books in the fire.

Our town is so small that the all-night diner closes at 7:30.

I'm a little worried about our town bank. Yesterday, one of my checks came back marked Insufficient Funds. Now what bank doesn't have $25?

Our town is so small that the statue at the courthouse is a private.

We held our talent show last week. It lasted a minute-and-a-half.

Our town is so small, our zip code is a fraction.

The road map is actual size.

Salunga is so small we have a 2-H Club.

Our fire company consists of 18 midgets with Waterpiks.

We used to have a local beauty pageant, and it was so pathetic. There was one girl with buck teeth, thick eyeglasses, knock knees and pimples--and every year she used to enter it. What made it pathetic was--she won.

Our town is so small that our Howard Johnson's has only one flavor.

Salunga is so small that the last one in bed each night has to turn out the street lights.

We're spraying my hometown for fruit flies. We have a guy in a hang glider with a can of Raid.

I've just been named Grand Marshal of the Salunga Beef Jerky Festival.

Our town is so dull that the tour bus doesn't even have windows.

Salunga is such a small town that the train only stops once a month-- for laughs.

I used to be a dog catcher in Salunga for two years, and then I lost my job. I finally caught the dog.

Once a guy in Salunga tied his wife to the railroad tracks, and she starved to death.

A visitor was staying a week in Salunga, and it was rainy and miserable the whole time. He asked a boy, "Doesn't it ever stop raining around here?" The boy replied, "I don't know. I'm only eight-years-old".

Our town has a ten o'clock curfew so that people will stay up longer.

We got confused in Salunga last year. Election day came close to Thanksgiving, and we stuffed the ballot boxes and voted for turkeys.

We don't have a jail in our town. If someone commits a crime, we make him stand in the corner.

Our town is so small that the town charter is written on Smurf stationery.

Our only heavy industry in Salunga is our 250-pound Avon lady.

Our town is so bad that Charles Kuralt once drove through Salunga with his eyes shut!

Our town is so small that at our four-way stop sign, only two directions go anywhere!

In Salunga you can always spot a funeral procession. The lead tractor always has its light on.

Our town is so small that the school crossing guard only has to look one way.

In Salunga, bubble gum cards are a part of the great books series.

Our town is so small our bowling alley only has seven pins. A perfect score is 211.

In my hometown even the yogurt has no culture.

We hired a guy as traffic commissioner. Next week we're going to go out and get some traffic for him.

What's the smallest book in the world? Who's Who in Salunga.

Recently they held a beauty contest in Salunga, and nobody won.

What's the smallest building in the world? The Salunga Hall of Fame.

On weekends we watch reruns of the Lawrence Welk show and count the dancers who dip.

In Salunga, cottage cheese is found in the gourmet section of our supermarket.

Salunga is the geographic center of the surrounding area.

Salunga may be a small town, but its mortality rate averages just one per person.

The Salunga Aquarium was forced to close. Our clam died.

I don't know about this year's winner of the Miss Salunga pageant For her talent, she pulled a piano across the stage with her teeth.

A truck ran out of control and smashed right through the walls of a suburban home. The embarrassed truck driver couldn't think of anything to say, so he asked the old lady, who was sitting on the couch, "How do I get to Fernwood from here?"
The calm, old lady said, "Go straight past the dining room table and make a right at the piano."

We used to have two windmills, but we took one down. We only had enough wind for one.

Our town is so small that we don't call policemen fuzz. We call them lint.

If your house catches on fire, our fire department offers ashes in rare, medium, and well-done.

On Saturday we'd go down to the Foto-Mat and watch the changing of the clerk.

We don't have crime in our streets. Well, let me clarify that. We have crime. We just don't have streets.

The bully in our high school always used to pick on me. But I got even. I married her!

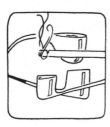# SMOKING

Do you realize that if it wasn't for coughing, some smokers wouldn't get any exercise at all?

He wanted to try the new smokers' tooth polish but he couldn't get the stuff lit.

# SNAKE CHARMER

A snake charmer and an undertaker got married. Their towels were marked hiss and hearse.

Do you ever feel like a Hindu snake charmer that's working with a deaf cobra?

SNOW

I just saw the abominable snowman. It was a kid who charged me $10 to shovel the walk.

I just can't stand to see my wife shovel snow--so I pull down the shades.

There's no chance that my car will be snowed in this winter. I've got front wheel drive, snow tires, anti-freeze, a shovel for the driveway and a son with a girlfriend downtown.

SOLAR ENERGY

I'm not so sure about the potentials of solar energy. My son has spent most of his life on the beach, and he has less energy than anyone I know.

SON'S ROOM

My wife keeps worrying about cockroaches in my son's dirty room. I told her, "Cockroaches? Do you think a cockroach would go in there? Never in the history of the world has there been a kamikaze cockroach."

Spring is here and it's time for us to make our annual decision about our son's room--either clean it and sweep it, or plow it and plant it.

I'm really concerned about our ten-year-old son. I don't know what's come over him. Last night I caught him in the bathroom experimenting with a strange, new chemical compound--soap!

SPANISH

Our daughter took Spanish in school this year, and this past Saturday she thrilled us all by translating the label on a bottle of Taco sauce.

SPEAKER

I'll never forget my first speaking engagement. It was for a group "on a tight budget that can't afford much for an honorarium." But they more than made up for it by not listening very closely.

A long-winded speaker, presenting a travelogue said, "There I stood, drinking in the scene, with a giant abyss yawning before me." One lady interrupted and asked, "Was the abyss yawning before you got there?"

He's going to speak his mind because he realizes he has nothing to lose.

Unfortunately, our speaker, who was to have spoken on the topic, "How to Solve World Problems," cannot be with us this evening. He couldn't find a babysitter.

An ideal speaker is one who has a plane to catch in twenty minutes.

He's a veteran after-dinner speaker. All you've got to do is open his mouth, drop in a dinner, and up comes a speech.

Normally during this part of the program, we would have our speaker field a few questions. But since our speaker is a (losing team's) fan, we'll just have him boot a few around.

(toastmaster to speaker at dinner) "Shall we let the crowd enjoy themselves a little longer, or shall we have your speech now?"

I gave a speech last week that will be remembered for a long, long time. It was to a group of elephants...

He's got rapid delivery. He can tell six jokes in one minute. That's true because his is never interrupted by laughs.

A host told a speaker addressing a Texas audience, "You're on a rigid time schedule. Don't go over twelve minutes."
When the speaker hit his thirteenth minute, he heard the click of several guns. He paused and said, "Surely you wouldn't shoot a guest speaker?"
"No, sir, that would be downright rude," said a man in the audience. "We're a gunnin' for the man who invited you."

"Must you fall asleep while I'm speaking?"
"No, sir. It's purely voluntary."

An American on business in Hong Kong was seated next to a Chinaman. During the course of the meal, the American inquired, "Likee soupee?" The Chinaman grunted, "Yes." Next he asked, "Likee meatee?" Same response. After the meal, the Chinaman got up and gave an eloquent speech for a half an hour, using perfect English. When he sat down, he turned to the American and asked, "Likee speechee?"

Subbing for a great speaker reminds me of the sign in front of a southern church which read, "Annual Strawberry Festival. All the delicious strawberry shortcake you can eat--$2.50. Everyone welcome." Then at the bottom, a small notice had been tacked on: "P.S., due to the severe drought this year, we are serving prunes."

I don't mind when people look at their watches while I'm speaking, but it does bother me when they start to shake them.

A master of ceremonies introduced a speaker with a lengthy eulogy, filled with platitudes. When the speaker got up, he said, "After such an introduction, I can hardly wait to hear what I am going to say."

An emcee is a man who eats a meal he doesn't want so he can get up and tell a lot of stories he can't remember to people who have already heard them.

I'd rather hear him speak than eat. I just heard him eat.

"The speaker we had last year really made a hit."
"Oh, really? What did he speak about?"
"Oh, about ten minutes."

He can take any dull and boring topic and render it drab and lifeless.

He puts a lot of fire into his speeches...now if we could only talk him into putting his speeches into the fire...

(after speech) Well done, Bill. Those of us still awake salute you.

The Getty Law of Public Speaking: If you don't strike oil after the first five minutes, stop boring...

Thank you. He just always seems to have so many words left over after he has run out of ideas.

Thank you. Whatever that speech lacked in content, you more than made up for in length.

Tonight he's going to give his famous "Stockyard Speech." A point here, a point there, and a lot of bull in the middle.

(when room is too hot) They said that this room would be air-conditioned, and they were right. I've never seen air in such condition.

I get hundreds of requests to speak. One just poured in today.

Speaker to audience: "As I understand it, it's my job to speak and your job to listen. If you get finished before I do, please let me know."

He's known for his after-dinner speaking. After dinner, you can always find him speaking on the telephone when the waiter brings the check to the table.

I've been informed that this is an express podium for speakers with ten thoughts or less.

He once gave a banquet speech, and after five minutes there wasn't a dry eye in the house. Everyone had nodded off into the soup.

He used to practice with marbles in his mouth. Then one day he got the hiccups and broke two mirrors and a picture window.

I feel like a mosquito in a nudist colony. I know what I'm supposed to do, I just don't know where to begin.

That was certainly a speech to be remembered. Not repeated...remembered.

"I have only ten minutes and hardly know where to begin."
"Good, begin at the ninth."

He's a speaker that has never gone back on his words. It'd be too long a trip.

Speakers are a lot like mushrooms. You never know if you're getting a bad one until it's too late.

(if you're addressing a group of TV repairmen or other profession) I don't know why I was asked to speak to you. I don't know anymore about television repairing than you do.

The other night I overheard a woman say to her husband, "That certainly was an inspirational speech, wasn't it?" Her husband said, "Yeah, but thirty minutes of rain would have done us a lot more good."

(when you have a laugher in the crowd who laughs prematurely) "Not yet, Evelyn, wait till the punchline."

I was up all night thinking about this speech. Wouldn't it be ironic if the speech that kept me awake puts you to sleep?

First rule of public speaking: Nice guys finish fast.

The world's best after-dinner speech is, "Waiter, I'll take both checks."

In just a couple of minutes we'll be hearing from the guy with the super-tough tonsils. He's backstage right now gargling with starch.

(after speech) Of all the speakers we've ever had, he's certainly one of them...

(after speech) Of all the speakers we've ever had, you're certainly the most recent.

Mr. Chairman, thank you for that introduction. I certainly admire the way that you didn't let the facts interfere with what you had to say...

Do not photograph the speakers as they are addressing the audience. Shoot them as they approach the podium.

He's been making audiences laugh for 11 years. Unfortunately, he's been in the business for 16 years.

I'm certain that our next speaker will give us a lot of food for thought-- and I'm certainly glad. The chef sure didn't give us any food for eating!

As a speaker, he's not a total loss. He can always serve as a bad example.

You're much better than our last speaker. He talked for over an hour and a half and never said anything. You only took fifteen minutes.

I've practiced this speech all week and I feel pretty good about it. So, if you can just manage to look a little more like the bathroom mirror, we'll get on with it...

There are only two things more difficult than making after-dinner speeches. One is climbing a wall leaning toward you, and the other is kissing a girl leaning away from you.

The speaker got up to the podium with a large band-aid on his chin and remarked, "I was thinking so hard about my speech while I was shaving this morning that I cut my chin." After the long talk, an audience member said, "He should have kept his mind on his chin and cut his speech."

Before coming to speak tonight, we negotiated a price and settled on $1500. So I wrote a check for $1500 to your organization, and they let me speak to you.

I have two talks, a 15-minute talk and a half hour talk. They're both the same speech. I lose my place a lot.

I haven't exactly made the greatest impression in my field. You've heard of "Who's Who"? I'm in "Who's He?"

The program chairman told me the essence of a good speech is to have a beginning and an end, and keep the two as close together as possible. So, in conclusion...

(if the microphone is low) Who were you expecting? Mickey Rooney?

(take a drink of water) As you can see, this is a prepared speech. All you add is water.

I will not make a long boring speech introducing _____ He will... I love this place. I've come here for the last six years, and I look back on them as the best years of my life. Which will give you some idea of what a miserable life I've been leading.

I don't want to seem immodest, but last night after I had concluded my speech, the program chairman said I really ring the bell. Well, he didn't exactly say that. What he said was that I was the biggest ding-a-ling he had ever heard.

Heckler: Tell 'em all you know. It'll only take a minute. Speaker: I'll tell 'em all we both know. It won't take any longer.

Whenever I hear a speaker say, "I just don't know where to begin!" Some small voice within me says, "Near the end."

He couldn't get a standing ovation if he finished his speech with the Star-Spangled Banner.

(opening remarks) My publisher called and gave me the good news that I had just sold my millionth book. The bad news was that there are still 999,999 left.

At my first speech I was so nervous that I bit my nails so often that my stomach needed a manicure.

Everyone was on the edge of his seat. Later on I learned that they were just mustering the courage to get up and leave.

I told the audience that my book would be read long after Homer and Plato had been forgotten. Someone in the audience yelled, "And not until then."

My humor is like history...it repeats itself.

I sent a manuscript for my joke book to the publisher, and he said that his side ached because of it. I said, "Did you find it that hilarious?" He said, "No, I fell asleep on top of it."

He said that the only way my joke book would get in front of an audience was if it was ground up as confettti. He said, "If you throw it in a fire, at least you'll hear the fire roar."

The most difficult thing a speaker needs to learn to do is not to nod while the toastmaster is praising him.

Always remember the first rule of public speaking. Be brief, no matter how long it takes.

There's a 1978 Buick on the parking lot with its headlights on and the radio blaring. Would the owner please report to the parking lot attendant? They want to hold a memorial service for your battery.

I only have two problems tonight. This suit isn't mine and the jokes are.

You can tell this is a rented tuxedo. Have you ever seen such a fit? Looks more like a convulsion.

(after applause) Was I really that good, or are you just trying to keep your hands warm?

After the meeting we're all going to get together and toast marshmallows on the air-conditioner.

I don't know what it is that makes our meetings so dull, but whatever it is, it works.

Always remember that being able to express your opinion without fear of reprisal is what distinguishes democracy from marriage.

It's a great honor to be here tonight having satisfied the two philosophical requirements of the program chairman: 1-He believes in free speech, and 2-He believes in free speeches.

(to emcee) You remind me of that famous Chinese philosopher, "On Too Long".

You can thank three people for shortening my speech: my partner took a 45-minute speech and made it 30 minutes; my wife took a 30-minute speech and made it 15-minutes, and my secretary took a 15-minute speech and lost it.

A speaker stopped abruptly during the course of his speech to arouse a sleeping man in the audience who was snoring loudly. "Just how long have you been sleeping?" asked the speaker. "Just how long have you been speaking?" came the reply.

During a two-hour speech, the speaker kept taking sips from a glass of water. After the speech, an old-timer remarked, "What do you know. That's the first time I've ever seen a windmill run on water."

I told the program chairman, "Sure, I believe in free speech." He said, "Good, because that's what you're going to be giving."

He's not going to bore you with a long speech. He can do it with a short one.

I predict that tonight's speaker will be interesting and entertaining. I also predicted that the (losing team) would win the Super Bowl.

This will be short because the program chairman informed me that you as an audience have a great way of making long speeches short. You leave.

(after applause) Thank you for that applause. It's always wonderful to appear before an audience that has good taste.

When your entertainment chairman phoned me to do this, I gladly accepted the charges.

A good speech to be immortal, need not be eternal.

Brevity is the heart of a great speech. Step in, step up, step out.

The following speech has been edited for television. I've cut out twenty minutes so that we can all get home in time to see the movie on channel six.

Tonight we were to have a speech on home safety, but our speaker was putting up a television antenna at his home and stepped back to admire the job.

(receiving an award) Thank you for this great award. You have just provided me with the maximum adult daily requirement for joy.

I really don't like giving speeches, but it's the only way I can afford to eat out.

He tells me that this is only the second after-dinner speech he has given. The first was last night when he yelled at his kids at Burger King.

Speeches are like lawns--best when they're kept short.

Here is a reason why we have chicken so often at banquets. Speeches, like chickens, seldom get off the ground.

He's a forthright speaker--about every fourth word is right.

I've learned a lot since I've been on the banquet circuit. For instance, before I started giving after-dinner speeches, I always thought mashed potatoes were supposed to be served hot.

When we announced our speaker for the banquet, we did a turnaway business. People heard his name and turned away.

When he gives a speech, there are no wasted words. He uses every single one of them!

There are two reasons why I am speaking to you tonight. Your program committee was looking for a speaker who is intelligent, entertaining, profound, and irresistable, and they found him. The second reason is, he became ill and they called me.

I made a bad mistake last night. The speaker said, "In conclusion," and I left. I was told today that I missed two-thirds of his speech.

 **SPEED LIMIT**

I think we should all be thankful for the national speed limit. Cars going 55 m.p.h. are so much easier to pass.

SPORTS

When he retired, they didn't give him a testimonial dinner, but some of the guys in the front office had a testimonial snack in his honor.

A couple was given two complimentary seats to a game. The crowd booed as the home team made miscue after miscue. The fellow got up and started walking out. His wife asked, "Where are you going?" "To the box office to buy two tickets so we can boo with the rest of the fans," he said.

Our team's been packing the rafters. We haven't been putting many in the seats, but we've sure been packing the rafters...

Rowing has to be the worst sport. You sit down while playing and go backward to win.

Our team questionnaire says "Bank". One player wrote in "Piggy".

The hardest thing about learning to roller skate is the ground when you come right down to it.

When I got off the plane, there were 20,000 fans pushing and shoving to get near me. If you don't believe me, ask Doctor J. He was standing right next to me.

The team was so bad that they could have played before the "What's My Line?" panel and stumped them.

We lost ten in a row and then went into a slump.

(fat coach) He kept his players in peak condition by having them run laps around him.

Our sprinter was so fast that at the end of a race he had to wipe the bugs off his glasses.

Outside our arena is a sign that reads, "Occupancy of this place by more than 18,000 is unlawful," and might I add, unlikely.

One of our fans was told that we had only two tickets left for the big playoff game, and that they were standing room. He said, "I'll take them if they're together."

Yesterday the newspaper printed the names of 25 people who won't be attending our games anymore. It was the obituary column.

My skiing is really improving. I can now get on the ski lift without falling down.

He really does burn up the track. I looked down after the race, and the track was nothing but cinders.

If people don't want to come out to the ballpark, nobody's going to stop them.

Being a track coach would be so simple. All I'd have to say is, "Okay boys, keep to the left and get back as soon as you can."

Better yet, I'd like to be a cross-country coach. There you just fire a gun, and they all run into the woods.

A guard we scouted was so fast that he could ring his front doorbell, go to the back door, and run through to the front of the house in time to go and let himself in.

"If you were the coach, how would you have played the final quarter of the last playoff game?"
"Under an assumed name."

In a crowded football stadium, an off-balanced fan yelled every two minutes, "Hey, Gus!"
Five rows down, a man would get up, turn around and tip his hat. By the third quarter, the man got up, turned around, and said, "Quit yelling at me. I'm sick and tired of standing. And besides, my name's not Gus."

On our team questionnaire, a line reads: "Length of residence at present address."
One of our players penciled in: "About 40 feet, not counting the garage."

Philadelphia is a great sports town. And the greatest sport of all, is competing to find a parking space.

When I was in college, I helped Wake Forest beat North Carolina three times.
Oh, really? Which team were you on?

I got a useful pamphlet with my new skis. It tells how to convert them into a pair of splints.

"Please send me two tickets to Wednesday's game. If it's good, I'll send you a check."
"Please send us a check for two tickets. If it's good, we'll send you the tickets."

The coach signed a lifetime contract with the university. After two losing seasons, the university president called him into his office and pronounced him dead.

He was asked, "How much pressure do you feel going into the World Series?"
He answered, "Thirty-two pounds per square inch at sea level."

Have you noticed how many major league teams are using mascots to give their fans a laugh? The Phillies have the Phanatic. The Pirates have the parrot. The Indians have their starting lineup.

Colleges are cutting back this year. I heard of one college team that's on such a tight budget, they may have to use students.

I still think our team could play 500 ball if they didn't have to win half of their games to do it.

A referee defines the typical fan as, "A guy who screams from the bleachers because he thinks you missed a call in the center of the interior line, then after the game, he can't find his car on the parking lot."

I've always been quite an athlete myself--big chest, hard stomach. But that's all behind me now.

I've decided to cut back on Sunday TV snacks. My wife saw me getting ready with Pepsi, chips, chip dip, peanuts and pretzels, and said, "Well, here he comes. The wide world of sports."

He had so many operations that his knees look like he lost a knife fight with a midget.

One thing great about playing for this team (cellar dwellers) you don't have to worry about having an off-night.

But remember, professor, if you can get 10,000 people to pay $5 each to cheer your English class, you too, can make as much as the basketball coach.

My high school basketball team was really bad. Sometimes, to avoid embarrassment, the entire team would foul out in the first quarter. Our fight song "Brahm's Lullaby".

Guys begged him to join the team. He was a wide-receiver on the archery team.

Basketball coach: "The trouble with officials is that they don't care who wins."

Coach: "The penalty for being good is that you have to be good every night." In New Guinea some of the tribes have the custom of beating the ground with clubs and uttering spine-chilling cries. Anthropologists call "primitive self-expression". In America, we call it golf.

How can a guy who signs a contract for $3 million be called a free agent?

One of our players was recently asked what the biggest detriment to an N.B.A. player is: ignorance or apathy. He replied, "I don't know and I don't care."

Athletes must learn that they can't stay up there on top forever, as I was telling our waiter tonight, Mark Spitz...

A football running back: "Our offensive line was so good our own backs couldn't even get through it."

One player on a cellar-dwelling baseball team wanted to play all the games on the road because: "We get to hit more than any other team. We always get to bat nine innings, and they only get to bat eight."

This year our basketball team plans to run and shoot. Next season we hope to run and score.

A football coach prior to the draft: "What we need in the draft is a 5-foot 6-inch, 130 pound fullback. That's the biggest hole our offensive line makes."

In college, I used to be a cheerleader for the golf team. I'd go around saying, "Sh-Sh."

We have a great bunch of outside shooters. Unfortunately, we play all our games indoors.

When he underwent a brain transplant he made sure he got a sportswriter's brain. Then he was sure that it hadn't been used.

One of our players was nervous at practice, and the coach asked him why. "My sister's expecting a baby," he replied, "and I don't know if I'm going to be an uncle or an aunt."

The best three years of a sportswriter's life are usually the third grade.

He's an exciting guy. After the big win he went out and painted the town beige.

When he played basketball in college, who will ever forget that magic moment when his teammates lifted him on their shoulders and carried him off the court saying, "And don't come back 'til the season's over!"

We were talking in the locker room about fame and prestige. One of the players said, "To me, prestige is when everywhere you go, people come up to you, call you by your first name, and ask you for an autograph."
A second player said, "No, to me, prestige is going to the White House and the President says, "Hi, Bill, how are Mary and the kids?"
A third player offered, "No, real prestige is being in the Vatican, talking with the Pope, and having the spectators asking, "Who's the man in the beanie with Williams?"

Our track team specialized in shot-put dodging and javelin catching.

That interview caused more commotion than a starving beaver at a log rolling contest.

The Cubs' highlight film for the past season has been nominated for an Oscar as the best short feature of this year. It runs one minute and twelve seconds.

The tickets he got me were so high up in the stadium, I didn't have an usher. I had a stewardess strap me in my seat before the game.

On opening day, only two people showed up for the game. And then the next game attendance really dropped off.

Attendance wasn't great that first year. We had ten players on the team and two more than that in the arena.

I would like to say a few words about last night's thrilling playoff game, but I never speak with my mouth full. And right now, my heart is in my mouth.

There really is such a thing as a natural athlete, but nobody starts out that way.

My salary finally reached five figures this year. After taxes, I earned $599.27.

$40 million dollars for a quarterback! Why I know a doctor that doesn't even make that much!

When I played college basketball, my coach presented me with a letter in my freshman year. The letter suggested that I switch to the chess team.

One of our forwards was so slow that if he ever got caught in the rain, he'd rust.

The crowd at last night's game was so small that each fan had something he'd never had before. His own personal usher.

We lost 15 in a row and then went on a one-game winning streak.

Our team gunner missed practice. Coach said, "We worked on a new play. One where you pass the ball."
The player says, "I'll never be able to learn that one, coach."

I asked the recruit, "What do you run the mile in?"
He said, "Shorts and a T-shirt."

You've been learning for seven years now, and you can only count to ten. What will you become in life if you continue this way?
A referee!

The rookie was so young that he autographed everything in crayon.

I told one of the players, "You smell good. What do you have on?" He said, "Clean socks."

He's such a good bowler that he recently had a gutter named after him.

He stopped playing with the hockey team when they finally got a real puck.

He was once a football player. He wasn't a fullback. He wasn't a halfback. He was a drawback.

He had an aversion to physical contact. When he'd dive into the line on a fake he'd yell, "I don't have it! I don't have it!"

He played a key role in the pennant drive. He got hepatitis. The trainer injected him with it.

What can a coach say after his team's lost 20 straight games, Way to shave, men. Nice sweating, fellas.?

He wasn't a great athlete in high school. Instead of a letter, he got an apostrophe.

Our track team had a cross-eyed discus thrower. He wasn't that great, but he kept the crowds loose.

A kid ran cross country for a college in Texas, and they practiced in prairie land. The coach said, "The only problem with that is, it's so hard to explain to a mother that a coyote got her son."

It's a strict school. No one gets in without the required average: 20 points a game.

I visited my old coach at the nursing home. Found him in his room, sniffing prunes.

He was on the U.S. olympic team as a javelin catcher.

He got me seats for the game. From where I sat the game was just a rumor. I turned to the guy sitting next to me and said, "What do you think of the game?" He said, "How should I know? I'm flying the mail to Cleveland."

My only sports superstition is that it is unlucky to be behind at the end of the game.

Before bed at night I eat a bowl of Rice Krispies and read (sportswriter's) column in the (newspaper). That way, before sleeping I won't have anything on my mind or stomach.

He's so fast that he can turn out the light and jump in bed before the room gets dark.

I find that Superman comic strip hard to believe. Not the part about the x-ray eyes, or kryptonite, or leaping tall buildings, but when have you ever seen a 'mild-mannered' reporter?

The most athletic thing he's ever done has been jumping to conclusions.

He was named the second best college coach of all time.
"I'm flattered, but who was chosen first?" he asked.
"The other 2,011 are tied for first, " was the answer.

Our team folded so fast last season they named a lawn chair after it.

Almost winning a championship is like almost beating a freight train to the crossing.

During a timeout, a ref looked into the stands and saw attendants carrying a woman out on a stretcher. He asked our trainer, "What happened? Heart attack?"
"No," said the trainer. "You called one right and she fainted."

I wasn't much of an athlete in college, but I was waterboy for the swim team.

Hockey is definitely too tough. I mean, what other sport has a team coroner?

The first law for all Philly sports fans--"Don't just stand there--Boo something."

I've watched so much basketball, football, baseball, and hockey on television,I think I've developed Athletes' Seat.

My doctor advised me to stay away from crowds, so I followed his advice. Now I spend weekends at (losing team's stadium).

"My son had to leave a promising career due to fallen arches."
"Was he a basketball player?"
"No, he was an architect."

Our MVP last year said, "I can't begin to name all those who have helped me win this award..." And his teammates seated in the audience were whispering, "But try, please try!"

Unlucky? I got athletes' feet just from watching the Summer Olympics.

SPRING

This is the time of year when you find out who won last spring--the moth balls or the moths.

May is that time of the year when you experience that great feeling that comes from finishing that last piece of Christmas fruit cake.

I looked out the window this morning, and the flowers were so colorful, so fresh, so delicately formed, that you could almost smell the plastic.

Well, here it is, spring again. The time when the economy wrestles with three major surpluses--wheat, corn, and Girl Scout cookies.

STATUE

I was walking through a museum when I noticed a strange statue of a general. I asked, "Isn't that a rather odd pose for a general?"
"Yes," said the museum director. "But the statue was half-finished when the committee found that it couldn't afford a horse."

STOCK BROKER

My broker has a strange sense of humor. He called this afternoon and said, "I have some good news and bad news for you. The Dow Jones is down 50 points, your portfolio is down 60 points, and if you don't come up with $50,000 to cover the margin, we're selling out. And now--the bad news.

I buy Sweet Chariot stocks. The minute I buy them, they swing low.

Wall Street just voted my broker Man of the Year--for 1929!

He can really tell the turns in the market. Six months after every major decline he can be heard to say, "Well, there's another one."

I could be a rich man today. In the early 70's I had a chance to invest in Federal Express, but I thought it was just a 'fly by night' outfit.

One broker told me, "You'd be surprised how many people drive to my office in a Mercedes to take advice from a guy who came to work on the bus."

My stock broker leads a frenetic life. He tosses and turns all night. He calls it "aerobic sleeping."

STOCK CAR RACING

For awhile I was a stock car racer, but I didn't fare too well. I had to make 11 pit stops--six for gas and five for directions.

STOCK MARKET

And now, here's the latest market report. Empire Hemlines are up. 7 Up is down. International Harvester is stable, and Pampers remain unchanged.

I invested half my money in paper towels and the other half in revolving doors...I was wiped out before I could turn around.

"What's the latest dope on Wall Street, Weinstock?"
"My son, Irving," Weinstock replied.

I just wish that for once my stocks would split instead of just self-destruct.

My stock broker believes in seasonal symbols. Last December he hung mistletoe over his office door so that his clients could kiss their money goodbye.

My broker is probably not as bright as he should be. The other day I called him and told him to buy 500 shares of IBM, and he said, "How do you spell that?"

I know of one guy who made $100,000 in the market. He slipped on a grape and sued.

STRIKES

I don't know why school teachers want more money. Who do they think they are--TV repairmen?

SUMMER

I always worry about dumb things at a picnic. Like how many calories are in an ant?

Every summer I think what this country really needs is a vegetarian mosquito.

If you don't believe that this is the land of the free, just let your neighbors know that you own a summer cottage.

"Summertime and the livin' is easy." Try telling that to an earmuff salesman!

Hurricanes do a lot of damage, make a lot of noise, and man hasn't learned how to control them. No wonder they're named after women!

Each summer we send our kids to the most reliable, most secure and least expensive place we know of...Camp Grandma.

This is the time of year when millions of Americans go beyond the challenge of the Rubik's Cube to face the ultimate challenge--refolding road maps!

SUNDAY SCHOOL

Returning from church Sunday morning, the father criticized the sermon, the daughter thought the choir was off-key, and the mother said the organist played loudly. Junior said, "Yeah, Dad, but it was a good show for a nickel, don't you think?"

Small boy: Mom, the Sunday School teacher told us that we came from dust and go to dust.
Mother: That's right, dear.
Small boy: Well, I looked under the couch in the living room, and somebody's either coming or going.

 **SWIMMING**

Experts say that there are certain tell-tale signs when a shark is about to bite. For instance, if he swims up to you and begins to squeeze lemon on your leg, watch out!

DO-IT-YOURSELF SPACE.

WRITE YOUR OWN JOKE HERE!

TAX

My tax accountant is an understanding man. He has an office with a recovery room.

The IRS called a charitable organization and inquired, "Stevenson claims that he gave $10,000 to your organization last year. Did he?" Firm's fund raiser: "Not yet, but he will!"

Note from the IRS: "We sympathize with your problems, but they can't be programmed into our computer."

I've just discovered a great tax loophole, provided you're a 65-year-old student who owns an oil well.

It's getting harder and harder for me to support the government in the style to which it is accustomed.

The IRS auditor had the audacity to question my $10,000 deduction to the family of the unknown soldier.

You know you're in big trouble when your tax advisor calls and asks, "How much do you know about plea bargaining?"

He is honest. On his 1040 form he reported half his salary as unearned income.

I.R.S. agent to taxpayer: "I know you have six children, sir, but we just can't allow $125 as a deduction to the Tooth Fairy."

"We live in such a great country, we should pay our taxes with a smile." "I'd love to. But the government insists on money."

I asked a famous author, "Which of your works of fiction do you consider best?"
He said, "My last income tax return."

Washington is a place where they take the taxpayer's shirt and have a bureau to put it in.

They keep threatening to do something about junk mail, but I still keep getting these tax forms every year.

Income tax time is the time of the year when people who are poor wish they were rich so they wouldn't have to pay any taxes.

He lied on his income tax form last year. He listed himself head of the household.

I've invented a new tax form printed on Kleenex for those of us who have to pay through our noses.

I try to look on the bright side. I figure if I didn't have to pay all those taxes, I'd probably blow all my money on foolish stuff like food and shelter.

I feel there should be a better deadline for our taxes than April 15th. How about February 31st?

Psychiatrist to patient: "And when was it that you first discovered that you love paying income tax?"

They say that by April 15th, 60,000,000 tax returns will have been filed--not to mention all those that have been chiseled.

I know a fella who got one of those calls from the Internal Revenue Service. They asked him to come down to their office and bring his records. He brought his Barbara Streisand records, his Frank Sinatra records...

Fear is taking your kids to remedial math class and seeing your tax accountant there.

Name one person who has money left after April 15th. Henry R. Block.

I wrote a letter to the Internal Revenue Service and told them that I could no longer afford their service.

Withholding tax: Instead of taking it out of your hide, they hide it out of your take.

My accountant, H and R Bonkers says that if I'm audited, they'll stop by and feed my dog until I get out.

Short income tax form: (1) How much did you make last year? (2) How much do you have left? (3) Send the amount listed in #2.

I go to one of those income tax services that speaks up for you if your return is audited. What they say is, "Who?" Their motto is: "Skip the bother and skip the fuss, skip the country, don't come to us."

This year the IRS claims that the forms are so simple that even a three-year-old can understand them--that is if the three-year-old is a CPA.

I got so mad at the income tax form, you know the box that says "DO NOT WRITE IN THIS SPACE"? I dropped a big blob of bacon fat right in the middle. I figured if I can't write in that space--nobody else is going to write in it either.

I was called down to the Internal Revenue Service. They wanted to know why I claimed 50% depreciation on me. Actually, it was my wife's idea. She claims I'm only half the man I used to be...
They also disallowed my seven dependants. They claimed parakeets couldn't eat that much.

This year the government is really simplifying the form. It reads, "What did you earn last year? Send it!"

Why can't the IRS see things my way? I figure if I spend it before I earn it, then it isn't income!

A fellow walked into the IRS with a bandage on his nose. The collector said, "Did you have an accident?"
The man replied, "No, I've been paying through the nose so long it gave way under the strain."

It's hard to believe that this country was founded partly to avoid taxes.

Ask not what your country can do for you. If it does, you will certainly be taxed for it!

He went to a discount tax service that charged him just $5 to prepare his tax return. So, he saved lots of money. But, then again, how much spending money do you need in Federal prison?

I just got done filling out my income tax. Who says you can't get wounded with a blank?

The other day I went down to the Internal Revenue. Thank goodness. I'm all paid up through 1947.

He discovered a great way to avoid taxes. He doesn't work.

Every year I send those people a letter telling them not to renew my subscription, but they keep sending me the new edition of the 1040 form.

My wife always triples her spending in April. She figures I'll just throw it away on the government anyhow.

I must have done the 1040 form wrong. I can't figure it out. I still have 27¢ left.

How do you figure it? It's really bad when you need more brains to interpret the 1040 form that it took to make the income in the first place!

The IRS has a special toll free number for persons having problems figuring their tax forms. It's designed especially for those of us who like to listen to busy signals.

I just had a real scare. I mailed my tax form and a Valentine card on the same day, and I can't remember which one I signed, "Your Secret Someone".

TEENAGERS

I don't really need this job. I can always go back to my old job of explaining what clothes hangers are to teenagers.

Father to son: Do you mind if I use the car tonight? I'm taking your mother out tonight and I'd like to impress her.

Hungry? This kid eats like a babysitter.

I won't say that my teenager eats. But the other day he went to a Chinese restaurant, and the manager had to send out for more rice.

I went to a teenage wedding last week. The couple was so young that half of their wedding gifts were made by Mattel.

TELEPHONES

The breakup of AT&T has caused all sorts of financial problems. They just announced that next year, they will not be able to afford to put the phone book in alphabetical order.

I'll tell you how near-sighted I am. Yesterday I tried to dial the pencil sharpener.

Operator, I'd like to make a long-distance call. How far should I stand from the phone?

When I came home today, my wife wasn't in the house, but I knew she hadn't been gone long. The phone was still warm.

When she's too old to talk, the telephone company is thinking about retiring her telephone number.

TELEVISION

Television is an educational experience. Until I watched a commercial, I never knew that mopping the kitchen floor could be so much fun!

We owe a lot to daytime television. If it weren't for all those game shows and soap operas, millions of women would be out driving.

I just saw a new TV show about an Alaskan dog and an Idaho potato. It's called "Husky and Starch".

There's a new game show on TV for 90-year-olds. It's called "Groping for Dollars".

A new show, coming this fall, "The Incredible Bore". The story of an insurance salesman who traps an entire family in their home and reads them a complete policy.

On today's show of "The Young and the Silly", Marsha breaks her engagement with Bill when she discovers that he likes his toast black. Julie finally musters the courage to tell her parakeet that he's adopted. Lorraine refuses to forgive Sam for chewing aluminum foil in front of her mother. Mary breaks off with Myron because he refuses to stop winking, and Eileen makes the painful decision to sue her dog for defamation of character, slander and getting mud on the couch.

I just got a new trash compactor. It's a TV set with a three-inch screen.

I believe in things that endure--a mother's love, the beauties of nature, the plots on daytime television.

Tonight on "That's Incredible" they profile a taxidermist who stuffs Weight Watchers into taxis.

Television is a wonderful thing. You meet so many new people... particularly TV repairmen. I just met the town's richest man. He's a television repairman who moonlights as an air-conditioner repairman.

Daytime television is not a total loss...Seven states are now using it in place of capital punishment.

Warning! Before retiring, take a week off and watch daytime television.

Television is often referred to as a "medium" because it rarely comes well-done.

What TV really needs is a weatherman who takes requests.

I just got Gillavision--That's 24 hours of Gilligan's Island.

Television is very educational. Just think of all the TV repairmen's children it has put through college.

I use the services of Light Brigade Television Repair. Boy, can they charge!

There's too much violence on TV. Last night I turned the dial and saw punching and pounding and slapping and twisting. That's the last time I'll ever watch Chef Tell prepare bread dough.

TEXAN

They really do things big in Texas. I walked into a car showroom in Dallas, three acres wide and wall-to-wall with Cadillacs, Lincolns, Imperials. And over in the corner there's this little pile of Volkswagons with a placard: "TAKE ONE."

It's such a thrill driving from Fort Worth to Dallas. Where else can you see money belts drying on the line?

I heard of a rich Texan who bought his kid a chemistry set for Christmas--DuPont!

A Texan called his insurance agent and said, "I need you right away. I just hit a Cadillac, bounced off a Corvette, side-swiped a Porsche and hit a Rolls head-on."
The agent said, "My goodness. Was anyone hurt?"
"Just me," said the Texan. "I was parking in my own garage."

And how about the Dallas Cowboy who hated wearing glasses, so he had all his Cadillacs equipped with prescription windshields?

A Texan walked into an exclusive art gallery in New York and in fifteen minutes he bought six Picassos, three Renoirs, ten Cezannes and thirty Wyeths. He turned to his wife and said, "There, honey child, that takes care of the Christmas cards. Now let's get on to some serious shopping."

"You don't have any cavities," the dentist told the Texas millionaire. "Well, drill anyway, doc, I feel lucky today," the Texan ordered.

How about the Texan who was so rich that he bought his dog a boy?

A friend was admiring a Texan's new sports car. "Is it air-conditioned?"
"No, but I always keep a couple of cold ones in the refrigerator," the Texan answered.

He's so rich, he doesn't brand his cattle. He engraves them.

A Texan came into town the other day and wrote a check at our local bank. The bank bounced!

A kid from Texas walks up to Santa Claus and says, "What can I do for you?"

Texas rancher: "I'm tired of riding from one end of the ranch to the other. All you see is Mexico, then Canada, then Mexico again."

Two Texans walked out of their swanky club on a rainy day to go back to their offices. Unable to get a taxi, they took refuge from the weather at an automobile dealer's showroom next door. "There's no sense waiting any longer for a cab, I'll buy us a car," said the one to the other. "No, let me," his friend answered, "You bought lunch."

I knew a Texan who was so lazy that he bought his wife a yacht for Christmas so he wouldn't have to wrap it.

I know an unusual guy who is six-feet-four, wears a ten-gallon hat, cowboy boots, has lots of money, owns oil wells and a cattle ranch. What makes it so unusual is that he lives in Rhode Island.

I have a friend in Texas who collects minatures. He started with Rhode Island.

A Texas sixth grader lost out in the first round of his school's spelling bee because he couldn't spell the word "small".

He's so rich, he doesn't have his cattle branded. He has them engraved.

A Texan was arrested for reckless driving. He was driving without a chauffeur.

Californian: "Why, in my state, we grow a tree that size in a year. How long does it take here in Texas?"
Texan: "I can't say for sure, but I know it wasn't there yesterday."

A guy from Oklahoma is bragging to a Texan: "Why, in Tulsa, they start a 20-story building one day, and in a week it's finished."
The Texan countered, "I was going to work in Dallas Tuesday morning, and they were laying the cornerstone on a 25-story apartment building. When I came home that afternoon, the landlord was putting tenants out for not paying their rent."

A stranger talking to an old-timer in a small Missouri town, "I don't like the looks of those clouds...look just like some we had back in Texas just before a tornado struck."
"Was it a bad one?" asked the native.
"Bad? Why, man, I didn't want to come to Missouri!"

A couple of fruit growers from rival states met at a convention and started bragging about the size of fruits grown in their states.
A man from California picked up a melon and said, "Is this the biggest apple you can grow in Texas?"
"Please!" shouted the Texan. "Don't squeeze the grapes!"

A young cowpoke returning from his first ride was overheard to say, "I never knew that anything stuffed with hay could be so hard."

 # THANKSGIVING

We're having the same thing again for Thanksgiving this year-- relatives.

Thanksgiving this year is at my mother-in-law's house--she's stuffing a can of Spam.

Our last Thanksgiving turkey was so tough that when we shut the oven door it blew out the pilot light.

To counter the weight gain of a typical Thanksgiving dinner, we recommend you get up from the table and jog--to Anchorage, Alaska.

Wow, can my relatives eat! Last Thanksgiving I bowed my head to say grace, and when I looked up, my cousin was handing me an after-dinner mint.

The first Thanksgiving my wife and I celebrated together, she used a recipe that said, "Wrap the turkey in aluminum foil, and roast in oven at 375 degrees until brown. Sixteen hours later, that foil was still silver.

We had bad luck this Thanksgiving. We got the only turkey that went in for jogging.

We should be thankful that the Pilgrims landed in Massachusetts instead of Alaska. Did you ever try to stuff a whale?

I knew that we were in trouble this Thanksgiving when my wife asked me if I'd help her carve the Big Mac.

I crossed turkeys with kangaroos so that next Thanksgiving the ladies will be able to stuff them from the outside.

The trouble with Thanksgiving dinners is you eat one--and a month later, you're hungry again.

This Thanksgiving, let's Xerox our blessings and microfilm all our problems.

One year the turkey was unbelievable. I said, "Where did you get this recipe?"
She said, "It's a very good recipe. I got it out of a magazine!"
I said, "Which one? Popular Mechanics?"

My wife doesn't miss a trick. She stuffed the turkey with left-over tuna casserole.

I always stand in awe of people who sit down to Thanksgiving dinner and eat turkey, stuffing, mashed potatoes, gravy, carrots, rolls, butter, pecan, apple, and pumpkin pie, coffee and ice cream--and then they want to know if there's such a thing as Alka-Seltzer Lite.

We had a wild Thanksgiving last year and I won the wishbone pull and my mother-in-law came down with food poisoning. I never knew those things worked.

Research shows that the average turkey is one-inch longer than the average roasting pan.

The election and Thanksgiving came so close together and people got confused. In our town they voted for turkeys and stuffed the ballot boxes.

Thanksgiving is when mom stuffs the turkey in the morning and the family in the afternoon.

We were going to have turkey for Thanksgiving but _____ had other plans.

My neighbor was complaining: "Grateful? What have I got to be grateful for? I can't pay my bills."
I told him, "Well, be grateful you aren't one of your creditors."

I was going to go to the slums and invite a few people who were down on their luck to come home with me, meet the kids, meet the relatives, meet the in-laws, and then share our Thanksgiving cooking. I didn't do it. I figured they had suffered enough already.

He's not taking any chances on missing any of those holiday football games. He invited the TV repairman over for Thanksgiving dinner.

I'm 35-years-old and am really excited. This Thanksgiving, when I go to grandma's, I get to eat at the big table.

 **THEFT**

I didn't mind when they stole our black and white TV set, or when they stole our color TV, but when they changed the address on the TV Guide, that was going a little too far.

TOBACCO

Tough is chewing tobacco. Real tough is lighting it first.

I just tried chewing tobacco once and I really got sick. Nobody told me you weren't suppose to inhale.

TOUGH NEIGHBORHOOD

Our neighborhood was so tough that both sides of the tracks were the wrong side.

The government had a great plan for our section of town. It was called "Neglect".

Our school colors were black and blue. The team cheer was "Ouch!"

In our neighborhood we never thought about the future. When I was eleven, all I ever wanted to be was twelve.

Our neighborhood was so tough that the Good Humor man came around in an armored truck.

The toughest kid in our neighborhood was Rocco. Where Rocco would spit, the grass would never grow again.

You could always spot the guys from our tough neighborhood on the rifle range. After firing a round, they would take a handkerchief and wipe their fingerprints off the gun.

Our high school was so tough, the school newspaper had an obituary column.

She came from such a poor neighborhood that she got married just for the rice.

We were so poor that we couldn't afford a watch dog. If we heard a noise at night we'd bark ourselves.

I used to beat up all kids on the block except the O'Briens. Had trouble with them. They were boys.

Our neighborhood was so tough that all the tattooing was done by a stone mason.

Talk about quick hands. Their hands were so fast they could steal hubcaps off of moving cars.

We were so poor and my pants were so thin that I could sit on a dime and tell if it was heads or tails.

My neighborhood was so tough that if you weren't home by 9 p.m. the cops declared you legally dead.

I went to a very tough school. In drivers' education we were taught how to run roadblocks.

Our neighborhood was so tough we used to play 'Simon Says' on the expressway.

In my school they had recess every half hour...to carry out the wounded.

We had eleven kids in our family and had to wear each other's clothes. It wasn't funny either, I had ten sisters.

"Your money or your life," the mugger said. "Take my life," said the victim, "I'm saving my money for my old age."

Somebody moved into our neighborhood the other day and they were fired on by the Welcome Wagon.

We were so poor that burglars used to break into our house and leave things.

As kids, mom used to let us lick the beaters before she shut them off.

The first thing that you notice about the guy who comes to collect for the loans is that he's really big. I mean how often do you see someone wearing barbells as cufflinks?

He had his nose broken in four places, and you can bet he won't go to those places again.

Our neighborhood was so tough that when a guy got married the fellas used to tie old shoes to the car bumpers--with the people still in them!

Claims that my neighborhood is tough and unsafe are overblown. Why every night I take my pet python for a walk and no one ever bothers me!

Our neighborhood is so tough the surgeons used to do appendectomies with chain saws.

A bumper sticker in our neighborhood reads: Today Is The Last Day Of The Rest Of Your Life.

Tough? We used to play Frisbee with a live porcupine.

My neighborhood was so tough we used to have our Easter egg hunt on the expressway.

In my neighborhood you could walk twelve blocks without leaving the scene of the crime.

My high school was so tough, our school song was "Taps."

Our high school's favorite cheer was, "Give me a G...give me a U...give me an N."

Our high school was so tough, our creative writing teacher taught us for three weeks on "How to Write a Will."

Our high school was so tough, we had a tomb for the "Unknown Substitute Teacher."

Our neighborhood was so tough, the welcome wagon was a tank. We used to bowl...overhand! Every morning I would make two lists ... things to do...and the other was who I'm going to do them to.

We were so poor as kids we couldn't afford x-rays. The doctor just held us up to the light.

A very tough neighborhood. You know some neighborhoods have an Easter bunny? We had an Easter German Shepherd.

My neighborhood was so tough, our Avon lady was Rocky Marciano.

Our town was so tough that the candy store had a bouncer.

So tough that the most popular form of transportation was a stretcher.

When my parents planned the family budget, they allowed for hold-up money.

The Avon lady went door-to-door selling bullet-proof makeup.

Our school didn't have custodians. The students mopped up the floors with each other.

The kids were so tough in my neighborhood that they ate only the heads off of animal crackers.

My neighborhood was rougher than a stucco bathtub.

Our neighborhood had a tough seafood restaurant with a sign out front that said, "Where the Mobsters Meet the Lobsters."

I lived in a very tough neighborhood. Once I was held up by a guy carrying a chewed-off shotgun.

My grandmother used to sit on the front porch knitting bullet-proof shawls.

It was an Italian neighborhood. Very Italian. In fact, last month the Baskin and Robbins flavor of the month was garlic!

My family was so poor, I was born at home. My mother took one look at me and they had to send her to the hospital.

We were so poor, mom used to take in laundry and keep it.

In my neighborhood we had kids' names like Rocco and Spike. And those were the girls' names!

My neighborhood was really bad...after I moved the mayor tore it down and put up a slum.

UMPIRES

I just saw something that has me troubled. A large-print edition of HOW TO BE AN UMPIRE.

UNDERTAKERS

Did you here about the undertaker who closes all of his letters, "Eventually yours"?

UNIONS

Striker's picket sign: "Time heals all wounds. Time-and-a-half heals them faster."

DO-IT-YOURSELF
SPACE.

WRITE YOUR
OWN JOKE
HERE!

VACATION

This summer we had the best vacation ever. Each day we'd rise early and pile the kids, cat, picnic lunch and sodas into the camper--then we'd go back to bed and sleep.

The ship we took on our cruise was really old. It was insured against fire, theft, and falling off the edge of the world.

If you want to visit "those far away places with the strange sounding names," just let your wife read the road map.

Rain is caused by big, high pressure areas, cold fronts, warm, moist air, and the first day of your vacation.

A couple on a safari were going through Africa when a lion leaped out, attacking the husband. As the lion was about to put the man's head in his mouth, the victim yelled to his wife, "Shoot! Shoot!"
The wife called back, "I can't. I'm out of film!"

Remember, the family that travels together unravels together.

The ideal vacation formula is: Take half the clothes you usually do, and twice the money.

Vacations are no problem for me. My boss decides when I go, and my wife decides where.

My wife is like Noah. When she packs for a vacation, she takes two of everything.

Never go on a vacation when the kids outnumber the car windows.

People really go out of their way to be kind. I had such a rotten vacation that the clerk at the drug store gave me someone else's vacation pictures.

A fool and his money are soon parted. We smart guys wait until we go on vacation.

A true vacationer is one who travels one thousand miles to get a picture of himself standing beside his car.

A native Californian asked, "Well, isn't California the most beautiful vacation state you've ever visited?"
"Not really," said the tourist. "Take away your lakes, mountains, and climate, and what have you got?"

If you're traveling with three young kids in the back seat it really isn't a vacation. It's more like World War III with coloring books.

Every year, thousands of Americans take vacations that are filled with adventure, fun, inspiration and romance. Now if they could only convince the people who develop their slides.

I don't want to seem harsh, but I am convinced that all vacation slides are processed in a solution consisting primarily of Sominex.

A tourist is a person who travels thousands of miles to get a snapshot of himself standing beside his car.

I had an unusual vacation that lasted two weeks. I got in an elevator in a 70-story building right after a kid had pressed all the buttons.

My wife has a different philosophy about vacations. Most people try to get away from it all--she packs it all!

Whenever we go away on vacation, we want to make sure that the house looks lived in. We hook up an automatic timer to a tape deck and then we pre-record an argument.

I'm still a little puzzled about our vacation. How is it possible to visit eight different countries and every one of our souvenirs is from Hong Kong?

I got so seasick on that cruise that I now get queazy when someone just opens a box of salt water taffy.

We went mountain climbing. The guide said, "Don't slip. We're up 9,000 feet. However, if you do slip, look to the right on the way down. It's a magnificent view!"

We pulled into a service station in a remote valley and read the sign at the pump: "Don't ask us for information. If we knew anything, we wouldn't be here."

Post card: "Having a wonderful time. Wish I could afford it."

On my European vacation I saw so much poverty, I brought some home with me.

On our southern trip, we saw a road sign that said, "Take notice. When this sign is underwater, this road is impassable."

In America, there are two classes of travel--first class and with children.

Travel agent: "Aren't you afraid that the tropical climate might disagree with your wife?"
Traveler: "It wouldn't dare!"

"Knock knock."
"Who's there?"
"Fortification."
"Fortification who?"
"Fortification this year we're going to the mountains."

Nothing is quite so upsetting on a vacation as getting a call from the house sitter who asks, "Is it the custom to tip firemen?"

The perfect resort is where the fish bite and the mosquitoes don't.

A camping party was hopelessly lost. One of the campers turned to the guide and said, "I thought you told us that you're the best guide in Maine?"
"I am," said the guide, "but I think we're in Canada now!"

I was saying that this summer I'd like to get away from it all and go some place where no one would ever think to find me. The boss suggested my desk.

Vacations are great. You get up at 4 a.m., drive hundreds of miles to find a place with 'home cooking'.

The resort we stayed at was so dull that one day the tide went out and never came back.

Who will ever forget those immortal words of Sir Winston Churchill: "We will fight on the by-ways, we will fight on the beaches, we will fight at sea!" Forget them? That sounds like our last family vacation.

Most passport photos look like you really need the trip.

Vacation is when they close all the roads and open all the detours.

I just returned from vacation and I have a severe case of bus lag.

I went on one of those "no-frills" cruises. Ten days and no nights.

While in Hawaii, I asked a native, "How do natives pronounce it? Hawaii or Havaii?"
The native replied, "Havaii."
I said, "Thank you."
He said, "You're velcome."

He took one look at his passport photo and he looked so bad he decided he'd better stay home and rest.

I wanted to buy train tickets for a pullman car. The clerk said, "What do you want, the upper or the lower berth?"
I said, "What's the difference?"
"Well, the difference is ten dollars. The lower berth is higher than the upper one. The higher price is for the lower. If you want it lower, you have to go higher. We sell the upper lower than the lower. Most people don't like the lower upper, although it's lower on account of being higher. When you occupy an upper you have to go up to bed, and get down to get up."

While vacationing in Jamaica I saw a very rare tropical fish. It was swimming backwards to keep the water out of its eyes.

In Florida they use alligators to make handbags. Isn't it wonderful what they can train animals to do these days?

I learned a lot on my vacation this summer...like where an alternator goes...what a valve lifter does...and how much it costs for an overhaul in Des Moines.

We put mistletoe over the door of our summer cottage so that when we see relatives coming we can kiss our vacation goodbye.

He just got back from a vacation to Bermuda. I said, "How did you go? By plane or by boat?"
He said, "I don't know my wife buys the tickets."

Happiness is having a neighbor go on a vacation and take 400 slides with the lens cap on.

The surefire way to spot a workaholic on vacation? He's the guy who rushes to the beach, picks up a large conch shell, holds it to his ear and says, " Any messages?"

Last summer we vacationed at Lake Erie. We went sailing and it was really nice. If the wind died down, we could all get out and push.

We were going on a seven-island tour, but had to cancel. I couldn't afford the first part of the trip--the one to the bank.

Last year, we wanted to go to the Bahamas in the worst way--and this year we did. We took the kids.

I'm so proud of our new compact car. Last year, we drove it to Florida during the hurricane season and got 550 miles to the gallon.

We spent last night sleeping at the neighbor's. It wasn't that there was anything wrong at our house. We were just watching slides of their vacation.

 **VALENTINE'S DAY**

On Valentine's Day I always try to do a little more for my wife--like holding the door open when she goes out on her paper route.

My wife was touched by the beautiful inscription that was on the band of the ring I gave her. Three little words..."made in Taiwan."

I'm such a practical romantic. I gave my wife a heart-shaped box filled with two pounds of ground chuck.

Cheap? Who else do you know who gives generic perfume on Valentine's Day?

February is the month we sample the hardest substance known to man--Valentine candy.

My wife and I spent a wonderful evening out on Valentine's Day. We stayed all the way through the last tag team match.

 **VIDEO RECORDERS**

Thanks to video recorders you can tape every football game on Saturdays and Sundays and replay them at a convenient time. Now you can neglect your spouse all year round.

WASHINGTON (GEORGE)

George Washington never told a lie, because in those days, Presidents didn't hold press conferences.

Every year my wife celebrates Washington's birthday by going to all the department store sales. This year, I'm celebrating Washington's birthday by using an axe to chop up all her credit cards.

I have a son who's a freshman and he's already following in George Washington's footsteps. He went down in history.

George Washington had wooden teeth. He brushed after every meal and saw his carpenter twice a year.

George Washington never lied because he had no campaign promises to keep.

George Washington never told a lie. But then again, he never had to fill out an income tax form.

Washington had wooden teeth. He had to watch treats, brush after every meal, and see the Orkin man twice a year. He brushed after every meal with Lemon Pledge.

WATCHES

I finally got one of those digital watches that has a calculator, tells time in five zones, has a stop watch, day/date, second, is waterproof, shockproof. Just my luck, it caught on fire.

WATER POLLUTION

Water pollution is amazing. Yesterday we drove across the Schuylkill River. What's even more amazing is that we didn't use a bridge.

If George Washington were alive today, he could have rolled the dollar across the Potomac.

Want to know what water is like in the river? Wait, I'll get you a slice.

WEATHER

I have an idea that's going to increase the accuracy of the weather bureau 100%. It's called a window.

I'll tell you what kind of weather bureau we have. Remember when Noah got on the ark? Well, they predicted, "Slightly cloudy."

Don't complain about the weather. Without it, most of us wouldn't be able to start a conversation.

Indian weather forecast: Summer squaw followed by Apache fog.

Let a smile be your umbrella and you'll get a mouthful of rain.

The summer sun may burn a bit, but you don't have to shovel it.

The water shortage is so bad in New Jersey that they can't even take baths. My son wants to move there.

I don't think the sun's gonna come out today. I mean, would you come out on a day like this?

I think it's going to be a rough winter. I just saw a squirrel burying a can of Sterno.

The good news is that it'll be in the upper 60's today. The bad news is that that's the wind velocity!

It was so cold last night that my teeth chattered all night. And we don't even sleep together.

The weatherman predicted showers last night and he was right. I know, I took one.

The smog was so bad that I opened my mouth to yawn and chipped a tooth!

It was so foggy this morning that I missed the freeway ramp and got to work 20 minutes early.

I think it's going to be a tough winter. Yesterday I saw a squirrel caulking his oak tree.

"How did you find the weather today?"
"Well, I went outside, and there it was!"

It was so hot that our Tupperware lady got stuck to her samples.

Conclusive proof that heat makes things expand and cold makes them contract. That's why summer days are longer and winter days are shorter.

How cold was it? I'll tell you. By November 23rd, all the turkeys were jostling in line in order to be the first to go into the oven.

It's really been a cold fall. I know that leaves are supposed to turn colors in the fall--but blue?

It was so hot yesterday that I saw a dog chasing a rabbit and they were both walking.

The first time they saw snow in Atlanta, they thought there had been an explosion in a grits factory.

Snow is the rain that couldn't afford the air fare to Florida.

(following a wicked tornado) "Joe, was your barn damaged badly in the tornado?"
"We don't know. We haven't found it yet."

Our weather man gave a terrific forecast. On Tuesday, he predicted a 95% chance of Wednesday.

"How close did it come to you?" gasped the farmer, running up to his hired hand who had almost been struck by lightning.
"Well," drawled the man, "I can't rightly say, but my pipe wasn't lit before."

WEDDING

I went to a vegetarian wedding last week. It was a very touching moment when the bride fed the groom the first slice of her bouquet.

They got married. Dad spent $6,000 on the wedding and they say, "He gave the bride away."

WHITE HOUSE

The President had a traumatic thing happen to him this week. He was taking a walk outside the White House, and a tourist couple came up to him with a camera and said, "Mr. President, we know this is a terrible imposition, but would you mind?"
The President said, "Of course not."
So they gave him the camera and posed in front of their car.

 **WIFE**

My wife bought seven overnight cases because she was going on a week's vacation.

"Another dress, hat and coat! Where am I going to get the money to pay for it all?"
Wife: "I have many faults, but I'm not inquisitive."

My wife goes to a sale and buys everything marked down. Yesterday she came home with two dresses and an escalator.

My wife is doing a better job of keeping her bills down. She bought a heavier paperweight.

My wife is struggling to keep up with the Joneses.
You're lucky. Mine tries to keep up with the Rockefellers!

My wife must be allergic to mink. She gets sick everytime she sees another woman wearing one.

When my wife told me she needed an outside interest, I bought her a lawn mower.

(auctioneer) "Sold to the lady with her husband's hand over her mouth!"

Before the department stores plan a sale, they always phone my wife to see if she's available.

My wife would make a great congressman. She's always introducing new bills in the house.

"Did your wife have anything to say when you got home so late last night?"
"No, but that didn't stop her from talking for two hours."

I call my wife "American Express" because she's always saying, "Don't leave home without me!"

(looking over bills) "The only thing to do is flip a coin. Heads I spend less, tails you earn more."

My wife is a cleanliness nut. At dinner she ties a pigeon around my neck so there won't be any crumbs.

(in fur store) "Will a small deposit hold it until my husband does something unforgivable?"

A wife ran to the fire department to report her burning house.
"Is your husband still in the house?" the fireman asked.
"Don't worry about him," she said. "He won't burn. He's taking a shower."

His wife is like life insurance. The older she gets, the more she costs.

Wives are like traffic tickets. No one complains about them until he gets one of his own.

His wife kept complaining about not feeling wanted so he went downtown and hung her picture on the post office wall.

Husband to spouse: "Light bills, water, gas, milkman! You've got to quit this wild spending!"

Wife to husband leaving party: "I was so proud of you, Bob, the way you stood your ground and yawned right back at them."

Caller: "Doc, my wife dislocated her jaw. Maybe if you're out our way in the next week or so, you could pay us a visit."

"My wife has a horrible memory."
"You mean she forgets everything?"
"No, she remembers everything."

My wife is amazing. She can go into a department store and come out loaded with everything except money.

"Do you think I'm going to wear this raccoon coat for the rest of my life?"
"Why not, the raccoon does."

His wife has him eating out of her hand--which certainly saves on the dishwashing.

My wife detests washing dishes. She says they rattle too much during the spin cycle.

I know that my wife is going to live longer than I do. She has a whole closet full of clothes that she 'wouldn't be caught dead in.'

My wife should go into earthquake research. She's the best fault-finder I know.

My wife bought her dress for $450, and the clerk guaranteed a fit. And she was right. I had a fit when my wife told me the price!

"I am not cheap!" I told my wife. "What happened to that $5 bill I gave you last week, serial number J678293F?"

My wife called, desperate for help. She said, "The car is stalled and I am now in a phone booth at the corner of 'Walk and Don't Walk.' "

My wife washes everything on the gentle cycle. She says it's more humane that way.

My wife always has the last word.
You're lucky, mine never gets to it.

My wife phoned the state park, "Are you the game warden?"
"Why, yes," the man answered.
"Good! Could you please give me some suggestions that would be appropriate for a six year old's birthday party?"

He and his wife had words...but he never got to use any of his.

My wife will go anyplace for a bargain. I mean, who buys contact lenses at a garage sale?

One time I accused my wife of not having a sense of humor.
She said, "Are you kidding? I have an official document that says I have a sense of humor. "
I said, "What document?"
She said, "Our marriage license."

My wife suffers in silence louder than anyone I know.

Let's be practical about this. The only time you should put your wife on a pedestal is when the ceiling needs painting.

My wife has a wonderful way of keeping all her pots and pans and cooking utensils spotlessly clean. She never uses them.

A wife read the fortune-telling card her husband got from the nickel-weighing machine. "You are a strong leader," she read, "with a magnetic personality and strong character--intelligent, witty, and attractive to the opposite sex." Then she turned the card over and added, "It has your weight wrong, too!"

Someone asked my wife what we have in common and she answered, "Well, for one thing, we were both married on the same day."

I walked into the stationery store and said to the clerk, "I'd like a nice fountain pen. This is my wife's birthday."
The clerk responded, "A little surprise, huh?"
I said, "Yeah, she's expecting a mink coat."

She thinks she's Teddy Roosevelt. She runs around everywhere yelling, "Charge!"

I'm really worried. I can't find my credit cards, which means either my wife has gone shopping or I've been pickpocketed, and a thief is using them all over town. Gee, I sure hope my wife hasn't gone shopping!

My wife recently had plastic surgery. I cut all her credit cards in half.

My wife really knows how to throw money away. Who else do you know who tips at toll booths?

My wife complained that the woman next door had a hat just like hers.
I said, "I guess that means you want another hat?"
She said, "Well, it's cheaper than moving."

They say that after many years of marriage, a man and wife begin looking alike--and my wife is very concerned.

Timid man to wife: "We're not going out tonight. And that's semi-final."

In Proverbs it says, "He that findeth a wife findeth a good thing." Tonight I brought my thing with me.

I said, "Look, you've overdrawn the checking account."
"I have not!" my wife replied. "You underdeposited."

My wife is always bragging about her family. For instance, she tells everybody her father has a large staff and directs thousands. And he does. He's a shepherd.

I asked my wife, "Have you seen tonight's paper?"
She said, "Yes, I wrapped the garbage in it."
I said, "But I haven't seen it yet!"
She said, "You didn't miss much. Just some coffee grounds and a few orange peels."

She's always complaining that she has nothing to wear. Friends, she has more clothes in her closet. It's packed so tight that there are moths in there that still haven't learned how to fly.

She said, "Next Christmas, let's get practical things like ties and furs."

His wife says that he's a big help around the house. Right now, he's taking the baby's nap for him.

She's the most efficient homemaker that you've ever seen. For instance, each night, after dinner, she gives the kids something to play with in the tub--the dinner dishes!

I told my wife, "I don't want to go to work. It's a jungle out there."
She said, "Don't sweat it. I put a banana in your lunch box."

My wife and I had an argument. She wanted to buy a fur coat. I wanted to buy a new car. So we compromised. We got the fur coat, and we keep it in the garage.

My wife is as sharp as a pin. She's pointed in one direction and headed in the other.

A wife went to a missing persons bureau and reported her missing husband. "Have you found someone short, thin, and bald with false teeth? In fact, most of him was missing before he was."

He hasn't spoken to his wife for three weeks. He doesn't want to interrupt her.

My wife is always breaking things...like fives, tens, twenties...

I'm so proud of my wife. She's just been crowned Mrs. Garage Sale for the entire state of Pennsylvania!

Thanks to the phenomenon of credit cards, my wife is worth her weight in plastic.

I just asked my wife not to buy anymore sale merchandise. It seems we're just not rich enough to save money.

My wife is extremely clever. She said to me, "I'd like to make one thing perfectly clear..."
I said, "What's that?"
She said, "The lawn," as she handed me a rake.

Every morning at six o'clock sharp, my digital alarm clock wakes me. My wife pokes me in the back with her finger.

My wife keeps me in touch with reality. The other night, I came home from a speech and she said, "How did you perform?"
I said, "I brought down the house."
She said, "So do termites."

It amazes me that airport security would take the time to check through my wife's purse. After all, if she can't find anything in there, how could they?

My wife never repeats gossip. You've got to listen very closely the first time she tells you.

My wife is overly cautious. Before she buys a hot dog at a baseball game, she makes the entire row get up, go out, and wash their hands.

My wife always talks to her plants. She went away for a week's vacation and I looked in the planter. The pansy is leaning over, saying to the begonia, "Hey, where's big mouth?"

My wife got a great buy at a garage sale. A set of encyclopedias with six volumes missing. I asked, "Why did you buy a set with six volumes missing?"
She answered, "Who needs to know everything?"

My wife's flying lessons are going pretty well. Last weekend the tower radioed for her height and position and she told them, "Five feet eight and in the front of the plane."

Keeping a secret from her is like trying to sneak daybreak passed a rooster.

She's very strange with a checkbook. Once she's started one, she can't put it down till it's through.

My wife has been with the kids too much lately. I took her out to dinner with my boss. I looked up from my plate, and there she was cutting his roast beef and wiping his mouth with a napkin.

My wife always keeps a bowl of wax fruit on the table just in case a couple of mannequins drop in unexpectedly.

My wife always knows when it's payday. I've got to hand it to her.

My wife knows how to save her money. She uses mine.

My wife has two closets full of nothing to wear.

We were planning a trip to Bermuda. The travel agent said, "Breakfast is from 6:30-11; lunch from 12-3:30, and dinner from 5 to 9."
My wife said, "If that's true, when will we get to see the sights?"

My wife called me at work today and asked if I'd bring home another mouse trap. I said, "What's the matter with the one I bought you last week?" She said, "It's full."

She'll never find my extra money. I hid it in a sock that needs mending.

My wife went to the bank to cash my paycheck. "It needs an endorsement," the teller explained.
My wife thought for a minute and then wrote on the back of the check, "Ken is a wonderful husband."

My wife exclaimed, "My checkbook balances perfectly! I'm overdrawn exactly what I'm short!"

Man pacing up and down maternity ward. Nurse comes out and says, "Congratulations, you're the father of twins."
The guy says, "Please don't tell my wife. I want to surprise her."

The way some women look in the morning. The neighbor lady ran after the garbage man and yelled, "Am I too late for the garbage?"
The garbage man replied, "No, jump in."

My wife loves to throw parties. Especially around this time of year. Like for the last three weeks, the bedspread in our room has been coats!

We had a party last night, and 35 minutes before the first doorbell, my wife called to me, "Where are you?"
I said, "I'm in the living room."
She said, "On the carpet?"
I said, "No, I'm hanging by my cummerbund from the chandelier!"
She said, "Good, don't make footprints."

My wife has a wonderful way of making a long story short. She interrupts.

I don't really think of her as a wife. She's more like my co-star in 20 years of home movies.

My wife is very thrifty. She didn't want to buy an Easter bonnet because she'd only wear it once. So she bought a mink coat suitable for all occasions.

When I woke up this morning my wife asked, "Did you sleep well last night?"
I said, "No, I made a few mistakes."

My wife calls it a purse, but I call it a portable attic.

There are some four-letter words that really bother my wife like cook, wash, dust, iron...

My wife uses her credit cards so often that she's using money that hasn't even been printed yet.

My wife treats me like a baby. I wanted to discuss it at dinner the other night and she said, "I'm not going to discuss anything with you until you've finished all your carrots!"

She's really neat. The other night I got out of bed to get a drink and when I got back, my side of the bed was made.

She couldn't afford a facelift, so for $80 they lowered her body.

My wife keeps complaining about headaches. So I told her, "Look, when you get out of bed in the morning, it's feet first."

I bought my wife a new dress. She claimed that everytime she wore the other one people threw rice at her.

Look for subtle signs that your wife might be dissatisfied...like when she vacuums up your stamp collection.

My wife is always buying clothes. I think that as a child she was once frightened by an empty clothes hanger.

His wife talks so much he's taken up speed listening.

He got his wife a gift certificate for her birthday, and she went out and exchanged it for a larger size.

I asked, "How did the car get in the living room?" She said, "Easy, I just made a left through the kitchen."

My wife's been wearing a mud pack. For two days she looked great...then it fell off.

What my wife doesn't know about money could fill a checkbook.

I wanted to take the same assertiveness training course my wife took, but she wouldn't let me.

"My wife doesn't understand me. Does yours?"
"I don't know. I've never heard her mention your name."

My wife says, "Okay, I admit I spend money. But name one other extravagance I have."

She had wanted a mink for months, and her husband gave in and got her one for her birthday, but on one condition. She had to keep the cage clean.

My wife had an accident at the bank last week. She got in the wrong line and made a deposit.

I met my wife at the travel bureau. She was looking for a vacation, and I was the last resort.

My wife's garage sale was over, and I was really discouraged. A lot of stuff hadn't sold, so I put up a sign. "Shoplifting Encouraged."

WIFE'S COOKING

I told her I wanted to be surprised for dinner, so she took the labels off the cans.

Talk about weird dinners. Before last night, I had never heard of chili-a-la-mode.

She's totally hopeless in the kitchen. She's the only one I know who can burn lemonade.

I helped my wife with breakfast this morning. Actually, she did all the cooking. I just put out the fire.

She's experimenting in the kitchen again. This morning she came up with something new. She calls it killer toast.

She's a terrible cook. I mean, really bad. In my house we pray <u>after</u> we eat.

The other day she made alphabet soup. The kids all spelled out H-E-L-P.

Before we were married, my wife used to dress to kill. Now she just cooks that way.

My wife considers dinner a success if she gets it all the way home without dropping it.

My wife idolizes me. She serves me burnt offerings every meal.

My wife's not the greatest cook. We went on a picnic, and the park ranger put flares around her picnic basket.

I can understand burning steaks, burning chops, burning roasts. But JELL-O?

My wife has just one problem with cooking. She burns everything. Like we were married three years before I realized there were other flavors besides charcoal.

"We've been married fifteen years," one woman said, "and every night after dinner my husband complains about the food."
"How terrible!" exclaimed the other. "Doesn't it bother you?"
"Why should it bother me," her friend replied, "if he can't stand his own cooking?"

She's one of those gourmet cooks. She make things like escargots. Have you ever taken a look at escargots? I'll tell you something. Before I'd touch escargots, I'd sooner eat snails!

My wife told me, "We're so poor that for the last five years we've been eating off paper plates."
I said, "Lots of people eat off paper plates."
She said, "The same ones?"

My wife tries to save money by getting cheaper cuts of meats. For instance, for the last few weeks we've had ankle of lamb.

The other night I came home and said to my wife, "I'm so hungry, I could eat a horse."
She said, "Oh, you peeked!"

The day after we were married my wife cooked her first meal. She said to me, "Honey, I have a confession to make. I've only learned to cook two things: beef stew and banana pudding."
I said, "That's alright, dear. Just one question. Which is this?"

My wife is such a bad cook, the flies in the backyard pitched in to patch up the hole in the kitchen screen door.

Her cooking is improving. The lumps in the oatmeal are bite-sized.

She's not the greatest cook, but she is practical. The other day she made me a hamburger, and I couldn't eat it. So, she used it to clean the sink.

I'm on the road a lot, and this morning I was served a breakfast of undercooked eggs, burnt bacon, stale toast, weak coffee, and it brought tears to my eyes. It's the first time in weeks that I've had a home-cooked meal.

She's the only girl I know who takes an hour and a half just to cook Minute Rice.

Can my wife cook? She's such a perfectionist. Yesterday she was in the supermarket squeezing cans of baked beans just to make sure they were fresh.

I wonder if Julia Child's husband ever looked up from the table and said, "Petite chaussons au Roquefort? Potage Parmentier? Filets de poisson poches au vin blanc? Haricot verts a la creme? We had that last night!"

My wife told me to take her some place on our anniversary she's never been before, so I took her to the kitchen.

I got my wife a microwave oven. Now she can burn the whole dinner in 47 seconds.

When I started to complain to my wife about taking out the garbage she said, "Just remember. I was on my feet for four hours cooking that garbage!"

Today she's making something special from a recipe out of her MR. GOODWRENCH COOKBOOK.

You know she's not the greatest cook when the handiest kitchen appliance is the fire extinguisher.

I even like her TV dinners now that she found out that you're supposed to warm them up first.

My wife complained, "I'm not just a wife...I'm a cook, a maid, a hostess, a babysitter. What would you do if you had to pay all of those?"
I said, "I'd fire the cook."

His wife can dish it out, but she sure can't cook.

She's a practical and efficient cook. She even serves Tums as after-dinner mints.

My wife served me a "Mustgo" for dinner last night. That is something that's been in the refrigerator so long that it's one day away from becoming a science project.

She burned the Thanksgiving turkey so badly that it could only be identified through dental records.

I miss my wife's cooking--about as often as I can.

She had a terrible accident in the kitchen the other night. And I ate it.

We just celebrated out tin anniversary...12 years of eating out of cans.

Nobody can cook like my wife, but they came pretty close in the army.

This morning my wife put instant coffee in the microwave oven and went back in time.

We punish the kids by sending them to bed with dinner.

My wife doesn't need to call the family to dinner. We know it's ready when the smoke alarm goes off.

Her meals have an indescribable taste--but rotten comes pretty close.

Not only should she throw away the leftovers, she should also throw away the originals.

"Your dinner is going to be better tonight, dear. A nice neighbor told me to add water to the dehydrated foods."

My wife is a creative cook. Yesterday she substituted milk of magnesia for white sauce in one of her recipes.

I'm not bragging, but my wife can make ice cubes that just melt in your mouth!

Ah, there's nothing like working hard all day and coming home into the kitchen to smell the aroma of boiling water and burning tinfoil.

She injured herself while preparing dinner the other night. She got a severe case of frostbite.

My wife serves greens every meal. The bad news is that the green is the bread.

My wife called me at the office and said, "I'm afraid that our dinner for tonight is a little burned."
I asked, "What happened? Was there a fire at Burger King?"

Wife: "I took this cake recipe right out of the cookbook."
Husband: "You did the right thing, dear. It should never have been put in."

Wife: "I made this pudding all by myself."
Husband: "That's great, dear. Who helped you lift it out of the oven?"

I'm sorry that I bought my wife a microwave. Now I have to eat her cooking twenty minutes sooner.

My wife gave me a dinner plate with a slice of American cheese on it. I asked, "Just cheese?"
She said, "Yes, when the chops caught fire and fell into the dessert, I had to use the soup to douse the flames."

A wife complaining to her husband about her old clothes said, "Look at these rags! If anyone came to our house, they'd think I was your cook!"
"Not if they stayed for dinner," the husband shot back.

The recipe called for diced potatoes, and when I walked into the kitchen, I saw my wife with a felt-tipped pen putting little dots on them.

My wife's meals aren't planned. They're premeditated.

My wife's idea of saving money on food is to look for a cheaper restaurant.

I asked him what his wife likes to make best for dinner and he said, "Reservations."

Where else but in America? The scene is a supermarket. A young mother is pushing a cart down the aisle with a four-year-old scouting ten feet ahead for his favorites. He rushes over to a display, pulls out a package and runs back to her with it. She smiles patiently and says, "No, Tommy, put it back. You have to cook that."

That's the trouble with girls today. All they can do is thaw foods. Why can't they open cans like their mothers did?

Now my wife's mad at me. She gave me a TV dinner last night--the fifth one this week--and after it was all over I said, "That was wonderful, my dear. My compliments to the oven."

She cooks soup just like the kind her mother used to make--right before they took her dad to the hospital.

She took a cooking course and finished in ten greasy lessons.

One night she awakened me and said, "Ken, there's a burglar in the kitchen, and I think he's finishing the casserole I made for dinner." I whispered to her, "Leave him alone. I'll bury him in the morning."

We haven't had oatmeal for some time now. I think she lost the recipe.

I don't want to say my wife's a lousy cook, but meat loaf shouldn't glow in the dark, should it?

My wife serves me a balanced diet every meal. Every beans weighs the same.

I can't describe how terrible my wife's cooking is, but the centerpiece on the dinner table is a spitoon.

Their party ended early last week when they ran out of ice...his wife lost the recipe.

Honey, what's this on the plate, just in case I have to describe it to the doctor?

She puts popcorn in her pancake batter so the pancakes will turn over by themselves.

The other night my wife made enthusiasm stew...she put everything she had into it.

My wife isn't much of a cook. Her meatballs explode on impact.

My wife just wrote a cookbook, and they're turning it into a TV series. It's going to be called The Survivors.

My wife's cooking never gives me an upset stomach. That's because she fries everything in Pepto Bismol.

My wife has a cookbook but I think she's waiting for it to be turned into a movie.

One of the earliest things I learned in marriage was to never ask my wife what she cooked for dinner--especially while I was eating it.

I used her leftover gravy as primer for my old Chevy.

I came home one evening and my wife was crying. I said, "What's wrong?"
She replied, "The dog ate the pie I baked for you."
I said, "That's okay, dear. I'll get us a new dog."

My wife wrote to the army cook to get all my favorite recipes.

Does she save leftovers? Yesterday we had a 14-pound meatloaf.

I walked into the kitchen this morning and saw my wife opening a grapefruit with a can opener.

She's not a great cook, but her cooking has broken the dog from begging at the table.

We have a great marriage. I bring home the bacon and my wife burns it.

I always know when we're having salad for dinner. I don't smell anything burning.

I've always said, "Where there's smoke, there's toast."

My wife is some cook! Every time I think of her bisquits, I get a lump in my throat.

Who else do you know who burns potato salad?

She used to make me toast every morning, and then she lost the recipe.

She serves roast beef, coffee, and ice cream--all at the same temperature.

My wife has a different way of calling the kids for dinner: "Get in the car, kids."

She's the one who puts the quiz in cuisine.

She signed up for a course to improve her cooking. The course title was "Advanced Defrosting".

With my wife, food has a way of starting out frozen and ending up burned.

I broke a tooth on my wife's cooking, and that was just the coffee.

When my wife's in a real hurry she doesn't even unfreeze the TV dinners. She just shoves a stick in them and we eat them like popsicles. You ought to try licking a Swanson Hungry Man Dinner sometime.

My wife and I make breakfast together. She makes the toast and I scrape it.

My wife specializes in preparing several dishes that are great provided that you don't put them in a warm place--like your stomach.

I'm having difficulty speaking tonight. My wife baked this afternoon, and I cut my mouth on a piece of her sponge cake.

My wife considers herself an expert in International Cuisine now that she's learned how to heat Polish sausage.

My wife is an imaginative cook. Last night she served us bologna shish kebab.

My wife believes in balanced meals. All her dinners contain the adult minimum daily requirement for heartburn.

No matter what my wife cooks, it always seems to turn out tough. At our house you get a soup knife.

Her idea of gourmet cooking is putting a bay leaf on a TV dinner.

When my wife says, "I'm fixing dinner," that's a signal to me that something will go wrong with the recipe and she'll have to fix it.

My wife's taking a great cooking course. Last week they learned how to pre-heat the oven, and this week they're going to put something in it!

My wife's cooking has earned her widespread recognition. In fact, the city's Department of Health has ordered her to register her cookbooks as lethal weapons.

She made me waffles that were inedible. Not to worry. I put them on the car as all-season radials.

WIFE'S DRIVING

My wife said, "Just look how close the numbskull ahead of us is driving!"

The officer stopped my wife for driving on the wrong side of the road. "Don't you know what the white line is for in the middle of the street?" She thought for a second and said, "Bicycles?"

My wife got a parking ticket, but she got out of it. She pleaded insanity.

His wife was in a car accident. The policeman said, "Let me see your license."
She replied, "I don't have a license."
"Well, lady, you can't drive without a license!" snapped the officer.
"So that's what's wrong," she replied. "I thought it was because I was near-sighted and nervous that I hit those two cars and that fire hydrant."

Officer: "Yes, ma'am, I know the gentleman stepped right out in front of you, but after all, it is his lawn!"

When the policeman handed my wife a ticket, she asked, "Now does this cancel the one I got earlier this morning, officer?"

The best way to stop a noise in your car is to let her drive.

When she puts her hand out the window, it means one thing. The window's open.

My wife backed the car out of the garage this morning, which isn't bad in itself, but I had backed the car in last night.

My wife took her driver's test and came home with three tickets---on the written part alone!

She's an imaginative driver. She even made a U-turn in a car wash.

She just got her license. Now all her accidents will be legal.

A guy yelled at my wife, "Why didn't you give a signal?"
My wife shouted back, "Why should I? I always turn here."

My wife was driving when she observed linemen working high up on telephone poles. "Look at those cowards!" she screamed. "You would think I never drove before."

My wife shows up at a garage with dented car: "Please take care of this for me. The fender's been acting up again."

"As I backed out of the garage, I hit the door, ran over my son's bicycle, tore up the lawn, hit our neighbor's house, crushed the stop sign, and crashed into this tree."
"Then what happened?" asked the policeman.
"Then I lost control of the car."

My wife was stalled at a traffic signal, as the light changed from green to yellow to red. An infuriated motorist, leaned out the window and yelled, "What's a matter, lady? Don't we have any colors you like?"

"Dear, I scratched the fender a bit on my way home tonight."
"Alright, sweetheart. I'll take a look at it."
"Thanks, honey. You'll find it in the trunk."

If your wife wants to learn to drive, don't stand in her way.

My wife was driving the other day and hit a tree. She claimed, "It wasn't my fault. I honked."

I went driving with my wife and she went right through a red light. I said, "Didn't you see that red light?"
She said, "So what? You see one red light, you've seen them all."

Our youngest daughter was screaming yesterday morning, "Daddy, Daddy! Mommy just ran over my favorite dolly with the car!"
I said, "Look, don't come complaining to me. If I told you once, I told you a thousand times not to leave your toys on the porch."

My wife failed her first driver's exam. The examining officer said, "Don't look upon it as failing. Think of it as increasing your life-span."

My wife called me and said, "There's water in the carburetor."
I said, "Where's the car?"
She said, "In the lake."

I bought my wife a car. Three weeks ago she learned how to drive it. This week she's learning how to aim it.

I don't want to say she's a bad driver, but yesterday the cop gave my wife a season ticket.

My wife told the mechanic, "My brakes don't work. Put in a louder horn."

My wife's been practicing backing into the garage. Next week she'll try it with the door open.

My poor wife--the time ran out on her parking meter, and she wasn't even done parking yet!

My wife's problem after parking is trying to decide which of the three meters she should put the dime in. Maybe the one under the car!

Look at the beautiful car I got for my wife.
Wow! Where did you make a trade like that?

A guy installed electric garage door openers for his wife. "Do they really work?" a neighbor asked.
"You better believe it," he answered. "She doesn't even have to push a button. When they see her coming the door flies open in terror."

People say that women are lousy drivers. That's ridiculous. I've known women who can drive better than men. But I've never known any that could putt.

My wife is learning to drive. When the road turns when she does, it's called a coincidence.

My wife's driving lessons just took a turn for the worse.

My wife was driving and knitting at the same time. The traffic cop pulled over alongside of her and yelled, "Pullover!"
"No," said my wife with a smile. "Just a pair of socks."

My wife has frequent accidents in the car, but they're really not her fault. Like the other day she was driving down the street, minding her own business, when a telephone pole cut right in front of her.

It gives me a real thrill to see my wife pull our new car into the carport. Relief is felt as well. You see, our carport started out as a garage.

I always let my wife drive on New Year's Eve. It's the only time of the year that her driving looks normal.

Yesterday my wife ran into a lot of money. She smashed into an armored bank truck.

My wife was going the wrong way down a one-way street when she was stopped by an officer.
"Didn't you see the arrow?" the officer inquired.
"Arrow! I didn't even see the Indians," my wife answered.

My wife's driving has improved. You know those signs that say "One Hour Parking"? Well, I'm here to tell you that she can park in 45 minutes.

My wife met me in the driveway and said, "I've got some good news and some bad news. The good news is today I rearranged the living room furniture. The bad news is I did it with the car."

My wife is a wild driver. Every month I have to take the car into the shop to have the horn relined.

 **WILL**

My uncle's will said, "Being of sound mind, I spent all my money."

Relatives were waiting expectantly as the lawyer read the will of a wealthy but eccentric man. Finally the lawyer said, "And to my nephew, Charlie Jones, whom I promised to remember--"Hi there, Charlie!""

Expectant relatives sitting at the reading of a will, were startled when the attorney read, "And so, being of sound mind, I spent every last cent before I died."

WILLIAMS, PAT

I was with the Phillies and was compared to Yogi Berra. My name came up and someone said, "We're not exactly talking about another Yogi Berra."

The P.A. announcer said, "No. 29, Pat Williams is batting for exercise."

The manager said, "Williams is now 22. In another ten years he has a chance to be 32."

I had a tendency to stretch triples into doubles.

My bubble gum card was worth two sticks of gum--chewed.

I was the only man to have my glove bronzed at the height of my career--and then I played with it.

I ran the bases well--the two times that I got on.

I was the only player that had to lose twelve pounds just to hit my weight.

I was so nervous my first game the manager came and told me, "In the pros you wear your underwear on the inside of your uniform."

Each time I was traded, the newspapers read, "This is a deal that will hurt both teams."

The fans were chanting, "We want Williams. We want Williams." Finally the coach said, "Williams, go out there and see what they want."

I could have hit better than Yogi Berra blindfolded. Unfortunately, Yogi never wore a blindfold.

I had deceptive speed. I was slower than I looked.

Ferguson Jenkins was asked, "Who's the toughest person you have to pitch to?"
Jenkins replied, "My catcher, Pat Williams!"

 # WINTER

It was so cold last winter that one player was late for practice because he was out trying to jump start a reindeer.

Winter has surely arrived. My neighbor just returned my lawn mower and borrowed my snow shovel.

It was really cold out there today--like a refrigerator. I know. I opened the front door and the little light went on.

It was so cold this morning that we had to spray de-icer on the boss's swivel chair.

What'd I tell you? The cold weather you prayed for back in August is finally here.

You know it's cold when the wind chill factor exceeds the speed limit.

You know it's cold outside when you're combing your hair and it breaks!

It was so cold this morning that I set a pan of boiling water outside and it froze so fast the ice was still warm.

Remember, if your car starts to skid on icy streets, turn your steering wheel in the same direction of the skid and jump out the window on the passenger side.

This is the time of year when people start going to places where they can pay $200 a day to experience the same kind of heat they were complaining about in August.

One nice thing about weather like this. It's easy to find a picnic table.

It's 60 degrees in Miami. Thirty in the morning and thirty degrees at night.

The highway department has been working all night spreading sand on the streets. That means that the streets are icy, or they're putting in a new beach for the tourist season.

What a weatherman! Last winter I spent three days shoveling "chances of flurries" out of the driveway!

It was so cold last winter that the candle froze, and we couldn't blow it out. Then when we were talking outside, our words froze, and we had to fry 'em just to find out what we were saying to each other.

It was so cold out there today he wore his toupee upside down.

It was so cold today, I saw hens laying eggs from a standing position.

One thing about living in Buffalo, it only snows twice during the winter. Once for two months and once for three months.

Our state has a great snow removal system. It's called August.

If you want to avoid colds this winter, take plenty of vitamin C--and take it to Sarasota and stay there.

Rescuers struggled through high drifts to work their way to a mountain cabin where they knocked on the door. "We're from the Red Cross," the rescuers announced.
The mountaineer replied, "It's been such a rough winter, I don't see how we can give anything this year."

Remember, when the roads are icy and your car starts to skid, turn your steering wheel in the direction of Miami Beach.

WOMEN

Women really don't like to repeat gossip, but then again, what else can they do with it?

Woman to frustrated sales clerk: "Now we're getting somewhere! That's the exact opposite of what I'm looking for!"

Women, generally speaking, are generally speaking.

My wife belongs to a women's hiking group. They call themselves the Walkie Talkies.

I like a woman with a head on her shoulders. I hate necks.

Ever wonder why we've never had a woman President? That's because a President must be 35 years old in order to take office.

(woman trying on mink says to sales clerk) "Now if my husband doesn't like it, do you promise not to take it back?"

A woman talking to her husband said, "Everybody is talking about Mr. and Mrs. Roberts, and how they're always fighting. Some people are taking her part, and others are taking his."
The husband looked up from his newspaper and said, "And I suppose a few eccentrics are just minding their own business."

Do you believe in clubs for women?
Only if all other means of persuasion fail.

A woman has to do twice as much as a man to be considered half as good. Fortunately, it isn't difficult.

A gossipy guest at a ladies' luncheon requested of her hostess milk instead of coffee. The hostess asked, "Would you like it in a glass or in a saucer?"

A woman walking downtown fell off her seven-inch platform shoes. She would have been injured, but luckily her eyelashes broke the fall.

WOMEN DRIVERS

If you don't like the way women drive, stay off the sidewalk.

I knew a woman driver who got only seven miles to the gallon in her economy car. I didn't know why until I watched her get in the car. The first thing she did when she got in was to pull the choke out all the way to hang her purse on it.

A lady hit a guy with a car and yelled, "Watch out!"
The guy cried, "Why, are you coming back?"

One day she drove into the side of a building and ran into another woman coming down.

WOMEN'S LIBERATION

They keep saying that women are smarter than men. But have you ever seen a man's shirt that buttons down the back?

I am glad there is sexual equality in all areas these days. Just this morning my wife was discussing this very issue with her Avon man.

I'm writing a book about men's liberation. It'll be published as soon as my wife okays it.

WORK

There must be some truth in reincarnation. Just look at the way some office workers come back to life after quitting time.

The trouble with being punctual is that nine times out of ten, there's no one there to appreciate it.

Reduce the number of mistakes you make at work--arrive late and leave early!

I don't have too large an office. People keep coming in and asking for brooms.

I'd rather work in Philadelphia than Los Angeles. I'd get paid three hours earlier!

No man goes before his time. Unless, of course, the boss goes home early.

I'll never forget the first company I worked for. This company was so small, when I was promoted from office boy to vice-president my duties didn't change.

If work is so great, how come they have to pay you to do it?

He's always given his company an honest day's work. Sometimes it's taken him a week to do it.

Before I go any further, I want to clear up a little misunderstanding. I did not say our company cafeteria serves the greasiest food in town. What I said was, "It's the first time I ever saw an oil spill with napkins."

If you hold your head up and chin in and put your shoulder to the wheel and your nose to the grindstone, you may get there, but you'll look pretty stupid.

Work is what people do--unless they're already employed by the government.

He worked all through the day and night Wednesday to get out an important job. Which probably explains why he slept through Thursday and Friday.

Remember, work like a dog. Eat like a horse. Think like a fox. Run like a rabbit. And visit your veterinarian twice a year.

WORLD CONDITIONS

I don't do jokes about current events because I don't get the newspaper anymore ever since my next door neighbor moved.

My plan to eliminate nuclear war is to make missiles so complicated that they can't be fired. This can be accomplished by having the instructions written by the same guys who write the tax forms.

Why can't nations solve their problems like husbands and wives? Just get mad, pout, and don't talk to each other for a couple of weeks.

I always read "Dear Abby" columns. It's wonderful to know that with all the problems in the world there are still some people whose biggest worry is how they should acknowledge a wedding present.

Those Arabs don't stand a chance against the Israelis, who have developed the toughest missile ever. A month-old bagel.

ZOO

Visitors to the zoo were surprised to see the exhibit labeled "Coexistence" containing a lion and some lambs. The zookeeper explained there was nothing to it. "All I have to do every now and then is add a few fresh lambs."

To develop your own joke file as an extension to this book, the following fine resources should be considered:

ORBEN'S CURRENT COMEDY
The Comedy Center
700 Orange Street
Wilmington, DE 19801

CONTEMPORARY COMEDY (radio service)
5804 Twineing
P.O. Box 271043
Dallas, Texas 75227

MAC McGINNIS
448 North Mitchner Avenue
Indianapolis, Indiana 46219

ONE TO ONE (radio service)
CreeYadio Services
Box 9787
Fresno, California 93794

QUOTE MAGAZINE
405 Sussex Place
148 International Boulevard
Atlanta, Georgia 30303

Special thanks to HAL RAYMOND, the Morning Mayor of WSBA-Radio, York, Pennsylvania, for trading material with us for this collection.

Thank you for sharing the inscribed copy of your book with us. We look forward to enjoying it now and shall retain it for inclusion in our future Presidential collection. We sincerely appreciate your thoughtfulness and we send our best wishes to you.

Ronald and Nancy Reagan
President & First Lady

I received your book, and I am sure I will enjoy it. I want to thank you for it now, because I am a slow reader. I hope your book is the success it deserves to be, and now with all this experience, your next book will probably only take you seven years. And the next one six years. Eventually you will be writing them as fast as I can read them. Okay, kids, lots of luck.

George Burns
Comedian

Nothing But Winners "is a winner". I loved it.

Milton Berle
Comedian

'It's a great book and is at the top of my pecking order. It's a license for laughter. It lays no eggs, has plenty of yolks and is everything it's cracked up to be.

Ted Giannoulas
The Famous Chicken

"I've been clowning around America for 40 years, and I've never seen anything like "Nothing But Winners." It's the finest collection of great jokes ever put together."

Max Patkin
Clown Prince of Baseball